UFOs:
EXOPOLITICS
&
THE NEW WORLD
DISORDER

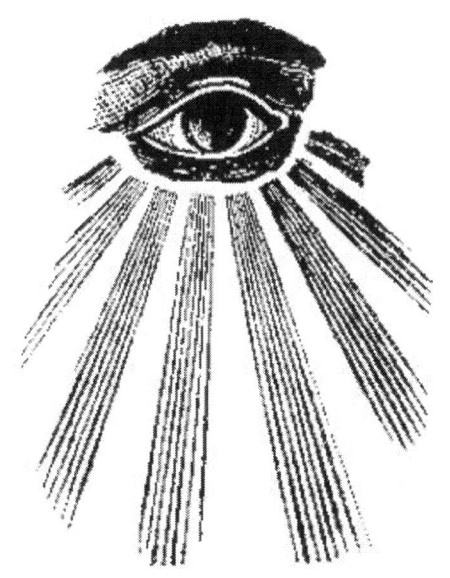

Written and Compiled by Ed Komarek

SHOESTRING PUBLISHING

Copyright © 2012 by Ed Komarek

3301 Hwy 93 S. Cairo Georgia 39828

ISBN-13: 978-1470077822

Library of Congress Number: 2012911236

In this book a large amount of the content is compiled by the author, but is not the property of the author. So the author and Shoestring Publishing can only claim copyright on the writings of Ed Komarek. Anyone wishing to use material from these other authors need to contact these authors and seek permission, especially material that is under copyright protection. Shoestring Publishing and Ed Komarek have made a good faith attempt to find and seek permission to reprint material, especially information that does not fall under the fair use laws and is copyrighted by the authors.

The author does not seek, nor does he expect personal financial gain from this work, but only to recover costs of publication and distribution of the electronic and hard copy books. The compilation of so much material and evidence accumulated over decades, as well as the author's limited resources, presents difficulties in regard to permissions and credit. People have died, have not replied to requests and some may have just fallen through the cracks.

The author feels very strongly that all this evidence should be organized and available to the public in the original writings, even though this format will most likely negate the possibly of getting a major publishing house interested in the book because of liability concerns. A complete rewrite would probably be necessary to get a major publisher interested if the author tries to go this route in the future, so the decision has been made to self-publish for now.

ACKNOWLEDGEMENTS

This author would especially like to acknowledge the long hours of hard work that Ash Staunton has dedicated to editing this book free of charge. Special thanks to Thomas Kemp for the final edit of the proof. I would also like to thank Ash and Clinton Bailey, creators of the excellent front and back cover.
www.theartistree.com.au

The author sincerely appreciates the contributions of all the following people whose material has been used in this book: Cherry Hinkle, Clifford Stone, Brent Raynes, Luca Scantamburlo, Berthold E. Schwartz, Stevens and Steinman, Tim Beckley, Dirk Vander Ploeg, Michael Salla, Len Stringfield, Bill English, Richard Dolan, Paul Hellyer, William Rutledge, Gavin Menzies, George LoBuono, Tom Fox, Jeff Adams, Robert Collins, John Edmonds, Derrel Sims, George Filer, Albert Rosales, Mr. Khoury, Michael Hill, Barbara Barbatelli, Chris O'Brien, Gary Bekkum, Steven Greer, Subhamoy Das, Sylvia Cranston, Bill Knell, Rodger Marsh, Dan Sherman, Lyn Buchanan, William Pawelec, Mary DeRiso, Richard Sauder, Kary Mullis, John Lear, Jorge Martin, Richard Boylan, Michael Lindeman, Don Phillips, Boyd Bushman, Bill Uhouse, Ben Rich, Donna Hare, Elaine Douglass, Philip Corso Sr., Jonny Sands, Udo Wartena, John Fontaine, Olavo Fontes, Charles Hall, Colin Andrews, Gene Ruegg, George Tyler, Hans Larson Loberg, William McDonald, Gordon Creighton, Philip Imbrogno, George Knapp, Colm Kelleher, William Baldwin, Linda Howe, Edgar Mitchell, Bob Lazar, Peter A. Bostrom, Lon Strickler, Gerald Light

Rise, and Rise again and again,

Like the Phoenix from the Ashes,

Until the Lambs become Lions, and

The Rule of Darkness is no more.

Maitreya

DEDICATION

This book is dedicated to all the courageous activists of the Occupy Movement, Alex Jones of Inforwar.com, and Ron Paul and the Tea Party, both the left & right, who are determined to resist the imposition by the Global Elite of the so called and deceptively named Orwellian, 'New World Order.' This dark perverted feudal vision for humanity is in reality an attack on and an affront to; an enlightened vision of a truly New World Order based on Republican and Democratic principles.

If our leaders had not failed us in the 1940s and 1950s, the positive vision of Star Trek could now have become our present day reality. In this book I will show that had our leaders embarked on a policy of openness and transparency in regard to extraterrestrial contact in the 1950s, rather than secrecy and cover-up, human evolution would have moved forward instead of backward and the earth's environment protected.

I will provide evidence in this book that the oligarchy starting in the 1940s chose to play to humanity's dark side, in deciding to selfishly protect its institutions and special interests and control over the masses. A UFO/ET cover-up was instituted and democracy and democratic principles subverted. Those leaders and individual citizens that opposed the oligarchy were discredited, harassed and even murdered.

Fantastic as it may seem, rather than lead mankind to an enlightened future offered to us by ethical extraterrestrial races and civilizations, our autocratic leaders agreed to secret Faustian treaties and technological transfer agreements with less ethical extraterrestrial races, thereby creating the greatest national security threat of all time. We can only imagine our future if overt space travel had become commonplace, with ethical ET cultural and technological exchanges bringing in a new age of enlightment along with exotic cheap non-polluting energy technologies.

NOTE TO READERS

If you are viewing this book with Internet access you can access the foot noted material by clicking on the footnote as you go along. If you are reading this in printed format, the footnotes and the Internet addresses are available at the end of the book. The footnote list will also be on my blog, so that the person reading this as hard copy can just click the links, instead of having to type them into the computer as they read along.

I, Ed Komarek, am available to lecture on this book. Where that is not possible, due to budget restraints, I have created a power-point lecture that can be delivered by others in my absence. I can be reached through my Facebook page or by email at: edkomarek@yahoo.com   Blog: exopolitics.blogspot.com/

TABLE OF CONTENTS

Preface   Page 10

Introduction   Page 14

CHAPTER ONE-   Page 29
Evolution on Other Worlds

CHAPTER TWO-   Page 74
Military Interactions with Extra-terrestrials

CHAPTER THREE-   Page 111
Breakaway Civilization, Secret Space Program

CHAPTER FOUR-   Page 146
The Wright-Patterson Electrogravitics Document

CHAPTER FIVE-   Page 171
Alien Resource Cartel

CHAPTER SIX-   Page 182
The Tall Whites

CHAPTER SEVEN-   Page 207
The Greys

CHAPTER EIGHT-   Page 252
The Celestial Human Mega-Population

CHAPTER NINE-   Page 294
Extraterrestrial Warfare

CHAPTER TEN-   Page 307
Paranormal Phenomena that Impersonates UFOs and ETs

CHAPTER ELEVEN-　　　　　　　　　　Page 321
Taking Back Our Future

CHAPTER TWELVE-　　　　　　　　　Page 345
The Really Big Picture

FOOTNOTES　　　　　　　　　　　　Page 358

PREFACE

As a young man I remember looking out the window of the passenger jet returning to college in Fairbanks Alaska in the dead of winter. Only hours earlier I had left home in the Deep South where the weather that Christmas had temperatures as high as eighty degrees. On the ground slowly passing beneath me, were dark, desolate, bitter cold landscapes of snow and ice.

When the plane made its descent into town, the University of Alaska on the hills above Fairbanks could be seen rising up though the dark grey blanket of ice fog that had settled upon Fairbanks, as was usual this time of year. With almost no sunlight and temperatures of sixty below zero, I wondered what in the world had possessed me to decide to go to College in Fairbanks. I must have been out of my mind! Looking back on my life now, it all makes sense, but then I had no idea who I really was and what my life was to become.

The University was a small college, and the courses were dull and uninteresting. I was barely making passing grades. I loved the outdoors, but in the middle of winter hunting and fishing had come to a standstill, except when it warmed to twenty below and my friends and I would go grouse hunting or ice fishing on the lakes south of Fairbanks. This time of year there was not much to do, so we kids drove the short distance downtown to a street lined with bars to drink beer and play pool.

I remember during my first Alaskan winter that I wandered away from the poolrooms to get a little fresh air and somehow stumbled on a strange unexpected anomaly, a tiny New Age bookstore hidden away on a side street. Upon entering, I remember feeling strangely at home with the wind chimes, beads, crystals and the smell of incense and bookshelves lined with books on reincarnation, Out Of Body (OBE), Near Death Experiences (NDE), psychic phenomena, UFOs etc.

This strange new world opening up before me was so much more interesting and exciting than dull university classes that included two years of French and the dissecting of dead cats drenched in formaldehyde. I could see that these courses had little relation to a degree in wildlife management I was pursuing. I was especially discouraged because I was part of a family of ecologists and had grown up and was mentored by some of the best early ecologists and wildlife managers in the world.

I found myself devoting more time reading material from the bookstore and studying less and less my college work. I began wondering if some of this is true, what does it all mean, what is life really about? Who am I? What is life? I developed a burning desire to know the truth. The more I studied what was to be my true calling, the further I fell into an existential crisis and deep depression. After my third year in academia with my old world falling apart and my new world yet to emerge, I dropped out of college to live life my own way. I never looked back. I had always disliked formal education as a young man, but it was not until later in life that I realized why.

I came to understand that skills based education was really an indoctrination program to stifle creativity and interest in order to create obedient wage slaves to serve elite masters in government, business, religion, and academia, etc. I now believe that a true educational system is one in which interest and creativity come first. If we find and develop the student's interest first, that student will naturally desire the skills to develop the interest further.

I believe that when skills are unnaturally forced on the student first, this has a perverse tendency to stifle creativity and interest, thereby dulling the students mind and emotions. As it turned out, once I dropped out of the formal indoctrination system, I subconsciously and then consciously pursued an interest based system the rest of my life.

In two or three years' time, I had extricated myself from this deep existential depression, and restructured myself through the practice of good mental and emotional hygiene that I had learned from books on Yoga and Buddhism. I was always one to apply to my life what I learned. It was not long before I began to concentrate on what evolved into my life's work, the understanding of UFOs and extraterrestrial life.

It has been an amazing life's journey. I find that my life has come full circle from an early interest in nature and ecology, to the study of exopolitics, then back down to earth to global politics. What I found was that in order to best understand Exopolitics, I had to understand the UFO/ET cover-up. I had to understand how a very few people could rule so many so well and even control national governments through global autocratic interlocking corporate networks. It turns out that the two ancient symbols of feudalistic power, the Pyramid and the Phoenix, are just as relevant today as in ancient times.

The Pyramid represents top down control of humanity by a few individuals at the top, while the Phoenix represents the inherent chaotic nature of autocratic, feudalistic power. Like the Phoenix, feudalistic civilizations are born of powerful, creative forces, yet as they evolve, sow the seeds of their own destruction and renewal. It seems that the original creative forces, when they become well established in a mature civilization, then tend to control and suppress emerging new creative forces out of self-preservation. The result is always the same, an eventual collapse of that civilization into corruption and mismanagement.

I now know that there is a better way, a better organizational structure for society, and that structure can not only be found among the more advanced extraterrestrial races, but very close to home in how the cells in our bodies are organized. If our bodies suddenly reverted to the way our society was organized, we would not live very long when one part of the body got fat and other parts starved to death. In fact, cancer cells seem to be an example of reversion back to a more primitive feudalistic organizational structure.

I have come to sincerely believe that both our bodies, and some of the more advanced extraterrestrial races, are pointing the way to a truly longstanding autistic society of continuous, stable, destruction, and renewal. Most of the cells in our bodies have short life-spans of a few days, as is the case with red blood cells, but they are continuously replaced without a total collapse of the body.

In us, if we survive, nature seems to be evolving a higher order of fractal! Somehow, through our electronic, soon to be quantum, social and communication networks, our individual minds will become one mind guiding our civilization forward. A truly New World Order is now becoming possible without the dysfunctional inequities of the Old World Order that cause the instabilities in our current feudalistic societal organizational structure.

In my sixties, I look back, and I can see how I have built my life to a great extent on the good works of others. I now seek to repay this debt to society by assisting others to better understand themselves, and the greater reality to which so many are so uninformed. I hope to return to a world that is a little better than I left it, because I have tried to live a life not just for myself, but for others as well. I do firmly believe that all is connected, and that we all do eventually reap what we sow.

INTRODUCTION

"Some of the biggest men in the United States, in the field of commerce and manufacture, are afraid of somebody, are afraid of something. They know there is a power somewhere so organized, so subtle, so watchful, so interlocked, so complete, so pervasive that they had better not speak above their breath when they speak in condemnation of it." President Woodrow Wilson.

"Three hundred men, all of whom know one another, direct the economic destiny of Europe and choose their successors from among themselves." Quote attributed to Walter Rathenau of General Electric, Germany in 1909.

"It is well that the people of the nation do not understand our banking and monetary system, for if they did, I believe there would be a revolution before tomorrow morning." Henry Ford

"The bold effort the present (central) bank had made to control the government...are but premonitions of the fate that await the American people should they be deluded into a perpetuation of this institution or the establishment of another like it." Andrew Jackson

In this book, I hope to define and clarify the newly emerging field of Exopolitics that is evolving out of the old UFO/ET field much like the field of ecology emerged out of the natural sciences. I have been privy to a front row seat in both emerging fields. As a child and young man, I grew up among some of the earliest ecologists, and now strive to move the newly emerging field of Exopolitics forward as one of the founders of the field of Exopolitics.

Exopolitics is simply defined as the politics of the universe. Exopolitics is about extraterrestrial races and civilizations, and how these advanced space faring cultures interact among themselves and with us. Some would argue that it is far too early to think exopolitically, but I and others disagree. In this book, I present my argument for Exopolitics along with the vast amount of evidence upon which this argument is based.

The writings and books of credible people in the UFO/ET field like Leslie Kean, Richard Dolan, Stanton Friedman, and Nick Pope are providing a solid public foundation for a credible popular book on Exopolitics that clarifies and defines the field of Exopolitics as a legitimate field of inquiry. Aldo Leopold did this for ecology in the Sand County Almanac, and Eric Drexler did this for the emerging field of nanotechnology with his book, Engines of Creation.

There is a great need for such clarification of Exopolitics because the field has entered popular culture and is being trashed by many characters of dubious distinction. These modern day sirens of the new age, with their sensationalistic false contactee and whistle-blower narratives, draw from the UFO literature and are ever ready to lure and pounce upon the unwary and undisciplined neophyte. Many are those who succumb and are lured onto the existential rocks, confused and discouraged.

We and our world are rapidly evolving into a spacefaring society, and contrary to what the public has been told by official groups and institutions, we are not alone and never have been alone. We who have dedicated our lives to the study of extraterrestrial reality have learned that the universe is highly populated, with very large numbers of intelligent extraterrestrial spacefaring races and civilizations, some which have come to earth for a variety of reasons, motivations, and agendas.

The truth is that in the past 70 years, our planetary civilization has covertly moved far into the process of integrating into extraterrestrial reality, to an extent that is far beyond the awareness and comprehension of the ordinary person. Ben Rich[1], former head of the Lockheed Skunkworks, was not joking when he said:

> "We already have the means to travel among the stars, but these technologies are locked up in black projects and it would take an act of God to ever get them out to benefit humanity…anything you can imagine we already know how to do."[2]

What authorities have done at the behest of the ruling globalist elite is to create a propaganda narrative that has diverged from the real narrative as to the true nature of extraterrestrial reality starting in the 1940's. The gap between the propaganda narrative imposed on the masses, and the real narrative that only the elite have special access to, creates a knowledge and technological gap that can be exploited by the elite to the detriment of overall society and the environment.

Knowledge is power, and special access to the real covert narrative allows the ruling families and their international corporations to exploit secretly, extraterrestrial knowledge and technology. The overt propaganda narrative is useful to the elite because it allows the elite to maintain their monopoly on UFO/ET technology, and prevents competition and innovation that threaten their global special interests in energy, transportation, medicine, and defense, etc. In my opinion this UFO/ET suppression and cover-up is causing severe damage to society and the environment and is destroying humanity's future.

In this book I attempt to organize the huge seventy plus years of almost unmanageable best accumulated evidence, in such a manner, that it is the evidence that proves my exopolitical arguments. I hope you the reader will give me that chance and stick with me through the duration, for I believe our very future depends upon the public becoming well informed on this.

If you have not paid attention to the evidence of extraterrestrial contact, or have only been exposed to silly fabricated UFO/ET stories at the local supermarket checkout counter, or on the Internet social networks, some questions may come to mind. You may rightly ask; if this is so, how come I and so many other people don't know this? Why don't the ET's just land on the White House lawn? If our governments know this, why have we not been told? Even if this is true, I don't see how it's going to affect me?

It's always a struggle to reduce complex problems down to their fundamentals. The best simple explanation I have been able to come up with is this: Contrary to what many people have been let to believe, American society and other so called free democratic societies around the globe, are to a very large degree not organized and operated by the people, but by a globalist corporate elite, that manage world populations through finance, politics, the military and the media.[3]

The truth is that feudalism is still the dominate organization structure in earth human society, even while it adapts to modern realities by becoming ever more secretive, covert, deceptive, and Orwellian. Democratic ideals and institutions are continuously being subverted and manipulated to maintain the feudalistic agenda of top down control over society. In reality, despite what the mass media would have you believe, democracy and republican ideals have yet to take root very deeply in a still very feudal humanity, albeit with modern technological trappings.

The globalists are promoting what they call, The New World Order, which they stole from the theosophists. The theosophists believed in an enlightened altruistic New World Order, but the globalists subverted the meaning of the phrase in order to deceive global populations, fraudulently repackaging the Old Feudalistic Order as The New World Order. In this book I intend to take back the concept and call the Old Feudalistic Order for what it really is today, The New World Disorder!

President Franklin D. Roosevelt said: "The truth of the matter is, as you know and I know, that a financial element in the large centers has owned the government ever since the days of Andrew Jackson." This is something that people in the Occupy Movement on the left, and the Tea Party on the right, are just beginning to figure out in mass.

Why Is There a Cover-up of Extraterrestrial Reality?

We really can't understand extraterrestrial politics without understanding global politics and the nature of feudal society. If we study feudalism today we can see it is still very overt in countries run by dictatorships, but has gone underground and become more covert in the so called democratic countries.

Feudal rulers overt and covert, must maintain control over their respective populations, and to do this they must control the society's resources, information, technology, industry, media, religion, science, etc. If rulers lose control over their subjects they are subject to being overthrown by dissenters.

It's a natural thing for rulers to suppress and control information relating to extraterrestrial knowledge and technology, as it is with other important information. Today's feudal rulers have had centuries to perfect the increasingly subtle means of control and suppression of truths that could lead dissenters to rise up and overthrow them.

The slave master only allows the slave knowledge to do his or her job and no more, because to know more would be to invite rebellion. This master-slave concept of need to know has been incorporated into modern day national security top secret classification systems, where the need to know and SAPs, Special Access Programs, are often not even controlled by governments, but by corporations which in turn are controlled by the globalists.

I believe our situation in regards to the globalist elite and the intelligent universe, is similar to that of the populations of North Korea in relation to its elite and the rest of the world. The only difference is a matter of scale. The North Korean tyrants have managed to isolate and control public access to technology and knowledge available through special access to other countries.

On one hand, the North Korean elite suppress and control access by their masses to the rest of the world, even to the point of starving the masses. Yet, on the other hand they exploit their elite access to the rest of the world to their advantage and live very well with the best technology the world has to offer, and to even use that superior technology to propagandize and suppress their people.

Throughout history autocratic regimes accumulate wealth and technological luxuries for the elite that are not available to the ordinary person. For instance, in Roman times the elite had running water, flush toilets and hot baths, all luxuries at the time, that have only became commonplace in the 20th century and yet even today many people still do not have these basics.

In a sense on a small scale the autocratic elite create a small breakaway civilization more advanced than the country as a whole in which they live. This breakaway civilization draws on the resources and the labor of the people in a parasitic manner, taking much more than is given back to the host society.

I think the reader as he or she becomes better informed; will come to realize that the global elite are doing the exact same thing to global populations as national elites have done to their individual countries. I intend to make the case, in this book, that the globalist elite have used their global networks of corporate trusts and monopolies to isolate global populations from knowledge about extraterrestrial reality in order to further their own selfish interests. There is nothing special about the elite taking such a stance; they are subverting all other aspects of global society and the environment for their self-interest.

The covert feudal elite have subverted UFO/ET understanding amongst global populations by creating and supporting a very effective secret policy of denial and ridicule around the UFO/ET subject through official institutions including the mainstream media which they control. It would be well to remember the words of the first director of the CIA, Admiral Roscoe Henry Hillenkoetter.[4] "Behind the scenes, high-ranking Air Force officers are soberly concerned about UFOs. But through official secrecy and ridicule, many citizens are led to believe the unknown flying objects are nonsense."

There exist declassified CIA documents that discuss the creation and implementation of this wall of ridicule and denial around the extraterrestrial subject. Investigator Jim Marrs author of the book; 'Rule by Secrecy' did a good job of summarizing how this official policy of denial and ridicule came to be in his article, UFO's Over Washington Prompted Policy of Denial and Ridicule.[5] Jim Marrs said, "With the CIA-dominated Robertson Panel, the U.S. Government thus began a conscious program of dismissal and ridicule regarding UFOs, which has continued; with only minor interruptions, to this day."

This national and international policy of denial and ridicule filters down into the public domain and we have to look no further than to Nick Pope. Nick now an advocate for disclosure, once headed the UK's Ministry of Defense UFO Office, and made the following public confession in this *Huffington Post* article.[6]

"I'm a little bit apologetic about this because obviously, when I was in MOD, I had to play this game myself. To really achieve our policy of downplaying the UFO phenomenon, we would use a combination of 'spin and dirty tricks.' We used terms like UFO buffs and UFO spotters. Terms that mean these people are nut jobs. In other words, we were implying that this is just a very somewhat quaint hobby that people have as opposed to a serious research interest." But Pope said the ridicule policy went much further than that.

"Another trick would be deliberately using phrases like 'little green men.' We were trying to do two things: either to kill any media story on the subject, or if a media story ran, insure that it ran in such a way that it would make the subject seem ridiculous and that it would make people who were interested in this seem ridiculous."

The UFO/ET cover-up is a very well-funded, organized, and orchestrated process, that began in the 1940's to divert and mislead public attention into a false NASA - SETI narrative that maybe ET is out there somewhere, but certainly not here in our own back yard where we are making trillions of dollars revere engineering ET technologies and suppressing exotic free energy technologies. Oh no, don't believe your lying eyes! Folks need to keep in mind that many of our early military and civilian leaders that created this false propaganda narrative were enamored of, and applied magician tricks to manage public perception and awareness on a mass scale.

The scope of the mass deception of the public mind is mind-boggling and requires huge resources and a coordinated effort organized covertly under the guise of national security. For example, NASA whistle-blower Donna Hare spent most of her professional life involved in the Space Program as a technical illustrator and held a Secret Clearance.

When a person signs a security oath, they essentially give up their individual rights and liberties in a free society, and henceforth the global elite feel they essentially own these people and they belong to the classified, covert breakaway society. When whistle-blowers talk about the fraud they come in contact with in the breakaway society, that is a sure recipe for harassment, jail and even death! Still these true heroes do speak out, even when they know that they could lose everything, but they are willing to take this risk not for personal gain, but for the good of humanity.

Donna Hare like so many other whistle-blowers opens a small window into the immensity of the cover-up fraud being perpetrated on the people. In an interview with Elaine Douglass, Donna asked;

> "Is it a UFO?" He said, "Well I can't tell you." And then I asked him, "What are you going to do with this piece of information?" And he said, "Well we have to airbrush these things out before we sell these photographs to the public." So I realized at that point that there is a procedure setup to take care of this type of information from the public."[7]

It is my contention that the military industrial complexes of the United States, Germany, and other allies, have operated a kind of Alien Resource Cartel or trust, to exploit and maintain their special access to ET reality and the advanced technologies involved. This corporate cartel or trust closely affiliated with the still classified MJ 12 organization, has been used to secretly accumulate trillions of dollars in wealth for it members, secretly inserting alien technologies into national defense and into the public marketplace. National security is being used as a means to fraudulently maintain the UFO/ET cover-up as long as possible, in order to prevent business competition and liability.

This process of secret technological insertion and transfer has been well explained and documented in Colonel Philip J. Corso's[8] book; *The Day After Roswell*.[9] Colonel Corso was a member of President Eisenhower's National Security Council and the former head of the Foreign Technology Desk at the U.S.

Army's Research and Development Department. On Corso's book jacket it says;

> "As Chief of the Army's foreign Technology Division in 1961, Philip J. Corso stewarded the Roswell, New Mexico, alien artifacts in a reverse-engineering project that led to today's integrated circuit chips, fiber optics, lasers, super-tenacity fibers and 'seeded' the Roswell alien technology to giants of American industry."

My contention is that like their smaller national elite counterparts in nations, the globalist fascist elite rule a very advanced, multi-national, classified, criminal enterprise, using fear, intimidation and greed, disguised in the name of national security, special access and need to know. Due to the extreme compartmentalization, most people involved in the national security apparatus of countries, don't see nor understand the big picture, for if they did they would revolt against this covert tyranny.

Many of us believe that the dark fascist world envisioned by George Orwell has now secretly become a reality. Don't forget that millions of Jews were secretly degraded by the German media and then murdered under German top secret classified national security programs. The German SS propaganda operations helped turned a whole nation into terrorist fanatics and or sympathizers. Many of the key individuals involved in SS propaganda and intelligence operations after the war were secretly incorporated into the heart of American fascist society by CIA operatives like Allen Dulles under Operation Paperclip.[10]

The German fascist leadership was not destroyed by the war. It was simply relocated, and then re-established in Germany and Italy after a few years. The globalist fascists networks were only temporarily disrupted by the war and have continued to grow and prosper unchecked in the economic, political, and national security organizations of world governments to the extent that the people of these countries have little real control over their governments and economic systems.

Critics just can't comprehend that if the German military industrial complex propaganda machine could turn a whole nation into terrorists, would it not be hard for the globalists now in control of governments to organize and orchestrate a global propaganda operation to cover-up the truth about extraterrestrial life? National security states can easily merge propaganda, security oaths, and crash retrieval teams to effectively discredit and plug whistle-blower leaks, and confiscate the hard evidence. This is a recipe for a formidable system of information command control.

So where is the money coming from to fund such operations? Many of us believe that trillions of dollars are being siphoned off by this covert, parasitic, classified world from the host society through black projects, drug running, manipulation of paper money, reverse engineering technology and reintroduction of that technology into society as original intellectual property for immense profit.

The extent of the fraud is so great that it is difficult for the ordinary citizen to grasp the immensity of the grand deception. No amount of credible collaborated evidence will satisfy the honest skeptic, unless they can comprehend the immensity of the globalist command and control apparatus in which the UFO/ET issue is embedded.

The Pentagon recently admitted that they had somehow lost track of three trillion dollars. Now where did that huge amount of taxpayer money really go, certainly not for 100 dollar toilet seats as they would have you believe! Ex-Canadian Defense Minister Paul Hellyer[11] did a very good job of explaining this global fraud in his article, *'Global Fraud, Global Hope'* that I publish in chapter eleven.[12]

Many former astronauts have spoken out publicly, but who is really listening?

Former NASA astronaut Edgar Mitchell[13] said;

> "A few insiders know the truth . . . and are studying the bodies that have been discovered," Mitchell, who landed on the moon

with Alan B. Shepard, also said; "A 'cabal' of insiders stopped briefing presidents about extraterrestrials after President Kennedy."

Buckminster Fuller[14] drives home the point that even the President of the United States no longer holds any real power, having been degraded to the status of globalist Cheerleader in Chief. The same goes for our Congress as well. No wonder peoples all over the world have lost faith in their governments. Fuller says;

> "The USA is not run by its would-be "democratic" government," "Nothing could be more pathetic than the role that has to be played by the President of the United States, whose power is approximately zero. Nevertheless, the news media and most over-thirty-years-of-age USA citizens carry on as if the President has supreme power."

I hope the reader can appreciate how interconnected are global politics, Exopolitics and individual sovereignty. Any of these in their own right, are difficult enough to understand and all have been almost impossible for the layperson to grasp. Still, there is hope for a bright future for humanity if citizens can overcome their fears and apathy, stop complaining and become an activist force to be reckoned with. Somebody somewhere said that thank goodness for the young, because they don't realize that it can't be done, so they find a way to do it!

I believe earth humanity is slowly evolving a higher order of fractal, from a feudalistic society into an altruistic society that will operate less like the predator/prey food chain and more the way our bodies are organized. Some extraterrestrial civilizations seem to have already made this jump in consciousness, while others are still in the same predicament we are in, hence the covert elite contact with extraterrestrial races much like ourselves.

We can learn a lot from contact with these other extraterrestrial civilizations. I hope the reader can appreciate that in order to accelerate our human evolution, we must have a free flow of extraterrestrial related information through all independent sovereign individuals, and not top down information flows that isolate and degrade individual sovereignty and keep us isolated from the rest of the intelligent universe. We must end the UFO/ET cover-up now!

Explaining Exopolitics

As I mentioned earlier, Exopolitics is a relatively new field of inquiry that just recently emerged out of the older UFO/ET field sometimes called Ufology. The emergence of Exopolitics has been remarkably similar to the rise of the ecological field out of the older natural sciences. I was fortunate to have been raised in a family of early ecologists and to have actually been mentored by one of the founders of ecology, Herb Stoddard, a close friend and mentor of my Dad, the first widely recognized fire ecologist in his own right.

Herb Stoddard was a close friend and associate of Aldo Leopold. My Dad was mentored first by an ecology founder Dr Allee, while at the University of Chicago, and then later by Herb. When I was a boy, Herb owned the plantation next door, and was like a grandfather to me.

In the 1920's museum collectors like Herb and my Dad and my Uncle, began to think beyond the accumulation and categorizing of specimens for natural history museums. They realized that the flora and fauna in nature were in dynamic complex interactions with each other. In the 1980's having investigated and studied UFO's and extraterrestrial life for over a decade, I and a few others in the public domain realized that humanity was in dynamic interaction with many extraterrestrial species.

When Alfred Webre introduced the term Exopolitics into the public domain over a decade ago, this galvanized into organized action several individuals who had been already thinking along these lines. These individuals were Paola Harris, Michael Salla, Alfred Webre, Tom Hansen, Steve Bassett, Manuel Lamiroy and myself. Other credible people soon became involved, including Neil Gould and David Griffin.

In such a manner the new field of Exopolitics came into existence, and now over a decade later it has spread to most countries around the globe with many new exopolitical leaders emerging too numerous to mention, due in a large part to Steve Bassett and the 'Exopolitics World Network' (EWN)[15] and Dr Michael Salla's 'Exopolitics Institute'[16] which I and several others helped create and develop.

Overnight Exopolitics became controversial, partly because of credibility problems among some of the founders who have promoted a mix of credible and not credible contactees, abductees, and whistle-blowers. Many credible important UFO/ET investigators have wrongly turned away from Exopolitics seeing the glass half empty rather than half full.

Exopolitics is still in the process of sorting out its true leaders, but critics have been guilty of throwing the baby out with the bathwater as well. On the other hand, a large part of the criticism has been unfounded due to the inability of many in the UFO community to comprehend and wrap their minds around the big picture.

Even the word 'Exopolitics,' like the phrase 'New World Order,' has essentially been stolen and subverted by unscrupulous practitioners and contactee frauds. I have been advised to drop the name Exopolitics altogether from this book by a very well respected individual from the aerospace industry, because the word has become so toxic in some quarters. Still there are many who are honest and credible in the field. I have decided in the book to take a stand for the truthful and the honest, and not retreat from the term, the disinformation operatives be damned! ☺

The battle to control language and information is a battle to control our minds and bodies. Words and concepts can be used for healing and as weapons of mass destruction. It's important to choose our words wisely in our communications with others.

I hope that the evidence I present in this book will cause the reader to at least think more deeply about Exopolitics. If I am lucky, perhaps I will be able to assist a few others in a personal transformation, as grand new vistas of human knowledge open before them, as happened with me in the past. Let's not forget we all stand on the shoulders of those that came before.

CHAPTER ONE

EVOLUTION ON OTHER WORLDS

"We find ourselves faced by powers which are far stronger than we had hitherto assumed, and whose base is at present unknown to us. More I cannot say at present. We are now engaged in entering into closer contact with those powers, and in six or nine months' time it may be possible to speak with more precision on the matter." The Father of Rocket Science, Werner von Braun, in reference to the deflection of the U.S. Juno 2 rocket from its orbit.

"It is my thesis that flying saucers are real, and that they are space ships from another solar system. I think that they possibly are manned by intelligent observers who are members of a race that may have been investigating our earth for centuries." Hermann Julius Oberth - One of the founding fathers of rocketry and astronautics. The American Weekly magazine, October 24, 1954.

After he said this, he was taken up before their very eyes, and a cloud hid him from their sight. They were looking intently up into the sky as he was going, when suddenly two men dressed in white stood beside them. "Men of Galilee," They said, "why do you stand here looking into the sky? This same Jesus, who has been taken from you into Heaven, will come back in the same way you have seen him go into heaven." Acts 1

NASA scientists involved with the Kepler planet-hunting telescope say that just our galaxy alone could be home to as many as 50 billion planets. This estimate is based on a sample of 1,235 found so far in a very small region of space. Of the 1,235 planets found so far, 54 of those are just the right distance from their sun where temperatures should be right for liquid water needed for organic life to develop.

The Kepler craft was launched in March 2009. Of the probable 50 billion planets[17] NASA speculates that at least 500 million reside in the habitable zone. We can see that with 500 million in the habitable zone in just our own galaxy, then just multiply that by the total number of galaxies in the known universe and the number become astronomical. Even as I edit this book NASA continues to up the count to hundreds of billions of planets in the habitable zone around stars in just our galaxy.

I have found it fascinating to discover, from the many cases of extraterrestrial contact and my own observations of the natural evolutionary processes on earth that these same evolutionary processes or laws also apply on other planets. Species seem to evolve using the same evolutionary strategies in environments similar to earth, resulting in insects, fishes, amphibians, reptiles, mammals, primates, even humans.

It would appear that one of the major determining factors as to whether an insect, reptile or mammal develops high intelligence on a planet, are environmental catastrophes that disrupt the evolutionary process. If the asteroid that hit earth had not destroyed the dinosaurs, except for the birds, earth may well have evolved an intelligent reptile instead of a mammal. If the hit had been even worse and only insects survived, earth might have evolved an intelligent insect. This is what extraterrestrial contact cases seem to be telling us.

I am not the first to think along these lines. Stevens and Steinman devote a number of pages in *'UFO Crash at Aztec'*[18] to this subject. They state:

> "A considerable proportion of the extraterrestrial human-like beings reported, fall into general classification quite different and distinct from Earth humanity. Walt Andrus at APRO's UFO '79 in San Diego gave a talk on extraterrestrial beings observed and described, in which he suggested that roughly 1/3 of the ET beings reported seem to be very similar to the contemporary humanity on this planet.
>
> He suggested that another 1/3 of the ET beings reported could be grouped in a similar way into a different category of human-like beings distinct from the physiology of Earth humans. The remaining 1/3 was a catch-all category including other physiological morphologies quite different from Earth humans, and of sizes both considerably larger and substantially smaller.
>
> What if the second largest category, which seems to have a number of similarities within the variety of the group, something like the general similarities among human species and types, sprang from a different evolution entirely? Do we have any evidence to support such a hypothesis? How different would they be? What would they look like? How does our observed evidence compare?
>
> Taking a cue from Dr Bernard E. Finch's article; *'Dinosaurs... Not Humanoids?'* published in *Flying Saucer Review* for January 1982, where Finch makes the interesting observation that an intelligent species having evolved from reptilian forbearers would develop "remarkable similarities to descriptions of the (UFO) aliens which are received from many sources," and statements by Adrian J. Desmond in his book *'The Hot-Blooded Dinosaurs,'* that the most intriguing Late Cretaceous inhabitants were the in-

telligent 'mimics' unearthed in recent years, wide-eyed ostrich dinosaurs, and dromaeosaurids like Deinonychus and Saurornithoides, with stereo-vision functionally mated to opposable thumbs.

These dinosaurs, capable of more skilled behavioral feats than any land animal hitherto, were separated from other dinosaurs by a gulf comparable to that dividing Men from Cows. The disparity in brain size is staggering—who know what new peaks the sophisticated 'bird-mimics' would have attained had they survived into the 'Age of Mammals?' Erich A. Aggen Jr prepared an article, *'Possible Reptilian Origins of Certain UFO Occupants'* for the *MUFON Journal.* Aggen argues; had the dinosaurs not died out, they quite likely could have become the dominant form of life on Earth.

Mammalian life succeeded only because the more aggressive and predatory dinosaurs were removed from the scene. On many other planets with more favorable conditions, Reptilian life could have survived and attained its full potential. An intelligent species evolved from reptiles would certainly possess many of the physiological characteristics we have come to identify in certain groups of UFO occupants."

In order to illustrate this concept of similar evolutionary development on other worlds, I present several contact cases to the reader, so that folks can draw their own opinion as to the validity of this idea. In later chapters I intend to build on cases such as these to roughly illustrate in much more detail, something of the motives and agendas of specific extraterrestrial races and their civilizations. I intend to concentrate specifically on the many human civilizations similar to our own, because I think that is where our humanity has the most in common. It is the greater humanity to which we are only one small part.

On the other hand certain non-human types or humanoids, with some human genetics, have had major impacts on our humanity for a very long time and bring up many issues, or imperatives of contact, especially national security, cultural and genome issues. It is increasingly obvious that we are not the top predators on this planet as is widely believed. There are more evolved very sophisticated predators that seem to prey on our earth human society way beyond our current range of perception.

Our common defense against these predatory ET types is limited but growing. Air Forces around the world in the 1950's were estimated to be losing an aircraft a day trying to intercept UFO's, and I suspect that this prompted Five Star General Douglas MacArthur who built extensive UFO/ET files in the 1940's to state in 1955 that; "The next war will be an interplanetary war. The nations must someday make a common front against attack by people from other planets." Fortunately this dire prediction has not yet come to pass.

I would place two autocratically organized races in this category, a species of the Greys, who have one of their bases at Nellis according to Charles Hall, and a seemingly degenerate faction of the Annunaki known as the 'fallen angels' of the Bible, the losers of the battle in heaven. Both these races or factions of races, while quite different, do seem to utilize very proficiently and subtly the skills of the predator, including secrecy, deception, fear, intimidation, confusion stealth, misdirection, perception management etc., to manipulate individuals and our society. Both of these races seem to be collaborating with the global elite, all having the common agenda to create an undemocratic and highly autocratic earth human society in which there would be little human freedom and liberty for the ordinary person.

Both of these civilizations have the technological abilities so as to appear human, or as any other animal for that matter, so this can confuse the investigators ability to sort out who is really human and who is not. One can get on the Internet and see that the military is making great strides in cloaking technologies so as to appear invisible or to appear as something other than what is. The radar image of a plane can be made to look like that of a bird for instance, or a human being almost invisible, or something else altogether, by manipulating light using holographic projection.

What follows are a few select cases of different types of extraterrestrials that give something of an idea of cosmic evolutionary history and a glimpse of very different agendas and motivations that will be brought up later in more detail.

Insect-like Extraterrestrials

Let's start with a type of insectoid extraterrestrial that has been seen during some abductions. Abductees often tell of Praying Mantis insect types of extraterrestrials. This first contact case illustrates this type of extraterrestrial Insectoid encountered in Sierakow, Poland. This was published in a UFO Digest Article[19] by Dirk Vander Ploeg.

"While camping near Sierakow Lake in the summer of 2001 a young 20-year old woman has a strange encounter. It was late in the evening when she began heading back to her campsite. She was walking beside the edge of a forest that led to the meadow that led to her tent. The meadow was approximately 200 meters (666 feet) in length. Suddenly, she saw a huge mantis like creature that appeared to bend over and picked up something. "When the entity heard me, it became scared and began fleeing," she said and added; "I stood there as if petrified when it crossed my path and stopped seven to eight meters a head (23 - 26.5 feet). Both of us were scared."

The young woman, who wishes her identity to remain anonymous, believes the creature she encountered was also a female. It looked like a huge insect and reminded her of a praying mantis with an elongated and skinny face and oval-shaped head. It was short and fragile being only 1.5 to 1.6 meters high (5.0 - 5.3 feet). It had skin that was gray or beige in color. This creature seemed to have wings or something resembling wings that were long and narrow and attached to the creature's back. Looking into the creatures eyes was terrifying according to the young woman. The eyes were dark and emotionless.

"That thing was looking at me and I knew that it was confused as well. Our meeting wasn't intentional. It was surprised." she added. The creature then disappeared back into the field. The next day she returned to the spot where the encounter has occurred and she found small footprints on the edge of the field. It is not known if photos or casts were made of the footprints."

A word search on the Internet yielded some more cases of insect type ET encounters. Researcher Vicki Cameron reported the following:

"Abduction researcher Brian Thompson claims that a nurse acquaintance of his reported that during 1957 in Cincinnati she encountered a 3-foot-tall (0.91 m) praying mantis-like entity two days after a V-shaped UFO sighting. This mantis-like creature is reminiscent of the insectoid-type entity reported in some abduction accounts. He related this report to fellow researcher Leonard Stringfield. Stringfield told him of two cases he had in his files where separate witnesses reported identical circumstances in the same place and year."

Abduction researcher Karla Turner, in her book *'Into the Fringe'*[20] reported that a man called David remembered an encounter with a giant mantis during a hypnosis session.

Linda Moulton Howe in *'Glimpses of Other Realities'*[21] describes some claims of alien mantis. The book includes the cases of Linda Porter and David Huggins. In 1988 Linda Porter remembered an abduction by alien mantis beings which she said took place when she was a child. In the same year 1988 David Huggins remembered an encounter with alien mantis that he said took place in the 1950's, when he was a child.

The book reports also the case of Jeanne Robinson, which said she had received messages by an alien similar to a mantis. According to Ms Robinson, these aliens are a branch of Greys. Vicki Cameron in UFO experience in Canada reported a case of abduction by an insectoid alien similar to a grasshopper.

Reptilian Extraterrestrials

This next case experienced by the Cherry Hinkle family illustrates a type of reptilian extraterrestrial species. The case is titled: *'Reptilian Encounter in the Nevada Desert'*[22] by Cherry

Hinkle, and I have permission to publish it here. She says this case is deeply personal and has had trouble with people taking her words out of context to discredit her and this case.

"Henderson, Nevada: The city of Las Vegas with its well-known Strip and glittering casinos, as well as the communities north of Las Vegas and Henderson, fill this crowded desert Nevada valley. Black Mountain looms over the desert community of Henderson situated on the east slopes of the valley. That dark mountain is the home of many television towers and other towers on the top. It is the home of mines and caves that pock the sides of Black Mountain.

Today, there are businesses and homes, and a freeway that cut into the slopes of that mountain, but in the middle of the 1970's there was just open desert from the middle of town to the mountain. More open undisturbed miles of desert inhabit the space up until sparkling Las Vegas. With the building boom, homes and businesses now crowd the once open desert.

In 1977, every kid in town knew the rules - do not climb or play on that mountain. All parents understood of the constant danger of the deep open mines and caves, but danger lures the younger set, and several deaths occurred on the slopes of Black Mountain.

It was on a pleasant day, and my thirteen-year-old son Marc and his friend Harry, roamed in the empty desert between my house, and the forbidden Black Mountain. Being adventurous boys, the chance to explore a cave and carry back a rock or two, and a lifetime of memories is enough to break the rules.

They hiked maybe the scant one mile across the desert and climbed the little hills in front of Black Mountain. On the backside of one of the little hills, Marc and Harry located a cave. They had to squirm into the narrow opening, and belly crawl through the cave to the larger room and turned on their small pocket flashlights. They saw a circular room roughly nine feet across. Near the back wall, they spotted a large deeper hole. They found several large branches that someone had dragged about a mile from the closest tree, and tossed the branches into the hole creating a makeshift ladder to climb down into the lower pit.

The pit was roomy, with a short annex. Occasional debris littered the rocky floor, like a tin can or two, a battered teen magazine perched on a small outcrop of rock that served as shelf. The boys explored the main cave, and then turned their attention to the short tunnel or annex.

Sounds carry in a cave, and the walls slightly vibrate if a loud voice reverberates throughout the small room. It was then, that the boys heard the sounds of voices and maybe the distance humming of machines. Intrigued by the thought that there was mining nearby, the boys went deeper into the tunnel. On the far end, they found a rusty metal door, and near the door a strange metal rod. The one-foot rod was lightweight and resembled aluminum, with a cap on one end and a few strange engravings on one side.

Marc weaved the rod through the belt loops of his jeans, focused the beam of his flashlight on the door, and tried the doorknob. He discovered a strong bolt secured the door from the reverse side. Harry shook the doorknob and pounded on it a few times. Startled, the boys heard the sound or guttural harsh voices talking, and the certain sound of approaching footsteps. They suddenly felt a wave of fear, knowing they were inside a forbidden cave, weaponless, and an angry animalistic growling voice attempted to open the door any second.

Marc, the taller of the two, pushed Harry up the makeshift ladder and scrambled up the wood branch to the upper level of the cave. They heard the metal door clank and squeak loudly as the door opened. The boys crawled as quickly through the narrow tunnel, and outside, the stood up and ran about the distance of a city block away from the cave entrance. They laughed at their dirty hands and faces, relieved they escaped from the unknown man with harsh voices in the cave. They looked at the strangely engraved rod, trying to figure out what language might include circles, ovals, swirls and triangles.

Without a warning, they heard a loud threatening growl. Harry and Marc looked back at the cave entrance and to their horrified eyes; they watched as a very large greenish humanoid struggled to force his big body out of narrow cave. The boys screamed and started running down the slope of the hill, running top speed! They didn't look back until they were near my back yard.

They slowed down, breathing hard and glanced back to the mountain.

To their shock and fear, the huge humanoid was trotting towards them! They started screaming again, put on a burst of speed, and ran into the house; Marc locked the door screaming: Mom! Mom! Help us Mom! He's going to get us. Alarmed, I ran into family room, and both boys threw their arms around me, crying. They both were shaking, not just their hands, but also their entire body shook! Wet tears left muddy tracks across their cheeks. Marc begged, "Don't open the door Mom, he going to get us!" Meanwhile, Harry added. "He is big, and looks mean! Don't open that door – please, please, don't open that door!"

Instantly I was furious with the man that generated such terror these young boys! At thirteen, boys are usually trying to impress everyone how brave they can be, so I know it took a lot of nerve to admit that much fear. I told them: "Boys, you go get a drink of water and let me go talk to this man," but they tightened their grip on me, screaming: "No, No, And No! That guy will kill you! He is not a man! Don't go out there Mom!"

I managed to coax one arm free from each boy. I looked into their worried eyes. "Boys – nobody is going to kill anybody, and you know I won't allow anyone to hurt you! Now – what do you mean he is not a man? Is it a woman that is threatening you?" "No Mom, it's a man, sort of, he looks like a man. But his face looks like a snake or Yeah, like a Lizard man! He's ugly and he doesn't wear anything. He's naked, except a wide belt with stuff on it."

I stared at my son, imagining some teenager wearing a Halloween costume. I laughed a little, and said, "Boys, it was just someone playing a joke on you!" Both boys started protesting again, both talking at the same time. I could hear the panic in their voices rising again, and finally Harry said, "That guy couldn't be wearing any costume, he could barely squeeze himself out of the cave, he would have ripped the costume into pieces!"

"What cave? Did you boys to up on Black Mountain even when you knew the danger?" I asked. "Mom, listen to me; it was a lizard man and he was naked. I've never seen a costume that shows everything, he was naked Mom, and it was not a costume! You know what I mean Mom?"

With difficulty, I untangled myself from the tight grip boys, and looked out the window. I peered carefully out the widow expecting the spectacle of a "Lizard man," but nothing moved, not a child, not a man and no lizard man. I reassured the boys the danger is in the past and the man was long gone.

It was at that point, I noticed Marc was holding a strange metal rod. "What do you have in your hand son?" Marc glanced at the rod and threw it on the floor as if it would burn his hand. I leaned to pick it up but Harry grabbed my arm, warning it was dangerous, maybe a weapon. I picked it up reminding them they carried it from the mountain safely all that time, so it couldn't be too dangerous.

The rod was approximate one and a half inch across, maybe a foot long with a slight indentation at one end and a plain grey cap on the other. I looked at the bizarre symbols engraved in a three-inch section of the rod. It was just symbols, from spirals, circles of different sizes, a few triangles, and a few unknown symbols. There were no levers or buttons, and the cap at the end didn't seem to move. The rod, with its professionally created symbols and smooth to the touch, I knew it was not a toy, but nothing I recognized.

It was late afternoon, and the long shadows cast ominous shapes in the yard, I knew Harry was still too nervous to walk home alone. Marc and I walked the distance of two houses and made sure he was safe inside before we walked home. That night, Marc was still nervous, peeking out the curtains often, expecting the worse. Marc played Scrabble with his sisters, anything to keep his mind busy. Near midnight, we went to bed.

It must have been around two in the morning when Marc shook me whispering harshly that someone is trying to get into his bedroom window. I hoped it was just a nightmare, or his nerves were still on edge. Quietly we slipped into his bedroom and listened to the sounds of scraping at the window edge! He was not mistaken – in the light of the moon I could make out the silhouette head and shoulders of a man.

I was alone with my four kids, no husband to protect us, so I grabbed my flashlight; suddenly tossed the curtains open to face the man. There was a glare from the flashlight on the window, but past glare that I could clearly see a large head with ridges on the top, other ridges on his cheekbones, and the glow of golden eyes. Marc and I stood still, unmoving, both fear and shock kept us frozen. The Lizard man didn't move either, his hand still poised in his attempt pry the window open. He hand was large, with webbed rough, gnarly looking fingers, with powerful claws.

After a couple minutes, not seconds, but long agonized minutes with our hearts pounding I knew I had to do something. One hand still holding the flashlight beam on his face and my eyes still locked into those golden eyes, I fumbled around in the dark with my other hand, hoping to find something to use as a weapon, is needed. He glanced at my hand, looked back into my eyes. He turned his head a little, as if he was asking a questioning, he slightly opened his lipless lips, displaying four of his pointed teeth, and suddenly he turned and ran off into the desert.

Marc suddenly closed the curtains, grabbed my hand and led my shaking legs to the edge of his bed. We sat there for a few silent minutes. We just sat there, trying to comprehend the incredible event, with little success. We started talking at the same time, and started checking the doors and windows repeatedly. His sisters were completely awake by then, and we all talked all night, going from windows to doors until full sunlight.

Later in the morning, we decided the reason the Lizard man was breaking in the house was to reclaim that metal rod. Marc and I hiked back to the cave and placed the strange rod beside the cave entrance. The Lizard man never again attempted to enter this house, and for that, I am relieved.

After a few days, I went outside and looked at that window. It was then that I found that that bottom edge of that window is close to six feet high from the ground. It was a shock to realize the lizard man must have been very tall, over seven feet tall! Inside the windows are high, but about five feet high, from outside there is no way no one could look through this window – unless they were extremely tall.

This event is real. "Harry" is not the real name, but since I have been unable to locate him and ask permission, I used a pseudo name. Marc's name is real, and he was my only son. Marc died in 1999. I still live in sight of Black Mountain. People living close to that mountain sometimes report underground rumbling at night when it is quiet. UFO's are often seen and photographed over Black Mountain, that shouldn't be too surprising; we live not far from Area 51 in Nevada."

In the article 'Missouri Caver Encounters Underground Reptilian Humanoid, [23] we find a remarkably similar reptilian case. Lon Strickler writes, "I received an intriguing typed letter in the mail from Jerry (not the witness' real name) who now lives on the US west coast. No contact information was given. A bit of personal information was removed in order for me to post and also preserve the witness' anonymity.

"Sir, this is the first time I am disclosing my experience to the public. My family has been previously informed of the details. At the time, I owned a small business which I had started after I finished a 12 year stint in the military. I was then living near Eldridge, Missouri and was raised in the general area and knew the terrain fairly well. I had spent time at the US Army Engineer School in Fort Leonard Wood, Missouri and some of the training included spelunking. When I left the Army I continued to explore caves as recreation.

In 1993 I helped form a local group of experienced 'cavers.' We would get together on weekends and explore some of the cavern systems throughout Missouri and Arkansas. The experience I am about to describe took place in the summer of 1995. I was on my own that day, which was not uncommon.

I had decided to check out a cave in Camden County, Missouri which was part of a fairly large system in the area. From what I could tell, this particular cave had not been explored for a long period of time. The entrance was very narrow and well hidden. After squeezing through the opening, I descended another 50 feet or so before the cave began to open up into a series of chambers. I moved through several of these chambers taking my time to examine the area for possible artifacts and formations. I finally reached, what I thought was, the end of the cave.

I started to hear a rustling sound that was echoing from a small opening near the top of the chamber. I assumed the sounds were bats and didn't pay much attention to it. But after a while I heard motorized sounds and talking. I stood and listened for several minutes wondering what was on the other side of this chamber. The opening was about 10 feet above me. I maneuvered my way up to the opening which was flat and narrow, but big enough for me to get a decent look into it.

As I positioned myself to the front of the opening, I started to see light at the other end. The passageway was only a few feet long, but it was just too narrow for me to move through. As I looked through the opening there was a very warm draft of air hitting my face. As well, the air had a very acrid vinegar-like odor. There was a very large and well lit 'room' with limestone walls. I noticed a small vehicle that looked like a golf cart but was very low to the ground and without wheels. I continued to observe until I started to hear voices that were getting louder and nearer. Something was making its way towards the vehicle. I had to rub my eyes because I didn't believe what I was looking at.

This 'creature,' because it was not a man, stood about 7 foot and had brown scaly skin. The face and head were shaped like a human with a flat nose but there were no ears or hair. The top of the head had a slight scaly ridge that extended down the back of the neck. From what I could see it had lips and regular sized eyes. The arms were very long and muscular with human-like hands. It also had a massive 4-5 foot tail that tampered to a point. It was dressed in a gold metallic outfit with long pants and shoes. It also carried an oval pack attached to its back.

I watched as this thing was looking at something on the vehicle. I had a high speed camera which I use to document my cave explorations. I was able to obtain a few distorted images of the being. For some reason while I was taking photos the creature stopped and turned, looking in my direction. I'm not sure if it heard me but it definitely knew of my presence. It then made a terrible 'hissing' sound as it continued to look in my direction. That was enough for me. I quickly started making a beeline out of the cave. When I reached the entrance I was shaking and hyperventilating. I finally reached my vehicle and drove home.

I continue to explore caves in the area. I have heard stories of people encountering strange underground beings, but I have never disclosed my experience. A few years after my experience I went back to the cave but was unable to get near it since the area is now government property. I can assume that I witnessed something that I was not supposed to see. It pains me to think what secrets are being kept from us. To those who say that there are no non-humans living among us, well, think again. They are here. I do have the aforementioned evidence of the experience but I do not wish to release this at the present time."

While these two accounts may be characteristic of some types of reptilian species, alien autopsy reports often describe that the skin and other characteristics on some types of Greys seems to indicate reptilian ancestry, other autopsy reports indicate maybe even amphibian ancestry, where the species has no digestive tract and may absorb nutrients through the skin or possibly intravenously.

It's clear that there are several species lumped together under the category of Grey and I think this will only be cleared up over time as more information becomes available in the public domain. It also would appear that artificial biological engineering could be involved because of the lack of a digestive tract on some of these species.

I did an interview with military whistle-blower and contactee Clifford Stone in April of 2011 and he told me that the skin on an alien he had communicated with since childhood had a chameleon type skin, which may or may not be the same as described below in an excerpt from Len Springfield's *Status Report 2*. The report interviews several medical doctors who did autopsies on ET bodies from UFO crash sites.

> "ET had large heads and were around 4 ft. tall. They have small noses and mouths with no ears or hair. The ET photo that I have was taken by an ET and has an eye diameter of an inch. He has his left hand raised in a salute. That hand has 4 fingers on it with one finger twice as long as either outside finger. The photo was taken at a range of 3 ft. from the waist up. Brain capacity is 1800 cc versus 1300 cc for the average human.
>
> The skin is grey or ashen and under the microscope appears mesh like. This mesh like appearance gives it the reptilian texture

of granular skinned lizards like iguana or chameleon. There was a colorless liquid in the body without red cells, no lymphocytes, no hemoglobin. There was no digestive system, intestinal, alimentary canal, or rectal area in the ET autopsy. "

The following case gives the reader further insight into military interactions and involvement with extraterrestrials called the Greys, whose evolution may be a combination of artificial and natural evolution. I have had trouble as to where I wanted to put this in the book because it would go well in the next chapter on military interactions with extraterrestrials as well. I settled on this chapter because of such detailed clear descriptions of the species known as the Greys. Dr Berthold E. Schwarz, M.D. was a highly regarded UFO/ET investigator and he did an interview with an American intelligence agent many years ago. This case is from Dr Schwarz's book, *UFO Dynamics, Book 2*, page, 536.

"The intelligence officer being interviewed said a conversation had come up with a fellow intelligence officer with high security clearances and his friend asked if he wanted to see the aliens and their crafts. He suspected this was some sort of test because his friend drove right through several security checkpoints and down underground without being checked. He thought maybe this was prearranged because of what appeared to be very lax security and that somebody was testing a battle tested intelligence agent to see how he would react cold turkey to such evidence of extraterrestrial life. The story follows.

It was several years ago. I was with the military intelligence unit in Arizona. I met a friend of mine who shall remain nameless, and as I happened to mention the subject of UFO's– experiences I had had overseas –he said. Well would you like to see some Aliens? I said he was joking, but when I saw he was not, I said OK. I did know that he was with a base in Arizona, so he drove me there, but I doubt if I could ever find that place again. There was a highway above ground that went over the base, and after a turn at the entrance, we went underground.

We violated every security code in the book. Because of this and the fact that I had a top secret clearance at the time I wondered if this was some kind of a set-up, that they wanted to put a man with combat experience in this spot and see what he does– to sow the seeds of doubt. It was too obvious. We used a staff car and not a private one. We entered a vaulted area. Now this was on a week-end and the security amazed me because it was so lax.

When we got in I observed five humanoid figures. I'll give a description as best I can. Remember I doubted what I saw. They were very, very white. There were no ears, no nostrils. There were only openings: a very small mouth and the eyes were large. There was no facial hair, no head hair or pubic hair. They were nude. I think the tallest one could have been about three and a half feet – maybe a little bit taller. As I recall there were three males and two females. The heads were large–not totally out of proportion–but large. Does that make sense? It wasn't exaggerated, in other words. Slender fingers, slender legs. There was a small bone structure. Can't think of what else?

Schwarz: Did you see the genitals? I don't remember seeing that in the men, or the female organs in the women. No, I don't remember seeing breasts on the women? Schwarz: How could you tell they were women? As I recall, he told me that the female of the group, the youngest female, was not there. Now he told me that they (the entities) were vegetarians. The teeth were smooth, flat and very small. When I saw the smallest female in the group I could see clear suture marks.

My friend said there had been an autopsy, opened with a Y incision. From all this they concluded that she was hundreds of years old. There was no bruising on the body. There were no signs of injuries to any of the bodies. I wanted out. I was scared. I wanted my security, and what protection did I have if I were caught? I had no right to be there. I didn't understand anything. You get in and you don't get out. I wanted to have a clean record.

They had a craft, and here's how they got it. He didn't give me a date, but it was seen on radar in this area (Arizona). The craft appeared on radar, and then it disappeared. It was slowly going from left to right in an arching, falling-leaf motion, slowly falling or descending. You could pinpoint it by crass-triangulation (on radar). There was no pattern to this descent. It just continued from left to right until it finally settled in the desert.

When they (the military) got out there and they started examining the craft the found a small hole. Evidently a meteorite had hit this craft, causing rapid decompression, and the people died from that. They were in their seats which were tilted to back on a seventy degree angle. I left my finger prints all over. I still doubt everything. They do have the craft but where, I don't know.
Schwarz asks; "You never saw it?" I saw something, but that wasn't that.

I saw other parts that they had taken from the machine and things like that from other craft. Schwarz asks; "Other craft?" "Crashes and things like that. He told me about one particular crash. Out of somewhere there was this horrendous explosion which almost knocked a tourist's car off the road. The tourist reported it as a meteorite strike and they went out and found a UFO half buried in the sand with absolutely no damage to it." Schwarz asks; "was this in Arizona too?" "No, this was in Nevada, and this craft was brought back to the site that I saw."

Amphibian Extraterrestrials

Singer Johnny Sands claims to have had a very interesting contact experience that seems to indicate contact with an amphibian extraterrestrial type in this interview with Brent Raynes.[24] I found some interesting stuff on aquatic gods.[25] I suspect this kind of case is rare but it seems to be an honest and detailed account by Johnny Sands. This case apparently has been well researched including lie detector tests. I also find it very interesting that the military and intelligence community found this case so compelling.

"Singer, Songwriter, Stuntman, Native American, and an Alien and MIB Eyewitness Johnny Sands gives the following abbreviated autobiographical description of himself.[26] He writes: "I have been 35 years performing in the music business as a singer/songwriter & performer on shows such as NBC's 'Today Show,' 'Grand Ole Opry,' and Las Vegas, NV. I worked many years with artists like Charlie Daniels, Razzy Bailey, Merle Haggard, and the late great Conway Twitty, just to name a few. (Some non ET material deleted)

Editor: Okay. So what happened in 1976? Johnny Sands: Sure. Well, actually we were on the record promotion tour and I was to be in Las Vegas to appear at the Sierra Hotel. I was working on the program there and we were going to radio stations and newspapers to get this program off the ground. Las Vegas was kind of the kingdom of entertainment and so I agreed to go there, and when I got there I was interested in sites. I had been in Vegas several times before. In fact, I used to work for a place called Old Nevada, and that was a Wild West town and I was a stuntman for them.

So the night that I got into town I decided that I would go and check out the Old Nevada western town, and somewhere along the way I got off track of where I was at and I realized that I was in the middle of the desert but I didn't know where. So about 14 miles out I turned the car around to come back toward town. As I turned the car around that's when I saw the lights in the sky. I noticed that it was about a thousand feet up. It looked like a cigar shaped object.

At first, I thought that it was a movie set. It looked like an oversized giant blimp, but with lights rotating around it. As I seen it, my car began to malfunction. I immediately pulled to the side of the road. I lost concentration of the thing in the sky thinking about what's wrong here. I thought I was out of gas. So I got out of the car and I went back and opened the gas tank and shook the side of the car just to see if I could hear gas, which I did. When I heard the gas, I went around to the front of the car and raised the hood.

As I raised the hood, I could see that the object was still hovering above me and as I looked up a flash of light descended to the ground in front of my car about (I don't know) maybe three or four hundred feet in front. As it hit, I could see from the brightness of the light two figures standing, and they began walking toward me. As they began walking toward me I realized that I was motionless. I couldn't move. It was like I was in a time lapse and nothing was functioning right for me.

They kept approaching, and as they got closer I realized that I wasn't going anywhere so I was there and so I needed to focus on what I needed to do. They got close and I could see that they were pale figures. They had no hair, no eyebrows, but they looked like human people. The only difference was that there was a growth coming out of the sides of their neck, which to me looked like fish gills. They had no ears, but they had a very wide nose.

The only thing that looked funny was that their mouth looked like they had no teeth, and that was the only part of them that looked old. As far as their physique they looked good. About 5' 7"/5' 8", very muscular looking. As he approached me, the first one came up to me close, and then he began to speak, but when he spoke I noticed that he wasn't talking from his mouth. It was like a telephone call long-distance. I looked down and he had some kind of device on his belly, like a belt, and it sounded like it was coming from it.

Still I was under the confusion and I was thinking; "Is this movie? Is something going to happen here in a minute? Am I going to be saying; What Ha! Guess what?!"

Editor: Smile, you're on Candid Camera!

Johnny Sands: Yeah! (Laughs) So I didn't know. My mind was there, but at the same time I couldn't move. So the first question that I asked them was, "Where did you come from?" And he pointed up there. He didn't say a word. He just pointed. Then when he spoke to me he asked me what I was doing there and I said, "I'm doing a record. I'm a country music singer." Like he understood all of that. I don't know if he did or not, but he seemed to understand what I was saying.

Then he reached behind him and pulled out a ball, which was only about the size of a grapefruit, silver colored, and as he held it in his hand it grew into the size of a basketball. Then he let go of it and it began to rotate in a motion with the circle and as it did that he would put his fingers over the top of it and like firecrackers would go off on top of this ball, and as it went off he said, "You see, nuclear explosions are causing a problem in the solar system. These things that you're setting off on this earth are causing troubles not only for you but for us and we cannot have this kind of thing to continue because it is going to upset the balance of everything that we intend for the future."

Well, I didn't know what he was even talking about. There was no talk about nuclear stuff back in the 1970's that I was acknowledged of, and if there was it was far out of the range of what I was thinking about because I was in the music business. But I listened to what the man said. I had a question and I asked, "But are you bringing harm to us?" And his answer was: "Harm comes from evil." That was his answer.

So I felt like "I am alive, I am still standing here, and so I hope and pray that you're not evil." So then I asked the question, "How old are you?" He said, "We are before the beginning of what you know as time." Well, that to me was saying a lot. I'm not a Bible scholar by any means but I've studied the Bible and understand the Bible and in Ezekiel they talk very much about a craft coming out of the sky with life-like figures on the inside.

So he's talking past that type and I realized that, and then I looked back at Sodom and Gomorrah and I realized that angels come to warn the people to move out of there because it was going to be destroyed. Now those angels that came did not have wings. They were in human form. They walked as humans and they walked amongst the people that are human.

I didn't know anything about what that meant at the time but I realize now 'Men In Black' represent that same kind of thing. They come in a human form, they look like us, they walk like us, they talk like us, but do we know whether they are from above or below?

We don't. So I asked them another question. I asked them if we were going to see them on any other occasion, and they said, "You will see us again." I said, "Why did you pick me? I'm a music guy. I don't know anything about science. I don't know anything about this." They said, "You will know, in time, the reason we picked you." I still don't know yet. But I did ask them, "Are you military?" They said, "We are not military, but your leaders know about us. They know us and know all about us."

So I believe that to be true because I talked to the Air Force in Las Vegas for a long period of time. When I got out of that desert man, I wanted to know everything and anything I could pertaining to this thing, because I thought maybe I was hallucinating. I'll be honest with you. Back years ago, I experimented a little bit with everything. I smoked a little wacky tobaccy in the past. I went to the hospital that night and I told them, straight up and straight across, I said, "Look, I smoked pot before.

I'm not smoking tonight. I don't know if I'm having some kind of delusions. I don't know what's going on with me. I really want to know." They admitted me and they ran all kinds of tests and they said, "There's nothing wrong with you." They said, "It seems like you're in a little shock from the situation that you've been in, but as far as you telling what you're telling, we believe what you're telling is true."

So they suggested that I contact the Aerial Phenomenon Research Organization in Tucson, Arizona. They listened to my story and they said, "Listen, we are interested. We're going to send some people in to meet you." So my first contact was John Remara. He was the director of the Sahara Hotel. John Remara is a very brilliant man. In fact, he's a marketing director for six gaming for casinos right now in Las Vegas.

I met John and John said, "I believe what you say is true, but in order to verify what you're saying I need you to take a few tests for us." I said, "What kind of tests could I take?" He said, "Well, a polygraph would be one. A voice analysis would be another, and there's a Dr Leo Sprinkle, who is a psychologist and a specialist in hypnosis, and we would like you to meet these three people." I said, "I'd be more than happy," because here's what I wanted.

Right now, I can't promote a record because everybody would think that I'm using that as a gimmick to promote my record. I can't do anything with my career. I'm on a stand still. Everybody wants to see me because it's hit the front page of the Las Vegas Sun, because they had had so many sightings that night, not by just me, but all over the state, New Mexico, Arizona, and Nevada. And see I didn't know this and they were all describing the same object, the same things, except they didn't meet the aliens.

Well, I'm not discriminating anybody, because I'm not wanting to say that I'm the only man who has seen somebody from outer space. But I do have a little bit of problem with some of the stories that I hear because I don't think those little balloony shaped headed people with green dotted eyes and crawl around and look like piss ants. I think their intelligence is far beyond that kind of look. They're not 3 foot high. These people I saw were intelligent people.

You could see wisdom in their face. You could see that strength in them. I mean, from an Indian Reservation, we know power, we know strength, and we know what the feeling of a spiritual feeling is all about, and I could feel that spiritual, that strength, that realism far beyond what most people can understand. I knew that I was talking to somebody who not only just knew what they were talking about, but knew far beyond what I could ever be talking about. I felt like a little pee on in a great big shell.

But I went through the tests. Dr R. L. Nolan was one of the best lie detector experts. He worked with the FBI for 27 years. He came in and he said, "I'm going to just take you right quick right now. You won't even get past me because when I get done with you I'm going to wash you out and you're going to be gone." I said, "Fella, if you can wash me out and I can be gone, that means that this story is all over with and I'll be very glad." He said, "I'm going to ask you several questions. Number one, did you meet two strange creatures in the desert?"

I said, "Yes sir, I did." He said, "Were those creatures pale and white, had no hair and no eyebrows, and had gills on the side of their face?" I said, "Yes sir, that's right." He said, "Let me ask you this one. This one is going to get you. Did they talk to you, and not use their mouth, and talk to you in a form of mental telepathy?" I said, "Yes sir, they did." He couldn't get past that part. There were people in another room with a glass window and he stood up and he said, "He's telling the truth. He's telling the truth." When I took the test it was a hundred percent in favor.

Then Dr Leo Sprinkle and the voice analyst gave their report as a 100 percent. Now they said that the only thing that was detected in what he was telling is that he's holding back a couple of things that they had told me not to tell and he said even under the psychologist's hypnosis he won't reveal that because that was the shock to his whole program, of his life, and because of that his subconscious won't let him release that, and for 34 years I kept that a secret.

Some of the things that I told you about the military, were they military, were they involved with the government, did the government know that they existed, all of these things fell around things that they had asked me not to talk about. I don't know why, but I think that it was because they just wanted to see the sincerity in what I would do and what I wouldn't do. They had me against the wall and didn't realize it because with the things that were going on, and because I was in this predicament and because I was promoting a record, I couldn't afford to make that kind of statement and jeopardize what my career was all about.

So that's where we landed, and then they took me into the Sierra Hotel, John Remara wanted to do an artist rendition of what the alien looked like, so they took me to their best artist that they brought in in the state of Nevada and they told me to describe it to him. I was there. A friend of mine named John Worth was also there. John Worth was a 17 year police officer in Philadelphia. He was a very smart man. He had busted Rinso and everybody, the Mayor, for drug stuff. So I've trusted John. He was a sparring partner with Leon Spinks out in Vegas, and quite a man. So I felt like I had a good body guard with me. So we went in to draw the picture and as the artist was laying it out he got down to the gills on the side of the face and he said, "I'm confused. They've got a nose but they have gills. Why do you think they have those?"

I said, "I really don't know." And two men walked up, dressed in black. One of the men, in an awkward lean, leaned over, almost like a robot, in front of my face, and he said, "That's because of where they're from." He said, "You see, there's a planet in the solar system of a star called Sirius and that planet is an aquatic type planet, which is half the time under water and half of it is on land, and because of the heat from Sirius and the sun, it's eight and a half light years from here, and he said that they would be part time under the water so that they could resist the heat.

The rest of the time they'd be on land where they'd breathe through the nose. They're kind of like a frog." I said, "Well, I don't know but it sounds good to me," and the artist said, "Well it explains it all to me," and he looked at me, this one in black, he patted me on the shoulder just like the alien did and he said, "We've got to go now, but we will see you again real soon.

" When he said that, John Worth was sitting beside me and he said, "Did you hear what he said?" I said, "Yeah, I heard what he said ." The security guard was standing there and I said "Would you follow them please?"

Now look, we're talking about the Sahara Hotel. The halls would normally be jam packed, but for some reason there was nobody in any of the hallways. Nobody except us. These two men walked down the hallway with security right behind them. He was less than 15 feet behind them. They went out two double doors and before the doors could close he grabbed the door and was pushing it open. When he went out, I saw him lean forward, look both ways, look across the street; he turned around and walked back. He was as pale as the alien I was just showing you on the picture. He said, "You won't believe this. Those people vanished in mid-air. There's no car, there's nobody on the streets." That's a broad street out there, and he said, "Let's look at this hallway. There's nobody here. Why?" He said, "They've gone."

Well, John Worth and I both began to wonder. We didn't know about any man in black stuff. We were worried about who the fellas might be, so I told John, "What should we do?" He said, "We're going to take some back alleys and get home." I was at his place. So we drove every alley, every alley all the way through Vegas out to his place and drove me into his parking lot and the minute that we stepped out of the car a long black Cadillac limousine drove down to the edge of the road, they rolled down two windows, a front one and a back one, and two men looked out the windows at us. It was those men that were in the casino. They looked at us, and then they turned their heads straight ahead, rolled the windows up and drove off. John said, "How could they have found us?" He was beginning to really wonder.

Well the next day, I got a phone call at John's house. Now nobody knew John's number. We hadn't given that out. The call was about how they'd like to meet me. They were Dave Dunn's filming production company out of Hollywood, California, and they had heard about this and wanted to do a documentary, and could they meet me. I said, "Can you get this program over with if I'll interview with you? I want it done." They said, "We think we can." I said, "Okay." So I brought John Worth with me and they told me what kind of a complex they were in and the apartment number. So me and John went down there. When I knocked on the door this Dave Dunn (or who said he was Dave Dunn) answered the door. He was dressed in a black/greyish turtleneck shirt, black pants, and as I came in the door I noticed that there were two more men. One standing in the back bedroom door looking out, not saying nothing, and one leaning against the bar.

The house was completely furnished with looked like New England furniture. Heavy duty big time stuff, beautiful fireplace, a mirror with hand painted murals on the glass. I sat down in the chair like I'm sitting here and we began to talk a little bit. He asked me about my experience and where it was at. The others were looking at him but not saying anything, and he said, "We need to write a song about this," and I said, "Well, I'm not really into a song right now." He said, "Well we need to write this about the aliens all pale white and about the headlights." He said, "You write this for me because I want to meet you tomorrow." I said, "Well I ain't never wrote a song quite that fast."

He said, "Well with my help you can." He gave me some lay outs and he said "You go home and work on it and we'll see you tomorrow." So I went home and because this guy was wanting me to do something I said, "Well I'll do it." So I wrote it and I came back and he laid out this and he laid out that and he said, "Say that the object was shaped like a sphere," and I said, "Okay, I will." He said, "Talking to you without using their mouth that's very important because that's mental telepathy," and I said, "Okay, I can do that," so I re-wrote it and he said, "That's fine. That's great. That's what we want."

So he said, "What we're going to do is tomorrow night we're going to meet you at the Desert Inn, in the lobby, and then we're going to go from there out to the site where this all took place and we're going to do our filming." I said, "Okay." So the next night I didn't go in my car I got John Worth to take his and when we got to the Desert Inn the parking lot was so full it was like a football field away from the casino that we had to park in the middle of the cars because we couldn't get there and I had to meet them in the lobby.

I told John that we had to hurry or we won't get there in time. So John said, "Let's go," so we opened the car doors in his vehicle and a car drove right up in front of us. A black Cadillac and out stepped Dave Dunn, or who said he was Dave Dunn, with a martini in his hand. He said, "Hello Johnny. Here's a martini for you," and he reached back in the door and he said, "And one for your friend." I said, "How did you know how to find us?" He said, "Because we were looking for you." John said, "That's a little weird there."

So what we did then we got in the back of that limousine. There was a man in the back seat and two in the front. Dave Dunn was on the passenger side. So I began to talk. I leaned forward and I looked at John. About that drink I didn't know too much about it. How could they have a drink already mixed, all fresh, coming from the casino which was way over here and find us and have it ready for us and not spill a drop was a little bit puzzling.

Editor: And he used his left hand to give you that drink? Johnny Sands: To give me that drink. Editor: Just like the guy with the ball. Johnny Sands: Yes. Same thing.

So what I did was I leaned forward to talk with him and as I did, I dumped the drink in the floorboard. John seen me do it so he leaned forward and dumped his. So we rode on toward the Blue Diamond Highway and as we rode out toward the Blue Diamond Highway I said, "I'll take you where it was at." He was talking up a storm. When we got to the location I said "Right here." He kept going. I said, "But right back there." But he kept going. They went on about five miles and then they made a turn like I did that night and they parked on the other side of the road, and when they did all kinds of lights hit me from all sides of the desert, and he said, "You stay in the car. We'll be right back."

He got out, the driver got out, and the guy in the back seat got out. Me and John was in the car. They walked across the street and then here come these figures out of the darkness dressed in black and this one particular man was standing up in front of them all and he began to talk to Dave Dunn and he pointed at me, and he kept pointing at me. So John Worth had the window cracked and John said, "He's talking about you and he says, 'He knows too much. This has got to end here and now.

John said, "You've got trouble." I said, "No, I don't have trouble. I'm going out there to see what the problem is." I was on the side next to the desert and I reached and grabbed the door handle and as I reached to grab it, I don't know if you've ever seen that show The Adam's Family, Cousin It, and the furry thing?

Editor: Yes. Johnny Sands: Okay. Cousin It come running at me, at my door, and I looked and it run so close to the door I slammed the door back and looked out and it stood right in front of my door. No face. Just fur. And I looked back and there was another one to the left of him, and I said, "John, do you see?" He said, "A cactus run into the door didn't it?" I said, "I don't know what it is." He said, "Are you getting out." I said, "No, I'm not." I backed up and locked the door and this thing went around the car and went over to Dave Dunn and this other man. I don't know what he said or what he done, but he came right back to my door and stood. In other words it meant don't get out. So I didn't move.

So anyway, after a long conversation they had, they came back and all got in the car and when they got in the car I said, "What's going on?" They wouldn't answer. All the way back from that 14 miles out on the Blue Diamond (the way they went it might have been twenty something miles) they did not speak one single solitary word and when we got back to John's car at the Desert Inn they let us out. They didn't say good night, thank you, good-bye, or whatever.

So me and John were all confused, so I said "John, turn around real quick. Let's go back to that Blue Diamond place out there and see who all them people was." So we drove back. Now all the way out to that location there was not a car that passed us. When we got to the location there was nothing. Nobody, no nothing. Then we turned around and came all the way back and not passed one car. When we got back to the Desert Inn I said "John, we're going to see them fellas in the morning, we're going to get to the bottom of this thing, and we're going to know what in the world is going on."

So we got up at daylight and went to that apartment and I was beating on that door and a maintenance man was coming up the hall and he said, "Excuse me, who are you looking for?" I said, "The people in here." He said, "There ain't nobody in there." I said, "Yes there is somebody in there and I want to see him right now. His name is Dave Dunn."

He said, "I'm sorry, you've got the wrong apartment." I said, "No, I haven't got the wrong apartment," and John said, "No, I've got it right here written down. This is right. We've been here three times." He said, "Sir, I'm not trying to be smart but something is confusing here because that's empty." I said, "No. It ain't empty. They've got all kinds of furniture in this joint." He said, "Let me take you downstairs," so he actually woke up the landlord and I explained to her and she said, "Sir, I'm sorry, but you've got it confused. Maybe there's another apartment building."

I said, "Mam, I'll tell you all about it," and I started explaining about all of this heavy duty furniture and then I got to the mantle, and when I got to the mantle being hand painted and all, she said, "Come with me," so we walked across there, went up the stairs and went in that apartment, on the second floor, and when we got there she stuck the key in the door and she said "Sir, I'm not going to tell you that you've never been here before, because you described the mantle, but the strange thing is" and she pushed that door open and she said "Where is that furniture at?"

I said, "Good God. They were here last night." She said, "It's impossible. With the kind of furniture and the many rooms you're talking about here, they would have had to have had a tractor trailer in here and several men moving this stuff. There's no way in the world they could have moved that much stuff in that many hours." I said, "Mam, they were here." She said, "I believe something went on."

Look we didn't believe nobody then. We knocked on doors after doors after doors in that apartment complex. "Did you hear anything? Did you see anything?" Nobody had seen anything. They never seen these men. I said, "Did you ever see that black Cadillac?" One person said, "I thought that I might have seen it at one time." But they disappeared. Now John Worth run an investigation, APRO run an investigation, trying to locate these people. They don't exist. They didn't exist then and they don't exist today.

So the story is one hundred percent true. I just told a man on the radio today "I don't care. There are skeptics in this world. I wish I hadn't seen it because I really don't understand it but I wish that I could see it again because I would like to get an explanation and ask questions about it because I didn't know what I was asking at the time. But I would be willing to take another polygraph test on the men in black because these men in black are the most extreme thing out of all of it.

They said 'somebody like us' or 'we will see you again soon,' and I believe that somebody like them was the men in black. I don't think that they were government people because even government people can't move that quick. They're good but they're not that quick. And government people, I don't believe with all of my heart, would dress in a manner like the men in black like a Will Smith and a Tommy Lee Jones outfit every time they went to do an investigation. I think they're too smart for this. I think they come in Bermuda shorts and sun glasses or T-Shirts, or they might come in underwear, but they wouldn't be in a man in black outfit.

And I think these creatures or these aliens or whatever we call them are much smarter intelligent beings than some of these programs illustrate them to be. I believe that they're far in advance of our knowledge. When they left me in that desert, when they unfroze me and I reached my car door I looked forward and the minute I looked forward in a flash of light they were gone and they were in that craft and that craft took off from a solid stand still to 4 to 5 seconds that sucker was completely out of sight. It was gone.

He said that our government is aware of them, and I believe that they are. From the soldiers I've talked to at Nellis Air Force Base they knew that kind of thing was real. The people that they seen in Roswell, New Mexico when that ship crashed was the closest re-enactment to anything like what I'd seen. They were pale, they almost looked human, they were body figured like a man, and they had fingers like a man. These other little things I'm just a little bit skeptical of. Not to call anybody a liar. Maybe they've seen something I haven't seen.

But I just see these to be very intelligent, supernatural human beings. I don't know if they're from heaven. I don't know if they're from hell. But I believe they're powerful. I don't believe that they're here to do destruction to us. I believe they're here to find out our directions and I don't know where we're headed but if you're a Bible believer we're headed for destruction and I think they're well-prepared and with knowledge to see and be aware and be prepared for the times of what is to come.

I may be wrong. I'm not a genius, but I do know this. It was told to me that it was eight and a half light years to Sirius. In the time that they told me the telescope to see Sirius had just recently been invented. They didn't know what Sirius was. Yet Africa, and even before the Egyptians, talked about the star Sirius and they said that life-like aliens came from Sirius and they rotated down in a thing like an ark and whirled down to the earth. There were thoughts that there were Gods that come from the Sirius to earth, far beyond what we even knew what the star was, they knew. They knew more about our solar system than we know today actually. How did they know that? It had to be because there were creations above us and more life with knowledge than we could ever imagine that we've got.

So what I'm telling you is true. It's not something that I'm making up. Yes, I wrote the song 33 years ago and didn't put it out 33 years ago. I'm 64 now and looking for more, so yes, I think I stood the statute of limitations with them, I think I was a good host to them, I hope that they come back and see me once again. I think I've been a gentleman with them and I'd like to be that gentleman again. I'd like to answer any and all of their questions and see them on a first-hand basis.

But the song told the story of my life, they helped me write it, and so I do have it. I have it on my web page. You can get the alien, you can get all the secrets of the story in a book that I wrote myself, and you get an 8 X 10 picture like I gave you absolutely free. I'm not selling it. All you pay is the shipping and handling. I just want all UFO collectors and people who are excited about it to see what my man looks like, to have a portrait of it, and the hope that we together and can see it sometime together.

Editor: Right after that happened, did you change in anyway spiritually, psychically, or anything like that? Johnny Sands: Yeah. I never did believe in aliens. But since then, every day of my life, every time I see something moving in the sky, or blinking in the sky, I'm outside looking up for it. My wife says, "Won't you come on in?" I'll say, "No, I'm going out here." And I talk to them. I talk to them! I say, "If you're up there, I'm still here. I'd like to see you." I don't know.

You see something and you don't realize that you've seen it then you've seen it and you know it's real and the more that they investigate it the realer it gets. I hate to see somebody destroy what's real about this thing.

It's a great thing. There is knowledge inside of this that we need to be able to capture. I don't think that they're here to harm us. If they were, they could have wiped us out a long time ago with the spirit and this power that they've got. But I believe that they are observing what we are and what we are all about.

As an Indian, we had spiritual beliefs. We seen things in animals that most people can't see. We seen gifts and reality with things that people mostly can't comprehend, but through those things there was a spiritual guidance that led us to a greater being and that greater being was a God, and that God was a God in heaven that was going to lift our spirit even through those sacred owls, or in some spiritual way to bring us to the being of the life everlasting.

And I think that these people are from that kind of a place. I don't see the devil. I know that the devil loves me because he's tried to kill me for years. He'd love to take me down and rip me up and tear me apart. These people would not do that. They helped me write a song. They took me out in the desert and kind of scared me a little bit because I had been in a place that most people haven't been. I can't walk up and down the streets every day and say, "Hey buddy, how are you doing? Have you seen any UFOs lately?" They'd think you're a kook! (laughs)

But I've been somewhere that most men and women would like to be, but for some unfortunate reason they've never had that opportunity. Was it a gift? Yes. Would I want to do it again? Yes. Am I glad that I am the man that got to see this? Yes. Why me? They said that I'll know someday soon. I'm looking up, I'm still hoping, and I'm still going to believe that it's going to happen, and I believe that there's a reason behind any and all things. We don't get big because we're smarter or greater than anybody; we get big because life pushes us to reach certain destinations because we're meant to be for the cause. What my cause is I don't know.

Editor's Note: We had finished with the interview, and then Johnny began sharing details about being miraculously healed. So I switched my tape recorder back on and caught the following:

Johnny Sands: I just made a cross, I said "It's gone," and my wife can verify it, the next day it was gone. I went to the Bahamas Islands and I got so sick I couldn't breathe. I came back and they said "You've got cancer. You're dying." I said, "Oh God. I've got to get my life straightened out before I die." And I went back to the doctor and he said, "Wait a minute. Let me do this one test." He did this test and said, "You've got tuberculosis." I said, "Oh God thanks a lot. One death to the other." He said, "No, no, no. We can cure that in eighteen months now." I said, "Oh well, good." So he brought me a sack of pills that was like a drug store and he said, "You've got to take these all day long, every day for eighteen months."

I took them for two days. My wife will tell you this is the God's truth. I said I ain't taking them no more. I said, "I'm healed." She said, "That doctor ain't going to buy that." I said, "Well I mean it." I went back to the doctor and I said, "Look Doc, I brought you these pills back." He said, "For what?" I said, "Because I'm healed. It's all over and its history." He said, "Oh I wish that it was that simple. But it isn't." I said, "Well just X-ray me." So he X-rays me, he X-rays me, he X-rays me and he says, "Listen, something is wrong with this machine. I'm sending you across the street to the hospital." So he sent me to the hospital. I come back and he clipped those X-rays in and he put the pills in the trash basket and he said, "You're absolute right. You're healed. I don't know how. I don't know what done it."

"How did they do it? Did they make that miracle happen in my own life? I don't know. It was from God. It was a gift. Still I'm alive today. I'm 64 years old. I've done 15,000 stunts. Hanging under helicopters, crashing through walls, been on fire. You name it, I've tried it. I walked across the Snake River Canyon, upside down, on a cable, 1200 feet in the sky without a parachute. I'm still alive. Most stuntmen my age are dead. They're not rocking, and that haven't even rode. I'm rocking and still rolling so I've been blessed. Things have been happening for the good, and I've got a wife I met 30 years ago. Everything ain't bad."

Human Extraterrestrials

The types of extraterrestrials that I find myself most interested in are the many different human types. I and many other investigators believe from the evidence, that our humanity on this planet is only a small fraction of the total population of humans scattered across the universe. I don't want to get too deep into these ET human contact cases. I would like to leave this to another chapter where I will get into human ET motives, agendas and our integration into the greater celestial human mega-population. But I thought the following cases would present a bit of an overview of human to human contact cases.

I think it is becoming obvious to people like myself that there is natural primate evolution on other planets, but the evidence suggests that the situation is further complicated by all the artificial genetic breeding and genetic engineering going on between species from different worlds from which we are not immune. Because our level of technology is still low, extraterrestrials can pretty much do what they want with us within limits, including mining and manipulating our genome. I am beginning to suspect that there are as many or more different breeds of humans as we have of dogs and cats.

Udo Wartena's Alien Human Encounter[27] occurred years before either Roswell or Kenneth Arnold's sighting and helps us to understand where some UFO's come from and why they are visiting our planet. This article's author states: "For more than two decades, Udo Wartena, a Dutch immigrant living in the Western U.S., kept what had happened to him one spring morning in May 1940 a secret, not even telling his wife. Before dying in 1989 he finally confided in two friends and then wrote the details of his experience down so it would not be lost.

Udo's incredible story remained completely unknown in UFO circles however, until the details were finally released by Australian researcher Warren Aston. Before we review what took place in this deceptively simple report we must remember that this is an unusually early case in the pre-1947 period, which has yielded only small numbers of UFO sightings worldwide, and almost no cases where the occupants of UFOs were reported.

Let us remember that in 1940, World War II still raged in Europe, the first satellite was still 17 years in the future and the sound barrier had not yet been broken. Udo Wartena's experience not only took place in daytime, but involved intimate and open alien contact with a reluctant witness. I have assembled the following from two handwritten accounts and one typewritten account by Udo and from verbal recollections through interviews with the handful of close friends and family members whom he confined in.

Udo's encounter took place mid-morning early in May, 1940 at his mining claim in the forest near the base of Boulder Mountain, a short distance from Canyon Ferry Lake, near the small town of Townsend, southeast of Helena in Montana. Udo, a 37-year-old miner of Dutch origin was working in the area part-time for the Northwest Mining Company. During the previous month he had found a glacial deposit at the base of the mountain, which showed indications of gold-bearing ore. He began working the site in his spare time and first cleared an old and neglected ditch, which ran around the mountainside, using it to divert the water he would need in his mining from a nearby stream.

While moving some large boulders, he heard a humming or droning sound, which he first took to be aircraft, which flew over the area occasionally from Great Falls base in the north. At first Udo took little notice of the sound, but when the noise continued he thought that a vehicle had driven up so he climbed up onto higher ground. A large disc-shaped object, measuring about thirty five feet high and over a hundred feet across, was hovering a short distance away just above the meadow where he had built his dam. Udo described it as like "two soup plates, one inverted over the other" and resembling "stainless steel in color, though not as bright and shiny."

As he stood watching, thinking at first that it was an airship, a circular stairway with a solid bottom forming part of the craft's hull was let down and a man who descended began walking towards him. "As I was somewhat more than interested," Udo later wrote, "I went to meet him. He stopped when we were ten or twelve feet apart. He was a nice looking man, seemingly about my age. He wore a light gray pair of overalls, a tam (a common term in that period derived from 'Tam O 'Shanter' - a circular cap) of the same material on his head and on his feet were slippers or moccasins."

The man came and shook his hand, apologizing that they had not known anyone was in the area, explaining that it was not their custom to interrupt or allow them to be seen. "He asked me if it would be alright if they took some water, and as I could not see why not, I said 'sure.' He then gave a signal and a hose or pipe was let down. His English was like mine, but he spoke slowly, as if he were a linguist and had to pick his way."

The man asked Udo what he was doing and this was explained. Udo, asked if he would be interested in coming aboard the ship, went willingly and without any sense of fear. As he got underneath the craft, Udo described the humming as "not loud, though it seemed to go through you." Once inside the ship, the noise was hardly noticeable except what came up the stairwell.

"We entered into a room about twelve by sixteen feet, with a close-fitting sliding door on the farther end, indirect lighting near the ceiling and nice upholstered benches around the sides. There was an older man already in the room, plainly dressed, but his hair was snow white. I then noticed that the younger man's hair was also white." Udo described him as being "young and strong-looking" and having clear, almost translucent skin. Perhaps this explains the curious fact that Udo seems to have asked their age, even before asking their origin. Clearly there was something about their appearance to prompt such an inquiry.

The men answered that one was; "about six hundred years old" as we measure time and the other was; "over nine hundred years" of age. They informed him that they knew over five hundred languages and were learning ours and improving upon them all the time. When asked why they wanted to take water from the stream and not the lake, the younger man replied that; "The water was good and was free of algae, (as if they had retrieved the same before) and it was convenient."

Many years later Udo indicated to a family member that hydrogen extracted from the water was in fact the fuel source for the craft. Udo then asked what caused the noise of the craft and was not only shown the mechanism that powered the disc, but also given what appears to be a full and open discussion of the key principle involved, in the following words: "As you noticed we are floating above the ground, and though the ground slopes the ship is level. There are in the outside rim, two flywheels, one turning one way and the other in the opposite direction.'

"He explained [that] this gives the ship its own gravitation or rather overcomes the gravitational pull of the Earth and other planets, the sun and stars; and through the pull of the stars and planets...to ride on like you do when you sail on ice." An interesting analogy, elsewhere Udo described the 'flywheels' or rings as being about three feet wide and several inches thick, separated by rods turned by motors and next to 'battery of transformer'-like units all around the inside perimeter of the circular ship.

Udo was told that the two revolving rings or wheels developed an electromagnetic force, a term he did not understand at the time and inferred from what he learned that the ability to develop a cheaper and more practical energy source was of the utmost importance to mankind.

He was also told that the craft was able to focus on a distant star and use its energy to draw itself through space at speeds faster than light, quote: "skipping upon the light waves." These 1940 explanations seem remarkably similar to the propulsion method Robert Lazar claimed to have learned while working on alien craft in possession of the U.S. government at 'Area 51' and also sounds very much like some of the theories now being advanced by physicists: The creation of a local distortion of space-time is expanded behind the spaceship, contracted ahead of it, yielding a hyper surfer like motion faster than the speed of light as seen by observers...

In essence, on the outgoing leg of its journey the spaceship is pushed away from Earth and pulled toward its distant destination by the engineered local expansion of space-time itself. Commentary on practical faster-than-light travel as proposed by Miguel Alcubierre, published in Classical and Quantum Gravity, 1994.

Udo then wrote "I then asked them where they got the energy to run such a large ship? They said from the sun and other stars and would store this in batteries, though this was for emergency use only. They carried another source but did not explain this to me..." Asked where they came from, he was told they lived on a distant planet and gave its name - unfortunately not recorded by Udo - and pointed in its direction. Udo asked what their object was for coming to Earth.

"Well." he said, "as you have noticed, we look pretty much as you do, so we mingle with your people, gather information, leave instructions or give help where needed." Explaining that they were monitoring the progression and retrogression of our societies, the man claimed that they lived among us from time to time, a clear statement indicating long-term covert alien surveillance prior to 1940. Udo wrote that he did not understand what was meant by them "giving help where needed" but he did not feel it proper to ask about it further.

When Udo asked if they knew of Jesus Christ and about religion he was told that they would "like to speak of these things but are unable. We cannot interfere in any way." The area of religion and belief systems was to be the only question the aliens refused to discuss. During his time on board, Udo was invited to be examined for impurities in his system by an "X-ray like machine" which passed over him. Little was recorded about this examination however and Udo seems to have attached scant importance to it.

While talking with the two men, a light had come on which Udo believed indicated that the water had been taken care of. He mentioned that he felt it was time for him to leave. The alien's response was to ask if he was interested in going with them, to which Udo responded: "I said that I thought it would be interesting, but felt it would inconvenience too many people. Later I wondered why I said that."

Sometime later, Udo recalled an incident about two years previously where a young man had vanished nearby without a trace, despite days of searching by a sheriff's team. He wondered if the young man had met the same craft and gone with them.

As he started to leave the ship, they suggested to Udo that he; "tell no-one, as no one would believe me at the time," but in years to come I could tell about this experience. When I walked away from the ship they raised the stairway, and when I got a couple of hundred feet away from the ship I turned around. "A number [of] more portholes had opened up and though I could not see anyone, I felt sure they could see me, anyway I waved at them. The ship then rose straight up until it cleared the trees, then while circling slightly; it practically rose straight up and in a very short while was completely out of sight."

"As I didn't have a watch, I did not know for sure how long I had been with them, but according to the sun it was around noon, or somewhat around two hours." Udo later related how some type of "energy" had permeated the area and that he lost his strength for several hours and was unable to walk. When his strength finally returned he went over to where the huge craft had hovered, finding only crushed grass where the stairway had rested. Later, still feeling overwhelmed by his unexpected experience, he walked back to his base camp.

A Second Extraterrestrial Contact Case

This second human contact case called; Humanoid Dies in Sweden, is one of my favorites, in that it is a moving account that illustrates so well the humanity of other human extraterrestrials and that they are really not that different than us. They are just more technologically advanced. The title of the article is; *'Humanoid Dies in Sweden,'* and the translation is by John Fontaine. The article was published in Tim Beckley's *UFO Universe,* which is no longer in publication.

"One morning when several schools were visiting the stand, I noticed a distinguished gentleman, about 60 years old, who listened to the lecture several times and became extremely interested each time the slide-show came to the section about humanoids, a series of slides produced on the basis of a substantial number of interviews with witnesses. Even though the lecture was interesting, I could not understand why an ordinary listener would attend it several times, so my curiosity was aroused, and I started to talk to the man.

At the beginning he was very reserved, and did not want to go into details, but when he saw that I took him seriously, he eventually told his story. For an hour he told about his experience while I took notes, and indeed, it was a strange story: "I once saw and talked to a man like the one shown on the slides. In 1955 I was working as a lumberjack in the Gulf of Bothnia in Vestra Norrland in Sweden with two brothers who supplied timber to a sawmill in mid-Sweden. One early morning in July, about six o'clock, we were busy cutting trees, when we heard a sound like a big animal thrashing its way through the forest, or like branches breaking and rattling.

A moment later we saw a cigar-shaped object flying haphazardly in between the trees and branches as leaves were falling to the ground. My immediate thought was that it was a small airplane, which had lost its wings and was now preparing, without control, for a crash landing. Approximately 300-400 meters away flowed a river, which the aircraft evidently was heading for.

It was obvious that the aircraft would hit the ground within a few seconds, so we started to run in the direction where it had disappeared. 15-20 meters before we came out of the forest, the aircraft crashed in a clearing 30-40 meters from the river. I don't know what we had expected, maybe a deafening crash, when the impact of the aircraft with the ground caused the petrol to explode. But it did not happen. Not a sound was heard, but a gigantic flash of light engulfed the whole area like a vast flashbulb, so that the sunlight almost disappeared.

The light was so intense that we in fact could see through the trees. For a second I could see the grains of the trees and these were more than one meter in diameter, like an x-ray. Seconds later came a vacuum wave sucking everything towards the center of the light. All three of us tumbled forwards, branches and leaves flying past us. It all probably lasted only a fraction of a second, but I still remember how I crashed into a tree, time stopped, and my whole life was reviewed in my mind in flash. Even the normal sound of the forest had stopped. When we had recovered somewhat, we went out into the clearing to see what had happened. Nothing was to be seen at the point of impact, only a few piles of timber were scattered around. We looked bewildered at each other and decided to return to work.

At the entrance to the forest one of the brothers suddenly shouted: "Here's a dwarf dressed in uniform." Obviously the plane has crashed in the river and he must have been hurled out. "For a while we stood paralyzed gazing at the lifeless body. He was small of build, about 110-120 centimeters tall. Around his body a white light vibrated like a halo. One of the brothers tried to touch the man to see whether he was still alive he retreated with a scream. He was deadly pale and said he felt as if he had received an electrical shock. At the same time the stranger opened his eyes and said in perfect Swedish: "Do not touch me, it will only bring you difficulties."

His Swedish was so perfect that the brothers who spoke a Swedish dialect could not understand very much from what was later said. "Now you know who I am," he said. He knew it beforehand what we were going to answer and just demonstrated that his question was correctly grasped. Suddenly I became quite calm and studied him closely. He was no dwarf. He was very well-built with broad shoulders and normal features. His skin was yellowish like that of an Asian. The eyes were deep socketed and black, without any white around.

His face was badly bruised with a couple of big wounds on the chin and on the forehead. It did not bleed but the skin watered around the wounds. The top of his head was slightly downy and the hair almost white. The earlobes were one with the neck and resembled a shark's fin. The lips were wrinkled, narrow and colorless. When he smiled reassuringly, which he did a lot, he revealed a row of small teeth in the upper as well as the lower part of his mouth. I especially noticed that his canine teeth were flat and as broad as two of our front teeth. His hands were small with five slender fingers without nails and when he moved his hand it looked as if the ring finger had grown together to the little finger, if not they moved synchronized.

His uniform was of a reddish metal and appeared glued to his body closely. Head and hands were free, but at the feet the clothing continued into a couple of closed shoes, size 35-37. The footsoles were ribbed and vibrated, and for a moment I thought of caterpillars on a tank. The stranger looked at me and nodded slightly. There was no doubt that he knew what I was thinking. With those shoes he could roll forwards and backwards without moving his feet. Around the waist he had a broad silvery metal belt with an unusually large buckle, which shone slightly in a light-blue shade, which later when he was dead, turned dark blue. In the middle of the buckle was a sign in yellow - UV - it looked like a V which was incorporated in a U.

He knew I was studying him, and he said; "It is because of the clothing I can stay with you a while. Internally, I am destroyed." His right hand disappeared into his clothing at the hip, where no pocket could be seen. He brought out a rectangular object. It was of the size of a box of matches with 12 small indents. With a slate pencil attached to the object, he engaged the different indents several times. When completed he tried to throw it a few yards away.

"Don't touch it," he said smilingly. "It will tell my fellow men what has happened, so that they don't come looking for me. Where I come from somebody is waiting for me." The stranger lay for a while as if asleep. His hands were tightly clasped, and it was evident he went through great pains. Suddenly the brothers became somewhat confused, looked at each other, and then went back to the forest without a word. Later, years after when recalling the incident, I am convinced that the stranger one way or the other asked the brothers to leave, without saying a word.

I sat talking and listening to him for two hours before he died. What they talked about for those two hours I could not get the witness to reveal. I begged and urged him, but there was nothing to do, just a few fragments like these. The stranger came from a place in the vicinity of the constellation we call 'The Eagle' (Aquila). Several races from space have visited us, some so far advanced, that we could only see them when they materialized or dematerialized to visit a parallel universe in the orbit of earth.

Some visitors kept people on earth under surveillance and had done so for thousands of years. Others took samples of the earth, with a view to later settlements. Still others have had contact with mankind for centuries. In this context it is rather immaterial what was talked about even if it would have been interesting with further information about this conversation. I could understand from the witness that it had not been what was normally being told in connection with other encounters of this kind.

The witness continued: "Just before the stranger died, he gave me a folded bag from the invisible pocket and said: "When I am dead, the light will disappear from my body and with the help of the other two men you shall put me in this bag and carry me out into the river where I shall disappear. Then you shall rinse yourself thoroughly in the water, so that you don't get ill."

"He was now breathing heavily, and I could see the end was near. The halo around him became weaker and gradually disappeared. His light blue buckle gradually got darker. He looked at me for a moment and smiled. Then he said something in a language I have never heard before or since. Suddenly he switched into Swedish, and I got the last couple of sentences... "You have come without any wish to and depart against you own wish. Our life is like vapor."

"He said a few more worlds, but his voice was so weak that I did not catch them. I am convinced he prayed to some deity before dying. I was very moved. With the help of the brothers we got him into the bag and carried him out into the river. The bag smelled of sulphur and burned our hands as if they were raw flesh. He was quite heavy between 90 to 100 kilos.

When the bag came into the water, it started bubbling around it and we realized that some chemical process had started. After 5 minutes nothing remained, and I thought that maybe the stranger had hoped to crash in the river to a quick death, instead of lying for a couple of hours suffering, whilst a minor in the mind asked some silly questions. He would probably have preferred to die alone, thinking of his home light years away.

"I think that was all." said the witness and prepared to take leave. "I stayed for a couple of years with the brothers, but we seldom talked about that special day. I think, however, each of us went through it every day. The brothers are dead now, but I remember it like it had happened just yesterday. Years later I knew him immediately from your slide. It is strange; I thought I was the only one who knew this type. Over the years I have seen many pictures and drawings of visitors from space, but I've seen nobody like him until today."

The witness produced a piece of metal and held it to my nose. "Look" he said. I looked bewildered. It resembled a bit crochet hook. "What is it?" He laughed knowingly. "A couple of days after the incident I wandered around where he had been lying. The rectangular object was gone, but the pencil slate was lying in the grass shining. I have kept it as a proof that I was not dreaming."
He left, and while I gazed astonished after him, he disappeared in the crowd. This anonymous man with his story and pencil slate could hit the front page on the world's newspapers.

I believe that only because the story is true, it is possible to carry it alone for so many years. A psychiatrist could possibly determine that a slide picture opened up for a long subdued incident, suppressed of fear for ridicule. There are probably many stories like this which are unfortunately never known."

A Third Extraterrestrial Contact Case

The Villas-Boas Case (1957) sticks in my mind because it clearly shows evidence of human extraterrestrial interest in hybridization between themselves and us. The case in its entirety is a 23 page report which was submitted to APRO by Dr Olavo Fontes, Professor of Medicine at the Brazilian National School of Medicine. It includes a verbatim report given to him by Villas-Boas and recorded by journalist Joao Martins and translated by Mrs. Irene Granchi. Included below is a summary from that detailed report.

Antonio Villas-Boas was cultivating a field on a tractor when he was chased and captured by four small men that came up to about his shoulder. The first one grabbed him by the shoulder and Antonio in a state of panic gave this man a push that sent him reeling and started to run but was attacked and grabbed by three more men of slightly larger size. They lifted him up and dragged him back to their ship. He yelled and cursed and cried for help. When they got to the machine he was lifted up and shoved up a ladder which was very difficult because the ladder was flexible and was made for only one person at a time. (Note there is a lot more detail in all this and I am just giving a brief description of this case.)

He said that the little men when they talked amongst themselves, they sounded like dogs making little howls that varied in pitch and frequency. After this howling talk amongst themselves, the little men forcibly undressed poor Antonio and smeared a liquid all over his body as he struggled and screamed.

Antonio was taken to a square room where blood samples were taken with two very thick rubber like pipes that took blood but only leaved an area that itched and burned later. (Many details are omitted as to the dress and description of occupants of the craft.)

He got sick, was left alone for a while in a room until a nude ET woman walked in. "She walked slowly and seemed amused at Villas-Boas's open-mouthed amazement at seeing her. Her blonde, nearly white hair, big blue, slanted eyes and even features contributed to an unusual beauty. The hair was smooth, not very thick, less than shoulder length and was parted in the center and turned up slightly at the ends. She wore no makeup, her nose was straight and small and her face fine-boned. The contour of her face, which showed very prominent cheekbones and a severely pointed chin, as well as slit-thin lips, was the only outstandingly unusual features.

Villas-Boas noted that the prominent cheekbones made her face appear to be very wide, even wider than that of an Indio native (Brazilian). The woman's body was well built with high, separated breasts, small waist, flat belly, well developed hips and large thighs. Her feet were small, her hands long and narrow. Villas-Boas estimated her height to be about 4 feet 6 inches, he being about 5 feet 5 ½ inches. He later deduced that she was probably the smallest of the five "men" in suits who had been the first to grapple with him in the field.

The woman's purpose was immediately evident. She held herself close to Villas-Boas, rubbing her head against his face. She did not attempt to communicate in any way except with occasional grunts and howling noises, like the "men" had uttered. A very normal sexual act took place and after each one she breathed with difficulty. After the second act the woman began to shy away from the man and he became a little annoyed at this. The howling noises she made during the togetherness had nearly spoiled the whole act for they reminded him of an animal. At no time would she allow him to kiss her and his overtures in this respect were met by a gentle bite on the chin. Some of the physical features noted by Villas-Boas were the woman's very light skin.

CHAPTER TWO

MILITARY INTERACTIONS WITH ETs

"The next war will be an interplanetary war. The nations must someday make a common front against attack by people from other planets." Five Star General Douglas Macarthur 1955

"I can assure you that flying saucers, given that they exist, are not constructed by any power on earth." President Harry S. Truman

"It is true that I was denied access to a facility at Wright-Patterson Air Force Base in Dayton, Ohio. Because I never got in I can't tell you what was inside. We both know about the rumors (concerning a captured UFO and crew members). I have never seen what I would call a UFO, but I have intelligent friends who have." Five term U.S. Senator & Major General Barry Goldwater.

"Back in those glory days, I was very uncomfortable when they asked us to say things we didn't want to say and deny other things. Some people asked, you know, were you alone out there? We never gave the real answer, and yet we see things out there, strange things, but we know what we saw out there. And we couldn't really say anything. The bosses were really afraid of this, they were afraid of the War of the Worlds type stuff, and about panic in the streets. So we had to keep quiet. And now we only see these things in our nightmares or maybe in the movies and some of them are pretty close to being the truth." NASA Astronaut, John Glenn.

The thing to understand about life is that environmental conditions are always changing and all creatures have to adapt to these changing conditions else they suffer or even die. I am discovering that this is just as true for extraterrestrial beings with advanced technology, as it is for us the indigenous human species of earth. Retired Air Force Airman Charles Hall has written extensively about a species of human extraterrestrial called the Tall Whites who occupy and maintain a base in the mountains now encompassed by Nellis AFB.[28]

Charles told me personally that the extraterrestrial species known as the Greys occupy and maintain a base larger than the Tall White base at Area 55 also on Nellis, while a very human type of ET with 24 teeth have a base near a fiord in Norway. Charles claims to have met all three types in his life. Nellis is the home of the world renown Area 51 that is now part of global popular culture.

In later chapters I will get into more detail about the nature of other ET races like the TW and the Greys along with the supporting case history. I have found Charles Hall's claims compelling because of the detail and the fact that there are many additional witness to the Tall Whites. These other cases are completely separate from the Hall case. These people came forward before and after he published his books and did interviews.

I even travelled to Indian Springs, Nevada in the spring of 2011 and found a couple of more cases while investigating. I feel too many contactee investigators are getting duped and are having their credibility undermined by false contactees, because they go way out on a limb in support of an individual without this kind of collaborating testimony and evidence.

Charles Hall claims that the Tall White's base in the Nevada desert predates for hundreds of years modern human activity on this planet. He has stated that he believed that the Tall White base was there at least since the time Madison was president of the United States, because his female Tall White teacher had mentioned that the Tall Whites have watched the wagon trains roll through the Nevada desert. They had a front row seat from their small Nevada base and from the Spring Mountains looking down on Indian Springs and Vegas as ranchers and miners began to settle the area.

According to Charles the TW live about 800 years and his teacher had grown up in the region. For this reason this area of the United States was very dear to her heart as the Tall Whites spend a lot of R&R time in the desert and nearby Spring Mountains in the summer. This getting out and about helps account for the fact that we have all this collaborating testimony from people who have encountered them in the desert and in Nevada towns.

Interestingly, Charles has said that the Greys and the TW don't get along and are in a kind of longstanding cold war, even though their bases in Nevada are not that far from each other. There also is a lot of intense speculation in the UFO field that the Greys have a biological research facility underground near Dulce, New Mexico where they treat us like lab animals, but there is so much disinformation involved in this controversy, it's hard for me to determine if this is true.

Against this backdrop let's move forward a bit to 1947. In 1947 the American military had a Top Secret Army Air Force base at Roswell that was active during World War Two with the only Atomic Bomb Wing stationed there. Some investigators believe that by this time the American military and top governmental officials already had the remains of at least one extraterrestrial crash that happened in the early 1940's.[29] [30] During World War Two efforts seem to have been concentrated on short term technological solutions to winning the war, including the making of the atom bomb at Los Alamos, New Mexico.

It would appear that the Germans may have recovered a crash in 1938 and because of this head start were further ahead in research and development of exotic electromagnetic / electrogravitic technologies than the United States. This would soon change when the Germans lost the war and lost their top scientists to Russia and the U.S. along with the accumulated information on these advanced technologies.[31]

Sometimes huge shifts in society are triggered by relatively small acts by one or several individuals. World War I was triggered by an assassination and an international incident between the U.S. and Iran was triggered when some hikers strayed into Iranian territory several years ago. When I was in Roswell in the spring of 2011 and interviewed contactee and military whistle-blower Clifford Stone, he had an interesting story to tell me. Clifford has networked with both military and extraterrestrials over a lifetime, so even as a civilian he stays well informed about these matters.

Unknown to Clifford several months earlier, there was a mention in the Senior Research Engineer Boyd Bushman interview, where Boyd told that a friend of his said he shot down the craft that crashed at Roswell.[32] I really perked up my ears when Clifford began to tell me what he had pieced together from his military contacts. Some of Clifford's contacts must have been in contact with the Gray ET's themselves to get their side of the story. Clifford claims to have known personally several types of ET's.

Clifford told me that there was not just one craft that went down near Roswell but three! The first craft went down because of mechanical and communication problems. There is debate in the UFO field as to if more than one craft crashed because of mechanical failure caused by lightning, or because the craft ran into a high power military radar that adversely effected the craft's navigation system. From the documents of the period there is no doubt that the military was tracking these craft by radar at the time. Perhaps what may have happened was that one or more Greys had taken a little excursion out into the New Mexico desert, perhaps even from their base that Charles claims exists at Area 55 at Nellis.

According to Clifford when the craft lost communication, two other craft were quickly sent out to find out what happened and rescue the occupants if they were still alive. If I remember correctly, Clifford said that in one of the craft were experienced adults, but in the other craft were inexperienced Grey children or teenagers. I figure that a recovery only a few years previously, would have not been that difficult for the Greys because the technological capabilities of the U.S. military would have been very limited. There would not have been radar to track the craft, and the human population would have been smaller because many people had not yet moved into the desert who could report a crash.

Clifford said that he had been told that these two rescue craft had lowered their protective fields and were flying in close formation in order to better search for the suspected downed craft. At this time a military craft came upon these two craft and asked base to be allowed to shoot them down. It may have been vectored into the area with all three craft being tracked by radar, but Clifford did not mention this if memory serves me.

The Greys in their two ships were following these transmissions and when the pilot got the order to shoot, the inexperienced Greys in one of the craft panicked and powered up their craft too close to the other. This caused one craft to come down right away which must have been at the exact same time as Bushman's friend fired at the craft thinking he shot it down. The other ET craft travelled quite a distance before it too went down. Clifford said that the craft had not been shot down as had been assumed by Boyd Bushman's friend.

I would assume that such a series of accidents, a perfect storm, put the Greys into turmoil and meant that they did not have craft in the area to recover the bodies and craft, because the area was now crawling with U.S. military. This seems to have been an unmitigated disaster for the Greys, creating a real turning point of history. These crashes galvanized the military and top political leaders into action and the National Security Act of 1947 was signed in September, creating the CIA, NSA and MJ 12[33] the organization to coordinate ET activities for the U.S. government and private corporations.

By the end of the 1950's official contact seems to have been established with several extraterrestrial races including the Nordics, Greys and the Tall Whites and Nellis AFB was built to encompass at least two ET bases. Charles Hall talks about the creation of Nellis in his four books. He entered into the picture in the early 1960's when our government and TW were still in the very early stages of developing relations in an environment of extreme distrust and paranoia. Charles also told me personally that he had met a very scary Grey adult in the desert and others, including young Greys, who were not so scary at Area 55.

There is considerable evidence for extraterrestrial crashes beginning as early as 1936 in Germany and the early 1940's in the United States. It was not until the end of World War Two that the United States and its allies could really begin to focus on the problem and began interactions in earnest with extraterrestrial civilizations. In the 1950's serious compartmentalization, secrecy and propagandizing of the public was so pronounced that one part of the government often was not aware of what another part was doing in regard to integration into extraterrestrial reality. Only MJ 12 knew the whole story. It was at this juncture that President Eisenhower realized that the whole thing was getting out of constitutional control and into the hands of the military-industrial complex.[34]

The *Fontes Briefing* gives a good general overview of what some global governments knew about the extraterrestrial presence, but it would seem that direct contact and negotiations were already ongoing between political and military leaders by 1955. This is evidenced by information that has leaked into the public domain, regarding the then United States President Eisenhower's contact and negotiations with more than one extraterrestrial civilization.[35]

The following statistics tend to support parts of the *Fontes Briefing*. Researcher Colin Andrews states:

"Timothy Good tells me that in his revised paperback version of his book, 'Need To Know,' that the U.S. Defense Dept. Statistics record, in just four years, 1952-56, the U.S. AF and Navy had lost in crashes, a total of 18,662 aircraft of which 1,773 were caused by 'Unknown Factors' 'Destruction' or 'Disappearance' of military aircraft during interceptions of UFO's continued apace."

General Benjamin Chidlaw, former commanding general of Air Defense Command, told Robert C, Gardner (ex-USAF) in 1953: "We have stacks of reports of flying saucers. We take them seriously, when you consider we have lost many men and planes trying to intercept them!" Furthermore, the former Air Force intelligence officer and UFO researcher, Leonard Stringfield, was told by a reliable source in the 1950's, that the Air Force was losing about a plane a day to UFO's![36]

By the late 1950's, and early 1960's when Airman Charles Hall became involved with a human extraterrestrial race called the Tall Whites (TW), it became apparent from the testimony of Charles Hall and others that there was now active cooperation with at least two extraterrestrial races, the Tall Whites and those known as the Greys, who were not human.

It makes sense to me that contact was established with these races first because it appears that these two ET bases were not that secure and that the ETs might want to cooperate with our military for purposes of trade and security. I am not sure if there was cooperation with those Human ETs known as the

Nordics, because it would appear from one Eisenhower meeting, that the military generals would not accept some of the conditions required by these human extraterrestrials for cooperation.

Charles Hall also talks of another blond race that he calls the Norwegians with 24 teeth, who maintain a base up a fiord in Norway and I would assume there might be some cooperation here with the Norwegian authorities as that base also might be a small forward operating base like that manned by the TW. In fact, Charles said that this race's deep space capabilities were not as advanced as the TW. UFO/ET investigators in Norway might check Norwegian military bases and UFO sightings to see if they could pinpoint such an ET base surrounded by a Norwegian military base with a fiord within its borders.

I intend to get into this later in more detail in further chapters, but for now let's first start this chapter with the *Fontes Briefing* and other briefings, to give the reader an idea of the overall context of military interactions over time with several ET races. Dr Olavo T. Fontes from Brazil was a prominent and respected UFO researcher in the 1950's. He was given an informal briefing by two American Intelligence officials that he wrote up in a letter of February 27, 1958. The briefing clearly details the paranoid military mindset and the degree of military understanding in regards to extraterrestrial reality in the late 1950's. The briefing states:

1. They told me that all governments and military authorities through the world know that flying saucers exist and that they are craft from another planet. They have absolute proof of both things.

2. As a matter of fact, six flying discs already crashed on this earth and were captured and taken apart by military forces and scientists of the countries involved under the most rigid and ruthless security restrictions to keep the matter absolutely secret. One of those discs crashed in the Sahara Desert but was too much de-

stroyed to be of some use. Three others crashed in the United States, two of them in very good condition.

The fifth crashed somewhere in the British Islands, and the last one came down at one of the Scandinavian countries; these two were almost undamaged too. All these six discs were small craft – 32, 72, or 99 feet in diameter. In all of them were found bodies of members of their crews. They were "little men" and ranged in height from 32 to 46 inches. They were dead in all cases, killed in the disasters.

The examination of the bodies showed they were definitely 'humanoid' but obviously not from this planet. In some cases the cause of the crash was determined with accuracy; it wasn't apparent in the others. All ships had the general shape of a saucer with a cabin on the top; all of them were of a very light metal which was assembled in segments that fitted in deep grooves and were pinned together around the base. There was no sign of this on the outer surface of the ships. Some of the ships had portholes made of an unknown type of glass; many kinds of unknown materials were found inside the ships.

3. Examination of instruments and devices found aboard these discs showed that they were propelled by an extremely powerful electro-magnetic field. Evidence shows it is a rotating and oscillating high voltage electro-magnetic field. Such a kind of field obviously produces some type of gravity effect yet not understood.

4. All ships were carefully dismantled and studied. Unfortunately the more important problem was not solved; how these fields were produced and what was the source of the tremendous amount of electric energy released through these fields. No clues were found in any of the discs examined. Apparently they got their power from nowhere. There is, on the other hand, evidence that large UFOs use some type of atomic engines as power source suggests that they were able to transmit electric power through radio beams as we now send it through wires. Some of the devices found inside the small disks would well serve to receive and to concentrate the electric power coming this way. If this is right, a nuclear power-plant operated on a ship or satellite of large dimen-

sions, placed outside our atmosphere. None of these UFOs of greater size was captured till now.

5. Our scientists could build a ship propelled by a similar rotating and oscillating electro-magnetic field– if they knew some method to change the energy released into a nuclear-reactor directly into electric power. The problem is not solved yet.

6. These visitors from outer space are dangerous when apprehended and definitely hostile when attacked. We have already lost many planes attempting to shoot down one of them. We have no defense against them till now. They outperform easily any of our fighters, which have no chance against them. Guided missiles are also useless; they can fly still faster than any of them and can even maneuvered around them, as if they were toys; or they can interfere with their electric instruments and make the useless soon after launched; or, if they like, the can explode them before they reach their proximities.

They have produced the crash of military planes (propeller or jet type) and airliners by stalling their engines through interference with their electrical systems. (We don't know yet if this is a side effect or their powerful magnetic field, or the result of some kind of weapon–possibly a high frequency beam of some sort). They have also a horribly destructive long range weapon which has been used mercilessly against our jet fighters. In one case, for example, an U.S. Navy interceptor with a crew of two, scrambled to go after an UFO.

Their mission was, as usual, to make it land or to shoot it down– if necessary. They used their guns. The answer was immediate and terrifying: instantly all metallic parts of their plane were disintegrated, disrupted into thousands of fragments, and they found themselves suddenly seated in the air (non-metallic pieces or objects were not affected by the phenomenon). One of them was killed but the other lived to tell the story. We have evidence that this tremendous weapon is an ultra-sonic beam of some sort, which disrupts the molecular cohesion of any metallic structure. They have means to paralyze our radar systems too, to interfere with our radio and television apparatus, and to short-circuit our electric power-plants.

7. They have not showed, till now, any interest in contacting us. They are obviously preparing a planet-wide huge military operation to interfere against us. We don't know what kind of operation will be this. There are, however, three possibilities: (a) total war followed my mass-landings, to destroy our power, slave the remnant of our people and colonize the planet; (b) police-action to stop our plans for the conquest of space, and to avoid our dangerous progress in the field of atomic weapons; this would involve mass landings at strategic points with occupation by forces of limited areas of vital interest for their purposes; (c) "friendly interference" (followed by military intimidation) to make us agree with their plans for us–whatever they may be–avoiding open war or any other kind of direct interference; patrolling and eventual police-action only outside our atmosphere.

8. All military authorities and governments through the world are informed about the situation. There is an exchange of information through intelligence services, and top-secret military conferences are held periodically to discuss new developments on the subject. The Brazilian Navy, for example, receives monthly classified reports from the U.S. Navy and sends back to them any information available here. A similar contact exists among our Army and Air Force and several (similar) military organizations in other countries. Here in Brazil only the persons who work in the problem know the real situation: intelligence officers in the Army, Navy and Air Force; some high-rank officers in the High Command; the National Security Council and a few scientists whose activities are connected with it; and a few members of certain civilian organizations doing research for military projects.

9. All information about the UFO-subject from military is not only classified or reserved for official uses, it is top-secret. Civilian authorities and military officers in general are not entitled to know. Even our President is not informed of the whole truth.

10. Military authorities through the world agree that the people are not entitled to know anything about the problem. Some military groups believe that such knowledge would be a tremendous

shock–enough to paralyze the life in our countries for many years in the future. On the other side, the believe that flying saucer reconnaissance (as it is now) might last other 10 years–the people couldn't be controlled for so long a time and the danger of uncontrolled panic would be high.

Besides, the probability of UFO-hostile interference (described on item 7) is still estimated at 50%; there is yet a 10% probability that their hostility is only a consequence of our attacks against their ships; because of this possibility, we are attempting now to make them aware that we would like to make a peaceful contact– so, the orders now (now) are to avoid any further attack against their craft. This policy has been adopted generally, with the exception of some countries which still have fools in their Air Forces–who think otherwise. We don't know if UFOs will react to these measures recently put under operation. We still hope they will.

11. To conceal the truth from the public, a carefully planned censorship is under operation for several years. The policy to debunk the whole saucer-subject is the better weapon we are using for this purposed. Ridicule is an efficient tool against most people who attempt to inform the public, but other measures are sometimes necessary. Chiefly against persons who possess evidence that, if published, would open the eyes of the people.

In some countries force has been used to silence some of them, when this is not possible, all tricks had been used to make their evidence useless. In a few cases, unfortunately, violence had to be used; we regret this but we have no choice. We are going to keep this thing secret at any cost. We are not interested in the so-called 'inalienable rights' of the people. Right or wrong we– the military– are going to do our job and no one is going to stop us.

As we can see from the following article at least some ET races were not cooperating with our military, and I believe this still continues to this day, from my experiences with local contactees. It would appear there is still disagreement between we the indigenous people of earth and those ETs that are here as to who owns the earth and its environs. I suspect it is those races with advanced enough technology to maintain bases deep underground, under the oceans and from huge motherships that are outside global government's ability to enforce jurisdiction. The following article from the *Mercury Newspaper* recounts an extraterrestrial / military interaction that did not end well for our military.

Saucer Captures Jet

After supper on a warm Thursday in July, Gene Ruegg finally did what he had wanted to do all day. He went into the back bedroom of his apartment in a suburb of Memphis, Tennessee, and firmly shut the door behind him. His wife shrugged at the sound of the closing door and busied herself with washing up. Her husband's consuming interest in radio-telegraphy had long been a matter of indifference to Nancy Ruegg, as it was to most people in the small apartment block.

Occasionally there were requests that "Gene should turn down that awful noise" but usually he would pursue his hobby - which he did most evenings and weekends. He spoke to other radio hams as far away as Chicago and Florida on the sophisticated equipment that had cost him over 5,000 dollars to buy and assemble. But much of the time Gene Ruegg did something that he knew was technically against the law. He eavesdropped on radio transmissions from the nearby top-secret air force base at Southlands, Tennessee, and the squadrons of Phantom jet fighters which operated from the airfield.

For over two years Ruegg had listened in on routine transmissions between pilots and ground control, fascinated by a world which, as a maintenance manager of a haulage firm, he was never likely to share. But all that changed on the evening of July 9, 1968 when Gene Ruegg became central to a mystery which still baffles both scientists and psychic investigators. For that was the evening when he heard the capture of a jet plane by a flying saucer.... and made a tape-recording to prove it! Today, the tape is in the possession of the US Air Defense Command. Gene Ruegg's repeated requests for its return are courteously refused.. He doubts if he will ever see it again.

Flying saucer research groups who have studied the incident are convinced that Ruegg's story is true. And after continual pressure from researchers, an Air Force spokesman admitted that a Phantom jet did go missing from the Southlands base in July 1968 in circumstances which remain a mystery. Today, Gene Ruegg has only a copy of the tape and a typed transcript as proof of the 15 minutes when he listened incredulously to what seemed to be a real-life drama more incredible than anything in space fiction.

When I interviewed Gene Ruegg in Cleveland, Ohio, we he had been addressing an extra-terrestrial study conference, he gave a vivid account of the events of that July evening. "I had a call to make to an operator in Montgomery, Alabama, but I was a bit early, so I tuned into the Southlands base. At first it was just routine transmissions between the tower and aircraft on training flights and I was just about to switch over and call up Montgomery when I realized something pretty dramatic was happening. An aircraft coded Delta four-zero had disappeared."

For five minutes Ruegg listened fascinated as the operator called vainly to the aircraft with reply. Then, through the crackling static came a voice, "I am being attacked by unidentified objects. I think I..." The transmission went dead. Ruegg realized he was listening into something highly significant. Feverishly, he connected a tape recorder to his receiver. Seconds after he had finished, the set once again crackled into life.

He told me: "It was the voice of the pilot. This time he was near-hysterical and shouting. "They're closing in on me. I am unable to steer a course. Something is happening to the plane... I am being taken along by this thing. I require assistance. I require assistance..." "Then the voice of the controller came in and told him to pull himself together. Seconds later, he said that they had got him on the radar scanner and that they could see objects clustered about the plane. "Someone else came on the radio then and told the pilot that other Phantoms in the area had been alerted and would stand by." "Then I heard a strange, searing noise like scraping metal and the pilot shouted something I couldn't make out. Control tried repeatedly to re-establish contact, but they couldn't."

The tape on which Ruegg had recorded the drama was scrutinized by experts of the American Society for Unidentified Object Research, who claimed that it had not been tampered with and appeared to be 100 percent genuine. The Society contacted the

Air Force authorities on Ruegg's behalf and asked for details of the incident. But for the next six years the authorities denied there had been any mishap that day. Finally it was admitted; an aircraft had gone missing.

Over the years Ruegg has had visits from security men. He has been told to say nothing further about the incident and to hand over the copy-tape and transcript, but he has refused. "I am convinced that what I heard was a genuine encounter with a flying saucer," he told me. "I believe the plane was destroyed or captured by some alien spaceship."

The 1949 Los Alamos Saucer Case

The following material is drawn from George C. Tyler's report on Baron Nicholas Von Poppen, and his alleged photographing of a crashed flying Saucer at Los Alamos, New Mexico. Taken from; *'UFO Crash at Aztec.'*

The hero of this story (and I do mean hero, because of what he suffered) is a noted scientist by the name of Nicholas E. Von Poppen. As to our personal relationship, I was, 25 years ago, president of the Shale and Metal Company in Denver, Colorado, where we make the first successful shale oil mill in the United States. It worked successfully, but was not economical, at the time.

One day the Baron (the noble title of Von Poppen) arrived in Los Angeles at the head of a delegation from France. He had trailed me all over the country after being informed that I was the only person who had engineered such a mill in this country. The Baron wanted me to visit his land of Estonia, which together with Latvia and Lithuania, made up a population of 17 million, and build a shale oil mill, in fact many of them. His country had developed oil fields with fine shale beds, and oil was needed.

I was afraid of the rising tide of communism, which was beginning to wash against their borders on the east; but he assured me there was no real danger. I finally consented to go after he made his offer more financially substantial. He had their Reichstag elect me Premier of the little country, with full power to rejuvenate the commerce. On the strength of this move, they borrowed

30 million dollars in New York, bought an old steamer of large capacity, and loaded it with old cars, discarded radios, and so on, to be made over in their land by mechanics that at that time were out of work and starving.

Shortly afterward, however, and before I could get my affairs in shape here, secret service men of a certain people came to me with the information that the entire end of Europe would soon be conquered by the Bolsheviks, and that persons such as myself would be hastily liquidated. The information was so definite, that I backed out, much to the Baron's dismay.

He departed for his country at once. They carried out the plans as we had made them, or tried to; but all was brought to an end by the disaster I feared would happen. The Baron saw his beautiful wife cut to pieces and his two children dashed against the wall of a stone cellar, as he hid under some driftwood, wounded and helpless. The Baron was finally smuggled out of the basement and out of the country. He finally returned to the United States. He had dabbled in photography and continued that interest here, eventually making a profession of it. He finally became a top man in the field. Our paths finally crossed once again. I learned to love the personality of the frail man. Already a scientist, he had to do constructive work, so he became a scientific photographer, and his work grew to be so well recognized that he was repeatedly called upon for difficult work along this line.

I was a little surprised one day in November of 1949 when his voice came over the telephone, asking me to meet him in the coffee room of a downtown hotel. He said, "I have a matter I must discuss with you. Get there at once; it will take about an hour to tell you." It took not an hour, but several, before I left the meeting, my head was spinning. Here is his story as he told it to me, without many details, since these would require a whole book.

"Last week, two secret service men came to my home. They told me they had a photographic job to be done, to please go with them. We went by plane and landed inside the vast Los Alamos Field, where I was met by the superintendent of that part of the field. We walked to the fringe of a crowd of several hundred men who were milling around a large flat object lying on the ground. When a lane was opened, I was led through the crowd and found myself viewing, what one might term a Flying Saucer.

There it was, surrounded by an estimated 1000 men, technicians and experts of all kinds, the best that the government can hire. To say that I was astonished would be putting it mildly. The door was so finely machined that when closed it left no indication that it was there. I suppose this served to insure against any seepage of air, when in space. Inside, was a circular room 30 ft. across, a curving ceiling in conformity to the outside of the machine. Between the sides next to the chime, were very heavy cables, some of which looked like copper, the rest I couldn't determine, and nobody expressed an opinion in my presence. It was like that all the time, very much hushed up. All of them seemed to be afraid of each other, and almost of themselves.

Approximately in the center of this room was a panel control board, covered with push-buttons and tiny levers, somewhat similar to those we have on earth. Before this small panel control board were four swivel, bucket type seats. And in all four seats were men—strapped in and dead. The largest, which seemed to be the captain, was four feet, nine inches tall, and weighed about 35 pounds. The smallest and obviously the youngest was 23 inches tall and weighed about 22 pounds. They were white men, with very pale skin, as if they had come from a cold world with little air.

Their faces were intellectual and refined. I have never seen anything like them here on Earth. The captain's right arm hung down as he lay slumped over the controls, and his fingers touched what must have been the ship's log book, lying open on the floor. The exposed pages covered with glyphs, nothing like I had ever seen before. But the book was made of some indestructible material which was not paper at all, but could be written on.

On the floor were some 15 little machines, beautifully welded to the floor, with welds that left no indication that showed any difference in appearance with the rest of the floor. Even though I could see that they were indeed welds. I am particular about this, for here is some secret which an expert should be able to discover. The machines appeared somewhat like typewriters, beautifully made, though not so intricate as you would imagine. It showed me that these people have long ago passed through the period of technological development we are in now, and have again tended toward the simplification of life, thus eliminating the intricacies which tend to obscure the natural laws of being.

I concluded that the machines were the different pieces of apparatus which controlled the cosmic space motor which was made up, it seemed, of the big cables coiled around the inside of the ship's chime, and of some mechanism which they did not let me photograph. Beyond the central control center of the ship was a kind of garret, which I will try to describe. Against the sides were several Pullman like bunks, but suitable only for the pygmies.

Against the wall was clipped a water bottle, out of which we drew water. I drank some of it, and it tasted good. In fact, that was all they would let me have. You could tell no difference between this bottle and any water cooler that we have in our offices, except that it was not made of glass, but was nevertheless translucent. There was a toilet, with peculiar arrangements, all very modest.

One thing in this compartment that drew my attention above everything else, was what appeared to be a regular radio tube (or at least it looked like one of our tubes) clipped against the wall. Every now and then it delivered a BEEP! BEEP! Sound, which I judged was a call from space, since I had the idea that other ships connected with this one were anxiously trying to communicate with it. That went on all day until I was ready to leave." So ends the informative story that Von Poppen relayed to me on that rainy day in November of 1949.

A Crashed Saucer From Germany

There is a second interesting saucer story involving human occupants in this the book, *UFO Crash from Aztec*, where a saucer was found at low tide on a small German island called Heligoland. This story was by Norwegian Hans Larson Loberg a Prize-winner for physics in Hungary.

"From the waters arose to the surface during low tide the dome of a flying saucer." "The discovery has contributed to clear up a few obscure points on the mystery of the spacecraft and has served to confirm the existence of extra-terrestrial creatures, much distant from us and our actual life, whether in time or space. The revelations of Dr Loberg truly leave us thoughtful.

"The flying saucer half-submerged was of impressive proportions; it measured 30 meters in diameter and 23 in height. Externally it was a light color similar to aluminum, but there was no question of the metal. The material of which it was composed, resulted from exceptional solidity, being however extremely light. As proof of its casting a sample of such material resisted 15,000 Fahrenheit without melting. "In its construction, the disc did not present any traces of any screws, riveting or of soldering; it seemed coined in a single piece like a coin."

"The cabin of the giant flying saucer, hermetically closed, was provided with beds similar to removable reclining chairs, but no one was lying there." The crew because of the slope of the spaceship were stretched out in a corner of the cockpit in a macabre heap of carbonized bodies. Seven corpses were counted; all men from 25 to 30 years old, whose stature attained about a meter and 85 (6 ft.) In the judgment of Dr Loberg, the unfortunate pilots had found death in the precipitate descent of the Saucer, which had happened to find itself in the tremendous active ray of a hydrogen-bomb exploded during the frequent thermo-nuclear experiments. In their death contortions the poor souls showed a magnificent set of teeth."

"In the same cabin was found an ampoule containing a transparent liquid similar to water, but with a specific gravity some three times greater." "Two cylindrical jars were brimful with small discoidal-shaped sweets which one supposes to be composed of nutritive and energy-giving substances. In the saucer no other food at all for the pilots was found." "There was discovered, deteriorated and unserviceable, a microscopic radio-apparatus, some special maps and a few volumes printed in an unknown language.

"In the saucer no weapons of any sort were traced, but as regards this, Loberg affirms that Flying Saucers do not need offensive arms, in as much as they are protected by their powerful magnetic field, whose existence was confirmed. This magnetic field constitutes, however, the defensive armament of the saucer and its own motive force, since it was provided with motors and possesses uniquely a gadget for landing formed by a metallic tripod which can rotate in any direction."

UFO Shot Down Over Germany

In the early 1990's I- Ed Komarek, received the following narrated ET shoot down report in the mail. I had apparently forgotten about it, but found it about fifteen years later and put it up on the Internet to see if anybody else might have any information. I posted it to the Open Minds Forum where somebody noted that Colonel Corso had written about the shootdown in three different places in his book, *The Day After Roswell*. Corso's book came out several years after the author received this report in the mail. This was powerful confirmation of the account. Corso said:

> "Nor could I forget about the radar anomalies at the Red Canyon missile range or the strange alerts over Ramstein air base in West Germany. Our only successes in defending against them, back in the late 1950s and early 1960s, occurred when we were able to get a firm tracking radar lock. Then when we locked our targeting radars on, the signals that missiles were supposed to follow to the target, it somehow interfered with their navigational ability and the vehicle's flight became erratic."
>
> "If we were especially fortunate and able to boost the signal before they broke away, we could actually bring them down. Sometimes we actually got lucky enough to score a hit with a missile before the UFO could take any evasive action, which an army air defense battalion did with an antiaircraft missile near Ramstein Air Force Base in Germany in May 1974. The spacecraft managed to crash land in a valley. The craft was retrieved and flown back to Nellis Air Force Base in Nevada." "We hid the truth and the EBEs used it against us until 1974 when we had our first real shoot-down of an alien craft over Ramstein Air Force Base in Germany."

After the shoot down article had been on the Internet for some time, I received an email from (name withheld) the squad leader of an XM163 Towed Vulcan. He served from February 1973 to Nov 1974 at Ramstein AFB Germany, 4th Squad 4th Platoon in B Battery 2/60 ADA 32nd AADCOM. He confirmed that the event happened and that there were some errors and a little poking of fun at certain members of the team. He said because he was sworn to secrecy he would not explain the errors.

This informant asked that his name be removed from the report because he still held a secret clearance and was afraid of being blamed for this leak. He did confirm that the names were real. He also told me after he read about the widely reported UFOs over nuke bases, that nukes may have been used as bait setting up an ambush. This was speculation on his part, but he did say nukes were in the area.

It was the night of May 23/24, 1974 at the height of the Cold War. The men of the 4th Platoon, Bravo Company, B Battalion, and 2nd Regiment of the 32nd Air Defense Command of the United States Army were deployed in a mountain pass northeast of Ramstein Air Force Base in Germany. They were only a few kilometers from Landstuhl - a man-made mountain Adolph Hitler had created to protect his underground bunker/headquarters. Landstuhl was still in use in 1974 connected by an underground trolley to Supreme Headquarters Allied Powers Europe (SHAPE) at Ramstein Air Force Base. The men were also very close to a multi-storied German Government Brothel.

First Lieutenant Robert Cardeni of Long Beach, CA was the 4th Platoon Leader and Captain Michael J. Shestak was commanding Bravo Company. The men were all weary because they had been on this special duty for 10 days alternating every 72 hours with other units. Half of the men would be on duty while the other half slept. They alternated this pattern every 4 hours during their 72 hours of on-duty regimen.

These soldiers had been told the special duty was because the Russians and/or Warsaw Pact forces had been messing around trying out the western air defenses. This was a common tactic of both the NATO and Warsaw Pact alliances. Each would send aircraft into each other's airspace to see how quickly the radar sites would come on, where they were located and on what frequencies they were operating and how quickly the other side's fighter aircraft would intercept them. Usually the American forces would achieve missile and gun lock-on's on the hostile aircraft to scare them and armed American fighters would intercept the "hostiles" and give them the alternative of being escorted home or being shot down.

Up until that point in the Cold War, the Western response had always been to scare and turn around. But now there seemed to be a big difference as the urgency of the mission was impressed upon the men and the fact that they brought live ammunition for the cannons and live Chaparral Antiaircraft Missiles. In this eventful night, two Chaparral Missile emplacements were deployed in the valley not far from the whorehouse. The missile sites were linked by field telephones to observers on the mountainside.

Lieutenant Cardeni gave orders to the crews of the Vulcan 20 Millimeter Cannons to load canisters of live high explosive phosphorus rounds into their cannons and to maintain a steady alert. These orders were given about midnight local time. The Vulcan Cannons had the capability of firing 2000 rounds a minute through their six rotating barrels at a kill and accuracy range of up to 6000 meters.

On the north side of the pass at about the 1050 foot level the Vulcan Cannon emplacement was manned by Specialist Houston "Tex" Thomas from Indio, CA. "Tex" was a big, jovial black man. About 4000 meters south, the Vulcan Cannons across the pass at about the 850 foot level were manned by Private William Langdon from West Seneca, NY, the top gunner in the 4th Squad. Bill was of Quaker ancestry and was an enigma for not claiming 'Conscientious Objector' status.

About 12:45 AM, Lieutenant Cardeni gave orders that something hostile was incoming and that the gunners were to shoot down anything coming through the pass. He stated that no 'friendlies' would be flying below 2700 feet and anything else was to be shot down. At that point, "Bill" Langdon suddenly came in touch with his Quaker upbringing, left his cannon and went back to awaken his squad leader, A (name deleted), from the

San Francisco Bay Area of California. Langdon refused to shoot down anything with someone in it.

The Private said his piece and climbed into one of the auxiliary vehicles and went to sleep while (name deleted) shook himself awake and climbed into the Vulcan Cannon and began adjusting his eyesight to the bright moonlight. (Name deleted) then got on his radio and confirmed that Lt. Cardeni had indeed issued orders to shoot down anything flying under 2700 feet of altitude.

About 1:00 a.m. local German Time, (name deleted) had his chance as something came down the valley headed for the pass. He described it as a flattened ellipsoid with rounded edges, about 30 feet long and glowing with a silvery iridescence. He said it was moving at a rapid speed that was impossible to judge accurately as it was apparently trying to be evasive by zigzagging side to side.

It took a few seconds for (name deleted) Cannon's computer and Doppler radar to calculate a precise speed, range, and direction of travel and to achieve a lock on. When the cannon was locked onto the object and he was visually sighting the object through the reticule gun-sights he began firing. First a few rounds for effect and then three four second bursts of 110 rounds each into the side of the object which was at about eye level.

(Name deleted) was almost eye level with the object as he watched his rounds pouring into its sides. He was expecting to see the 'blooming flower' effect of the phosphorus rounds exploding but he did not, although he could clearly follow the trail of his shots pouring into the side of the object. "It was as if the shells were being absorbed or being vaporized at the explosion by some sort of force field." (Name deleted) said.

(Name deleted) perception was that the rounds were going into invisible tubes that contained the detonations, so that he saw only pie-tin sized explosions but not phosphorus blooming that he expected. This was quite a remarkable containment of shells having a 35 meter kill radius. (Name deleted) could observe "Tex" Thomas shooting down on the object from the higher elevation across the pass and he noted that Tex's rounds were trailing the object missing it.

At the same time as the shooting was going on, on the mountainside, Sergeant William McCracken from Pittsburgh, KS was inside the launch control console of a Chaparral Missile Battery in the valley was rotating his console according to directions supplied by his uphill observer (the operator in the launch console could not see out at night because of the reflections on the Plexiglas's bubble from the instruments on his control panel).

Up until that point, McCracken had not painted anything on his radar screen. When he had rotated to the 10 o'clock position (a heading of about 300 degrees), Sgt McCracken saw a green light flashing on his console and heard a warbling tone indicating an infra-red signature lock on. After tuning adjustments, the sergeant pushed the "launch" button and a bright fire ignited on one of the launch rails as a Chaparral Antiaircraft Missile streaked skyward.

The missile climbed to about 900 feet (near the minimum operating altitude of the missile), found the flying object, moved along side of it, turned close in front of it, and detonated its 75 pounds of high explosives warhead. The Chaparral, designed to bring down conventional aircraft with cockpits near the front. Always moved to the front of a target before detonating so as to potentially kill the pilots and disable a plane's engines by shutting off their air.

The gunners and observers on the two mountain sides, missile crews in the valley, and anyone else not currently known about, saw the target start wobbling and then stop forward motion and finally wobble downward to the valley floor in what the observers believe was a controlled descent.

The cannon and missile crews were ordered to immediately drive their artillery back to the Ramstein Air Force Base Motor Pool which was highly unusual because the artillery was normally stored in its own area for rapid reuse if needed. The crews were also told not to take time to pick up their expended brass - also highly unusual. The crews were told to quickly get the cannons and missile launchers to the motor pool and go right to bed and not to talk to each other about the incident and they would have the next day off. As the crews were packing, they noticed Air Force Personnel moving into the valley to secure the crash (or landing?) site.

As is expected when someone is ordered not to talk about something, the men couldn't wait to talk about what they had seen once they got back to the barracks. Specialist Thomas swore he was shooting at a MIG-25 and (Name deleted) held fast that it was not an airplane at all and neither could the other. Sergeant McCracken from the Chaparral mount said that for all he knew he could have shot down the Oscar Meyer "Wiener Wagon."

At the same time as the American Soldiers were shooting at something in Germany, other events were set in motion in the United States. Major Mike Andrews, from Silver Spring, MD, had spent a week on ready alert duty at McGuire Air Force Base, New Jersey, while his C141 Starlifter sat nearby, serviced and preflighted daily. The major was awaiting orders that would send him and his crew winging off to they knew not where. Now this was unusual because a transport like the C141 was not exactly a B52 bomber.

About 2025 hours (8:25 PM EDT), 1:45 in Germany, Major Andrews waiting was over as he was handed typed orders. Quickly gathering together his crew, checking the weather, and filing a flight plan, Major Andrews and his crew were airborne at 2100 and flying South Southwest. About 2200, they landed at Andrews Air Force Base, Maryland. They were met by an Air Force Brigadier general and a 50ish civilian bearing CIA identification.

Major Andrews was given sparse details of what was about to be his mission and was told he would be taking aboard air force personnel who would be arriving soon from Wright Patterson and Nellis Air Force Bases and that neither he nor any of his crew were to talk to any of the airmen they would be flying to Germany.

Shortly afterward, 26 airmen from Wright Patterson Air Force Base in Ohio arrived, carrying large cases of equipment. As they boarded the C141, Major Andrews noted that the airmen were all sergeants of one grade or another and that they all wore blue berets and white ascots and were armed, not with traditional .45 caliber automatic service side arms, but with ivory handled revolvers. Major Andrews was told that the officers had flown on direct to Germany in a faster jet. About a half hour later a jet arrived from Nellis Air Force Base, Nevada, carrying 6 officers who were going along. They were waiting only for a helicopter from Aberdeen Army Proving Facility, Maryland that was bringing the last 3 passengers.

About 2300 (11 PM EDT) three army officers from the Army Vulnerability Assessment Laboratory in Alamogordo, New Mexico arrived by helicopter from Aberdeen, Maryland. At 23:30, Major Andrews was airborne and soon was winging over the dark waters of the Atlantic Ocean carrying a strange group of passengers to Germany for he knew not what.

At 1030 German time, Major Andrews landed his C141 Starlifter at Ramstein Air Force Base in South-western Germany only about an hour's drive from Belgium. The disembarking passengers were met by a delegation of ranking air force officers including a few generals. The men of Bravo Company had been told they would have Friday, May 24, 1974 off to catch up on their sleep. They were a little edgy when they were awakened before noon for a 'debriefing.'

The soldiers who had a direct active part in the mission less than 12 hours earlier met individually with the debriefers. The first debriefing was handled by the three officers from the Vulnerability Assessment laboratory in Alamogordo, NM. They wanted minute specific details about every phase of the operation from what kind of shells were being used to opinions on what type of damage was being done to the target.

The debriefings continued the rest of Friday afternoon and Saturday morning by groups of Air Force Officers. One central theme was repeated over and over to the debriefers: "You weren't up there, nothing happened, and don't ever talk about this to anyone."

The men were warned that if they ever told anyone about what they imagined had happened that they would never work for the government or any government contractors and warned of unspecified dire things that would happen to them should they ever talk. They were told that in following years people would question them about the night and these people would be testing them to see if they would divulge any details and if they did; "Too Bad." Then the men were required to sign a security oath to never divulge the details of the night and if questioned in the future to deny it ever happened.

The men of Bravo Company felt confused and very irritable for about a week after the incident. The soldiers noted that they did not recognize any of the Air Force officers who debriefed them and they felt that although the officers were all in uniform they did not act like military. Those debriefed felt that they were being questioned by civilians in Air Force uniforms.

More questions are raised about the incident than can be currently answered. Why had the men been on alert in Germany for a week and a half at the same time as a C141 crew was kept on alert in New Jersey for over a week? Why was the object, not picked up on the control tower radar at Ramstein Air force nor by the Chaparral Missile launcher? Was it because both used radio frequency radar whereas the Vulcan Cannons used Doppler radar? Why would the Army and air force risk showing secret wartime defense emplacements to an incoming MIG?

What could have totally fried the IFF receiver on the Chaparral Missile? (All NATO aircraft then and today carry radio transmitters that emit a specific signal on a specific frequency. Other friendly aircraft and defense emplacements are fitted with IFF (Identification Friend or Foe) receivers that interrupt firing mechanisms on the guns or missiles from firing at each other.)

Why was it that when the soldiers of Bravo Company first saw their weapons systems at the tactical site a few days later, everything had been overhauled and cleaned? (Name deleted) and 'Tex Thomas' Vulcan Cannons had been totally cleaned and the multiple barrels had been replaced so as no one could tell they had been fired. Sgt McCracken's Chaparral system was cleaned up and the burned up IFF unit replaced.

The official explanation for the incident was that a firepower demonstration was being conducted. But why would live ammunition be used in just a demonstration? Why would live ammunition and missiles be used near a civilian populated area? Why was a first lieutenant the only officer at the scene? It is obvious that a first lieutenant did not have the authority to order firing live ordinance in peacetime. Why had the army's chain of command been short circuited, and who gave Lieutenant Cardeni the orders to fire?

Perhaps the answers can be partially found on the afternoon of Saturday, May 25, 1974. Major Andrews and his crew were told to report to their aircraft which was then at a remote spot on the air base. Major Andrews was shocked to see that a set of metal supports had been constructed on the wings and fuselage of his Starlifter and that something large and ellipsoid had been attached to the supports. Whatever it was it was covered with olive drab green canvas tarpaulins with dangling ropes. The airmen returning to the US were already on board the plane.

Mike Andrews noted when he prepared for take-off that he had only a minimal fuel load aboard because of the weight on top of his bird. A motorized tractor called a "mule" towed the aircraft to a runway turn on position accompanied by armored security police vehicles with flashing red lights.

Once clearance for take-off was obtained, the tarpaulins were pulled away and Major Andrews began his take-off roll. His fuel supply dwindled rapidly as they took off with the heavy load. When they had achieved cruising altitude, a KC-135 was waiting to refuel the C141 with a much larger fuel load. Major Andrews' orders were that he was not to land until he reached Wright Patterson Air force Base in Ohio and that he would be met by refueling tankers at strategic points across the Atlantic.

It was dark in Ohio when Major Andrews landed to disembark the airmen - all but 4 who were to remain aboard and who then were carrying M16 rifles in addition to their side arms. The pilots and crew of the C141 were not allowed out of the plane while on the ground and they did not refuel. Taking off again with a minimal fuel load, they were once again met at altitude by another KC135 tanker and flew on direct to Nellis Air Force Base, Nevada where the crew was once again not allowed outside the aircraft as their wing-top cargo was offloaded and taken away again covered completely.

Upon returning to McGuire Air Force Base, Major Andrews and his crew were debriefed by an Air Force Colonel who told them they had just participated in a highly classified mission and they were never to talk about it to anyone. For eighteen years they did not nor did the soldiers of Bravo Company.

Three Star General Speaks Out

The following briefing clearly gives some indication of intense government involvement with various ET races and the extent of military knowledge by the late 1980's. The reader can see that by this time military integration into extraterrestrial realities is accelerating even as the public continues to be deceived, lied to and propagandized by world governments though the mainstream media and the tabloids. We can also see that military fear and paranoia of the Fontes Briefing has been dissipating over time.

Here I include portions of an interview published July, 1989 in Tim Beckley's *UFO Universe Magazine* under the title: *'Blowing the Whistle on the Governments UFO Cover-Up.'* The interview is with a three star general. This general presents some very detailed documentation and pictures to the person doing the interview. The general only allows the interviewer to see the pictures and secret reports which he then plans to return to a secret file in a safe before it is discovered missing.

The general had not been interested in the subject but the interviewer had gotten him interested and he made inquiries and pulled in some favors. His superiors wanted him to be part of the extraterrestrial awareness program and he refused. He eventually got into a lot of trouble and decided to retire.

The following is a little of the specific information in the article. The general states in the article:

"There have been several crashes of UFO's over the years. From all documentation and information available that I have seen with my own eyes as well as the physical evidence, this is in answer to your questions."

1. The aliens really do not have any sort of 'invasion' planned for this planet. Aliens have visited this planet off and on for thousands of years. Our U.S. guest is over 300 years old. There are both "good and bad" aliens just as there are good and bad hu-

mans. They are not all that different from us. The aliens utilize around 55% of their brain capacity or ability. The aliens do have DNA, just as we do. The alien which is the guest of the U.S. Government is 5 feet, 3 inches tall and weighs 96 pounds. Large head (no hair) large slanted eyes. Some of the alien's abilities include moderate telepathy and telekinesis.

The purpose of alien visitation to this planet is one of curiosity and scientific research, not world domination as some would have you believe. Cattle and humans have been used in alien and U.S. research for various biological applications. Most humans are not hurt in this research and experimentation. Some however have died due to complications and down-right carelessness. Several cross-breed 'young' have been born to both human females and alien females. We as humans are fully biological compatible with most visiting aliens. Some are not. More than one type or 'specie' of alien has visited this planet. They are listed by category... this information I could not retrieve.

2. The U.S. Government and the British have made secret treaty agreements with the aliens in exchange for technology and so-called 'recon' missions during times of human conflict. The aliens have basically agreed to not concern themselves with the wars or conflicts of humans. Not to interfere in society. Let the governments rule and decide. Exactly what the aliens get in return was not exactly made clear or available. Also, there are special 'teams' which eradicate, discredit, harass and 'trump-up charges' to control humans which experience any visitations from aliens, or make verifiable UFO sightings. This is one of the reasons I retired. It's too much for any government to impose upon the civilian population like this.

3. Many of the 'strange' happenings which people experience with UFO sightings can be one of two things. First, it can simply be an overactive and wishful imagination. Second and foremost is the influence of the vast mental power of the alien visitors. In the reports and experiments conducted with live aliens, they have an incredible power of 'telepathic suggestion.' Combine this with their telekinetic abilities and just about anyone can be some-what directed to do or think just about anything. The general has this

further to say, "Make no mistake, President Truman and later President Eisenhower gave specific direct orders to keep everything and I mean everything top secret."

The 'special group' assigned to oversee the alien situation and other government VIP's agree to gather all of the technology possible and put it to use for the benefit of the USA. I really wonder what other motives are there. Further on he makes these very disturbing comments. The questioner asks when seeing the documentation, "Why are children aboard these crafts? My God! You don't mean the aliens are snatching our kids, what for?"

The general says; "There are over a million missing children every year in the world. Now not all of them have been taken by aliens. The aliens take about 2,200 children a year from the United States and other countries. It's all right there in the report attached to the three photographs. The rest of the missing children are the result of Mankind's Dark Side." "The children are used in several ways: Biological, to educate and return, experimentation, disease study, the same as adults."

The questioner is looking at the report. "According to the report, implants are being used on the people that are taken aboard UFOs and returned. Some of these implants are microscopic in size (and smaller) and influence the growth, function and learning capabilities of the individual. This is a very detailed report. Could I have a copy?"

The general says, "No. Sorry but you know our agreement was that you did not get to keep or copy any paperwork. As well as the other matters we discussed. I warned you that this material is very serious and real."

Alien Shot and Killed At Ft. Dix

This is a very well researched case first by the highly regarded crash retrieval investigator, Len Stringfield,[37] and later by researcher Richard Hall.[38] The case is important because of the insight into military alien interactions and the exopolitical dynamics of integrating into extraterrestrial realties. Billy Booth did this summary of the incident, but if you want to see more detail and documents check out the links sited above.

"In the wee hours of January 18, 1978, several reports of UFOs were made by personnel of Ft. Dix and McGuire AFB in New Jersey. Soon, Air Force security was called to McGuire's back gate to allow the New Jersey State Police entry. One airman on duty that night we shall call Sgt Jones. He was told that Dix Military Police were chasing a low flying UFO, which had hovered over one of the M.P. vehicles.

The account given to Jones would take on another dimension when he was told that an alien looking being with a large head and slim body had appeared right in front of the M.P.'s car, with the startled patrolman shooting the alien several times with his .45 automatic weapon. The alien had managed to get over a fence that separated the two bases before dying on a runway.

Jones and company soon located the body. The area was roped off. Soon, a group of "blue beret" forces took over the scene. Although Jones had been removed from the main investigative group, he was still close enough to watch the action. Hours later, a group of soldiers from Wright-Patterson arrived upon the scene. They quickly crated up the body, and loaded it on their C-141 cargo plane.

Jones, along with the soldiers who accompanied him as the first group on the scene, were strongly warned to not discuss the incident under the threat of court-martial. Jones' group was taken to Wright-Patterson, where they were interrogated, and again threatened with court-martial if they ever discussed what they had seen. Jones would later reveal the names of the interrogators by recalling their names from tags on their clothing, and their identities have been verified.

Jones would return to McGuire AFB, and again be debriefed. Afterwards, he would hear nothing of the incident again. Soon, airmen involved in the incident were transferred to a base overseas. Jones himself was sent to Okinawa. He would subsequently talk about the incident on numerous occasions, and sign a deposition on the incident. Jones' life would suffer because of his knowledge of this unusual UFO incident, having trouble finding employment in the private sector.

George Filer (Major, Ret.), of Filer's Files fame, was another witness to some of the events surrounding the Ft. Dix-McGuire alien being. He was stationed as an intelligence officer at McGuire at the time of the incident, and though he was not on duty at the exact time of the occurrence, he heard talk about the "alien body" the next morning. He also saw a lot of unusual activity that morning.

In 1985, at a MUFON gathering, Jones would relate more details of the alien incident. Though the testimony is copyrighted, I can paraphrase some of the more important details. He stated that the skin of the unclothed being was wet, shiny, and snake-like. The entity would be about 4 foot tall, with a large head and a slender body. The overall color was a greyish-brown.

Although the Air Force has deemed Jones' report as a hoax, several well regarded UFO investigators that have come to know Jones well, know better. He has gained nothing from his story, and it has been corroborated by others. An investigation into this monumental case is still in process. Hopefully, more details will be forthcoming in the near future.

Grudge/Bluebook Special Report 13#

A fascinating case of possible military interactions with extraterrestrials is told by UFO/ET investigator Bill English. He claimed to have read the highly classified *Grudge/Bluebook Special Report 13#*. Reports 1-12 and 14 had been publically known to investigators, but there was always a question why was there not a Special Report 13#. Bill himself was only 95% sure that the document was legitimate and not some kind of disinformation. After Bill discussed the report with Stanton Friedman and others he became a very controversial figure in the UFO/ET community as one would expect.

Bill English is a son of an Arizona state legislator and former captain in the Green Berets. He claims that he was exposed to this Report when he worked at a RAF listening post at Chicksands in the UK where he worked as an information analyst. His exposure to this document caused Bill to become a dedicated UFO/ET investigator in order to gain an understanding of the big picture.

I first ran across this material in *UFO Crash at Aztec* where the name of the witness was not given, but Bill eventually went public, especially after claiming assassination attempts on his life. One really has to be wary of a case so dramatic and without a lot of supporting evidence. That said, those of us who have researched this kind of UFO/ET material in detail believe a lot of little bits and pieces that tend to collaborate the extraordinary detailed information in the document. I myself have not dug deeply into this case, but certainly invite the reader to do so for a very interesting ride. I also noticed that this Internet home page is a good resource for UFO/ET related documents.

There is very disturbing material in this report that is confirmed by other reports available in the UFO/ET community where humans have been harmed, killed and even mutilated by an extraterrestrial race known as the Greys. While there is other evidence indicating this, what I like is the extreme detail from the report that Bill English claims to be able to remember, some of it which seems unique to this case. Bill English reports on one mutilation case he investigated and reported in Viet Nam that ended up in the Special Report helping to confirm his belief that this document was real. What follows is an excerpt from Bill's testimony as to what he saw in the document.

"There were also what was then classified Close Encounters of the 3rd kind. It was made very clear that these people whom it was determined had genuine CE 3's were moved in the middle of the night by Air Force personnel and relocated to various sites in the Midwest and Northwest parts of the United States. In many cases these people experienced physical ailments from exposure to various types of radiation.

One case especially noted and remembered very vividly was entitled "Darlington Farm Case" out of Ohio. Case apparently took place in October 1953. Man, wife and 13 year old son were sitting down at dinner table. As they sat there the lights in the farm house began to dim. Dogs and animals raised ruckus on outside.

13 year old boy got up from dinner table to see what was going on. He called his mother and father to come look at the funny light in the sky.

Father and mother went out onto the porch. When they got out on the porch one of the dogs broke loose from leash beside house and came running around front. The boy began chasing it into the open field, as his mother and father watched the light come down from the sky.

They described it as a round ball of fire and it began to hover over the field where the boy and dog had run to. As they stood and watched, the mother and father heard the boy start screaming for help whereupon the father grabbed his shotgun which was right next to the door and began to run out into the field with the mother following. When the father got to the field he saw his son being carried away by what looked like little men, into this huge fiery looking object. As it took off the father fired several rounds at the object, to no avail.

They found the dog; its head had been crushed but no sign of the boy or any other footprints of the little men who apparently carried him off. Father immediately called the Darlington police and they immediately came out to investigate. The official report read that the boy had run off and was lost in the forest which bordered the farm. Within 48 hours the Air Force made the determination that the family was to be relocated and the mother and father were picked up by Air Force Intelligence and all personal belonging and possessions were loaded into U.S. Air Force trucks and moved to a north western relocation site.

The mother was in shock and had to go through a great deal of psychotherapy and deprogramming as did father. One interesting aspect about this case was classification under Air Force report which read it was a genuine CE 3 and that for the good of national security the mother and father had been relocated to relocation zones Z21-14. Not sure whether this indicated map grid coordinates or latitude longitude.

According to the report there were at least four relocation sites across the United States. Depending upon which type of encounter these people had, the report indicated that there were extensive medical facilities available at the relocation sites to deal with all medical emergencies up to and including radiation poisoning.

The report mentioned a site located in the Utah-Nevada area, but no indication of its purpose or what it was for.

Report gave clear indication of reports of human mutilations, most notably was a case witnessed by Air Force personnel in which an Air Force Sgt E-6 by the name of Jonathan P. Lovette was observed being taken captive aboard what appeared to be a UFO at the White Sands Missile Test Range in New Mexico. This abduction took place in March of 1956 at about 0300 local and was witnessed by Major William Cunningham of the United States Air Force Missile Command near Holloman Air Force Base.

Major Cunningham and Sgt Lovette were out in a field down-range from the launch sites looking for debris from a missile test when Sgt Lovette went over the ridge of a small sand dune and was out of sight for a time. Major Cunningham heard Sgt Lovette scream in what was described as terror or agony. The Major, thinking Lovette had been bitten by a snake or something ran over the crest of the dune and saw Sgt Lovette being dragged into what appeared to him and was described as being a silvery disk like object which hovered in the air approximately 15 to 20 feet.

Major Cunningham described what appeared to be a long snake-like object which was wrapped around the sergeant's legs and was dragging him to the craft. Major Cunningham admittedly froze as the sergeant was dragged inside the disc and observed the disc and observed the disc going up into the sky very quickly. Major Cunningham got on the jeep radio and reported the incident to Missile Control whereupon Missile Control confirmed a radar sighting. Search parties went into the desert looking for Sgt Lovette. Major Cunningham's report was taken and he was admitted to the White Sands Base Dispensary for observation.

The search for Sgt Lovette continues for three days at the end of which his nude body was found approximately ten miles down-range. The body had been mutilated; the tongue had been removed from the lower portion of the jaw. An incision had been made just under the tip of the chin and extended all the way back to the esophagus and larynx. He had been emasculated and his eyes had been removed. Also, his anus had been removed and there were comments in the report on the apparent surgical skill of the removal of these items including the genitalia.

The report commented that the anus and the genitalia had been removed 'as though a plug' which in the case of the anus extended all the way to the colon. There was no sign of blood within the system. The initial autopsy report confirmed that the system had been completely drained of blood and that there was no vascular collapse due to death by bleeding. Sub-comment was added that this was unusual because in anybody who dies of bleeding or in the case of a complete blood loss there is always vascular collapse.

Also noted was that when the body was found there were a number of dead predatory type birds within the area who apparently had died after trying to partake of the sergeant's body. There were a number of extremely grisly black and white photographs. From all indications the body had been exposed to the elements for at least a day or two. The New Mexico sun in the desert is extremely hot and debilitating under normal circumstances."

I would like to point out as I end this chapter that what I have presented here is only a very small amount of the evidence available that provides a suitable foundation for Exopolitics and the military and intelligence community involvement, no matter what the uninformed critics have to say. For those that would like to build on a reliable foundation, would be well served to read Richard Dolan's books *UFO's and the National Security State 1 & 2,* These are rich in documentation as well as *AD, After Disclosure.* For a good source of declassified and leaked documents one can go to www.majesticdocuments.com

There is no need for me to get into all this background material in this Exopolitics book when there are already very good books on UFO's and documents easily available. Furthermore one can use the social networks to keep up to date on developments in the UFO field and in Exopolitics, if one is willing to stick with the credible people in the field and avoid those trashing up the field with wild unfounded speculations and scams.

CHAPTER THREE

BREAKAWAY CIVILIZATION AND THE SECRET SPACE PROGRAM

"We already have the means to travel among the stars, but these technologies are locked up in black projects and it would take an act of God to ever get them out to benefit humanity... Anything you can imagine we already know how to do...There are two types of UFOs – the ones we build, and the ones THEY build. We learned from both crash retrievals and actual 'Hand-me-downs'...The Government knew, and until a 1969 took an active hand in the administration of that information. After a 1969 Nixon 'Purge,' administration was handled by an international board of directors in the private sector." Ben Rich, former head of the Lockheed Skunk Works

"The real menace of our Republic is the invisible government which like a giant octopus sprawls its slimy length over our city, state and nation... At the head of the octopus are the Rockefeller-Standard Oil interests and a small group of powerful banking houses generally referred to as the international bankers who virtually run the U.S. government for their own selfish purposes" Former Mayor of New York John Hylan in 1922

Richard Dolan author of; *UFO's and the National Security State 1&2*, came up with the term 'Breakaway Civilization' to describe a separately evolving covert, technically advanced community of people with trillions of dollars of resources siphoned off from our host society. This very autocratic, even fascist elite society uses fear, greed and intimidation even murder, to remain invisible to its host society all under the guise of National Security.[39]

Anything that relates to this Breakaway Civilization is classified Top Secret or above with access by Need to Know and Special Access Programs (SAPS). While much of the Breakaway Civilization is centered in the United States, it has integrated itself into allied governments around the globe. It is what President Eisenhower called the Military-Industrial complex in his farewell speech, just before leaving office, warning that it was breaking away from constitutional controls.

If a person really thinks about it, Special Access on a need to know basis, is how the plantation slave owner controlled his slaves, educating them just enough to do their jobs but no more. To educate them further than need to know would invite rebellion. The old plantation system promoted ignorance among slaves in tandem with methods of control based on fear, intimidation and reward. I think the New World Order (NWO) as envisioned by the Elite Military-Industrial Complex Globalists is no more than a more sophisticated version of old feudal society reintroduced into the modern age.

The NWO's wage slaves are not controlled by the whip or the withholding of food as in the past, but through the creation and control of paper money and the mass media. Money is created and distributed through private central banks disguised as Federal, in almost every country of the world. Paul Hellyer the Ex-Defense Minister of Canada gave a very good speech called *'Global Fraud, Global Hope'* that explains sophisticated mechanism of control and even slips a little ET information into the mix as well.[40]

I explained in the introduction to this book that there should be nothing surprising about the idea of elite breakaway civilizations. Humanities past is replete with instances where the ruling elite of a society overtly maintain a standard of living and technology in advance of what subjects as a whole have access to. What is different in this case, is that this system covertly hides behind a guise of National Security, while growing like a cancer to such size that it subverts and corrupts legitimate transparent constitutional governments all around the world.

I am going to provide the reader with evidence that supports the idea that much of this Breakaway civilization's advanced technology and its super-secret Space Program is based upon reverse engineering extraterrestrial technologies. These advanced exotic propulsion and exotic power technologies have been gained first through extraterrestrial crashes, and soon afterward from what are called Technology Transfer Programs (TTPs), negotiated between different ET civilizations including the Tall Whites and the Greys. Such negotiations imply embassies and ambassadors, and I recall Charles Hall stating that his female teacher in the 1960's was, 'The Ambassador's Daughter.'

This Military Industrial Complex is the real reason the UFO/ET cover up has lasted so long because the corporations involved profit immensely from maintaining a monopoly on

ET access or in the suppressing of exotic cheap energy technologies that would put the fossil fuels industry out of business. I call this loosely knit conglomerate of allied special interests the Alien Resource Cartel, which is a very important part of the overall globalist's network of criminal enterprises.

According to aerospace engineer Bill Uhouse and Ben Rich, this cartel was spun off of the MJ12 organization in a purge by the Nixon administration in the 1960's. These following quotes from Bill Uhouse' material provide a fascinating window into how, what he calls the Satellite Government, operates. As one can see from these quotes Nixon left a dark imprint upon society in this arena as well. In this early report Bill was called Jarod, but later the ET he worked with was called the J-Rod. Bill Uhouse states:

"Understanding how this social structure works is like trying to understand the internal relationships of a tight-knit family in some Asian culture." "If any area seems dubious, he asks his boss about it, who says either "Okay" or "Let's hold off on that a while." For example, his boss said it was okay to mention Nixon as the founder of the Satellite Government, because "Nixon is dead." Playing by the rules is very simple for Jarod. He is not working from any rule book or security classification system."

"Jarod says the satellite government lives by its own laws, completely separate from the conventional government except for an interface with the military. It is not controlled by any other agency, so it does not have to obey the security regulations of other agencies. The fact that Jarod is allowed to speak does seem to imply permission from a higher level than the supervisor, but perhaps a word from management, without any paperwork, is all it takes to make something secret or not secret. Security could be both more intrusive than in any conventional defense program and more informal to those who are used to the structure. Consider the special circumstances...."

"This agency was separated from the rest of the government over 40 years ago. Thus, it would have had an opportunity to evolve in its own way, adapting to the unique requirements of the subject matter." "The organization is largely composed of older

men who have worked with each other for decades. A worker's supervisor and his security officer are assigned to him for life."
"The organization is extremely hierarchical, especially given the needs of compartmentalization. A worker reports only to his immediate supervisor, and direct contacts with members of other departments and higher management are rare."

In my estimation one of the most important documents released by the United States Government is the declassified Wright Patterson 1956 paper on Electogravitics.[41] It's technical, but it provides a powerful foundation and basis for the technological development timeline to a present day Secret Space Program based on electromagnetic and electrogravitic propulsion and exotic power technologies. It also includes the names of corporations that became the major players in the Military Industrial Complex. I have included it in its entirety as the next chapter so that it is available to the technically inclined, but the lay person can just skip over it if they like.

Many researchers believe that this Secret Space Program and its Space Fleet is capable of not only rapid travel about our solar system with bases on the Moon and Mars, but is deep space capable as well as first was indicated by Ben Rich. This is why there has been no overt return to the moon because in the 1960's NASA became little more than an expensive and dangerous cover and public propaganda operation. Several NASA employee whistle-blowers have testified to being involved in airbrushing out any and all images of the ET presence from images of the Earth, Moon, Mars and even space.

There is so much evidence for this Secret Space Program and the Breakaway Civilization in which it is imbedded that I hardly know where to start. Maybe the best place to start would be statements that Ben Rich made in public and in private before he died.

Ben Rich Lockheed's CEO Admits on Deathbed: UFO.ETs Are Real

According to an article published in May 2010 issue of the *MUFON UFO Journal* Ben Rich, the "Father of the Stealth Fighter-Bomber" and former head of Lockheed Skunk Works, had released information that extraterrestrial UFO visitors are real and the U.S. Military can travel to the stars.

What he said might be new to many people today, but he revealed the information before his death in January 1995. His statements helped to give credence to reports that the U.S. military has been flying vehicles that mimic alien craft. The article was written by Tom Keller, an aerospace engineer who has worked as a computer systems analyst for NASA's Jet Propulsion Laboratory.

"Inside the Skunk Works (Lockheed's secret research and development entity), we were a small, intensely cohesive group consisting of about fifty veteran engineers and designers and a hundred or so expert machinists and shop workers. Our forte was building technologically advanced airplanes of small number and of high class for highly secret missions."

"We already have the means to travel among the stars, but these technologies are locked up in black projects, and it would take an act of God to ever get them out to benefit humanity. Anything you can imagine, we already know how to do."

"We now have the technology to take ET home. No, it won't take someone's lifetime to do it. There is an error in the equations. We know what it is. We now have the capability to travel to the stars. First, you have to understand that we will not get to the stars using chemical propulsion. Second, we have to devise a new propulsion technology. What we have to do is find out where Einstein went wrong."

When Rich was asked how UFO propulsion worked, he said, "Let me ask you. How does ESP work?" The questioner responded with, "All points in time and space are connected?" Rich then said; "That's how it works!"

Lockheed "Skunk Works" former CEO knew the Roswell extraterrestrial UFO influenced designs of Testor model kits for Roswell UFO models, and U.S. top secret aircraft. According to a CNI News report by Colorado resident Michael Lindeman, the design information was derived from forensic illustrations and numerous witness testimonies about the Roswell UFO, provided by William L. "Bill" McDonald.

In an e-mail, dated July 29, 1999, apparently addressed to Lindeman, McDonald referenced an excerpt of a discussion with Harold Puthoff, founder of the highly classified U.S. "remote viewing" program. McDonald said: "Well Hal, you asked for it! Now that legendary Lockheed engineer and chief model kit designer for the Testor Corporation, John Andrews, is dead, I can announce that he personally confirmed the design connection between the Roswell Spacecraft and the Lockheed Martin Unmanned Combat Air Vehicles (UCAVs), spy planes, Joint Strike Fighters, and Space Shuttles.

Andrews was a close personal friend of 'Skunk Works' CEO Ben Rich; the hand-picked successor of Skunk Works founder Kelly Johnson and the man famous for the F-117 Nighthawk 'Stealth' fighter, its 'half-pint' prototype the 'HAVE BLUE,' and the top-secret F-19 Stealth Interceptor. Before Rich died of cancer, Andrews took my questions to him.

1. There are 2 types of UFO's the ones we build and ones 'they' build. We learned from both crash retrievals and actual "hand-me-downs." The Government knew and until 1969 took an active hand in the administration of that information. After a 1969 Nixon 'purge,' administration was handled by an international board of directors in the private sector.

2. Nearly all 'biomorphic' aerospace designs were inspired by the Roswell spacecraft — from Kelly's SR-71 Blackbird onward to today's drones, UCAVs, and aerospace craft.

3. It was Ben Rich's opinion that the public should not be told [about UFOs and extraterrestrials]. He believed they could not handle the truth — ever. Only in the last months of his decline did he begin to feel that the "international corporate board of di-

rectors" dealing with the 'Subject' could represent a bigger problem to citizens personal freedoms under the United States Constitution than the presence of off-world visitors themselves."

Lindeman added that; "Bill McDonald received the above information from Andrews from 1994 until their last phone call near Christmas in 1998." Lindeman also noted "It should also be known that Dr Ben R. Rich attended a public aerospace designers and engineers conference in 1993 before his illness overwhelmed him in which he stated — in the presence of MUFON Orange County Section Director Jan Harzan and many others that – 'We' (i.e., the U.S. aerospace community/military industrial complex) had in its possession the technology to 'take us to the stars.' See the complete letter in May, 2010 MUFON UFO Journal from John Andrews and the hand written reply from Dr Ben Rich.

Lockheed Skunkworks Engineer USAF, and CIA Contractor Don Phillips confirms Ben Rich's statements, "These UFO's were huge and they would just come to a stop and do a 60 degree, 45 degree, 10 degree turn, and then immediately reverse this action." During the Apollo landing, Neil Armstrong says, "They're here. They are right over there and looking at the size of those ships, it is obvious they don't like us being here." When I was working with the Skunkworks with Kelly Johnson, we signed an agreement with the government to keep very quiet about this.

Anti-gravitational research was going on. We know that there were some captured craft from 1947 in Roswell, they were real. And, yes, we really did get some technology from them. And, yes, we really did put it to work. We knew each other from what we call an unseen industry. We can term it black, deep black, or hidden.

The knowledge I have of these technologies came from the craft that were captured here. I didn't see the craft, nor did I see the bodies, but I certainly know some of the people that did. There was no question that there were beings from outside the planet.

Are these ET people hostile? Well, if they were hostile, with their weaponry they could have destroyed us a long time ago. We got these things that are handhold scanners that scan the body and determine what the condition is. We can also treat from the same scanner.

I can tell you personally that we've been working on them. And we have ones that can diagnose and cure cancer. One of the purposes I had for founding my technology corporation in 1998 was to bring forth these technologies that can clean the air and can help get rid of the toxins, and help reduce the need for so much fossil fuel. Yes, it is time. I can tell you personally that it has already started."

The following is an article I wrote after I first heard the term Solar Warden being used as the alleged code name for the part of the Secret Space Fleet that operates within our solar system. I already had an interest in the Secret Space Fleet and had written material about what I already knew.

Here is an interesting little tid-bit folks, that Vince White our exopolitical poet in residence sent me yesterday that I think deserves sharing. People that have been following my blog know I have discussed this alleged allied space fleet in some of my articles.

Forwarded Message: "Subject: Solar Warden Date: 4/5/2009 Dear Jerry: I have verified a little about the Solar Warden that you asked about some time ago. It is the overall project identification for our Space Fleet Carrier program coming out of Regan's old Star Wars efforts. We apparently have one or more Space Carriers, like Aircraft Carriers at sea, but in deep space, that supports our Space Patrol efforts and house our American built flying discs that require no fuel and operate on free energy."

"The STS-58 video clip that was filmed from one of our space shuttles showed such an intercept and that footage was immediately suppressed and resulted in that free video from the shuttles being shut down. Gary McKinnon, the English computer nerd that lived with his mother in London, using a cheap home PC late at night, said that he discovered this project and that he found evidence of three such carriers and their names and numbers and even the names of some of the commanders in those black project files."

"Now you can see why our government is spending so much money and political clout to extradite that foreign national to our country for trial in our country for silencing and then elimination.

One has to wonder how much it took to persuade the English House of Lords to give him up to us. Regards, W."

After I posted the two articles on Solar Warden, Open Minds Forum (OM) management sent the following to me. It would appear that the code name Solar Warden first surfaced at OM before the Gary McKinnon affair. As far as I know Gary did not know of the name Solar Warden.

"You may come to find the information somewhat shocking and unable to understand. I pray the Almighty will look out for the inhabitants of this planet as the coming years will bring much misery. I pass on this information in the hope that you, as an unbiased observer, will make sure the public learns the truth."

"All space programs are a cover that exists to deceive the people of this world. We have a space fleet, which is code named; 'Solar Warden.' There were, as of 2005, eight ships, an equivalent to aircraft carriers and forty-three 'protectors,' which are space planes. One was lost recently to an accident in Mars' orbit while it was attempting to re-supply the multinational colony within Mars. This base was established in 1964 by American and Soviet teamwork. Not everything is, as it seems."

"We have visited all the planets in our solar system, at a distance of course, except Mercury. We have landed on Pluto and a few moons. These ships contain personnel from many countries and have sworn an oath to the World Government, also, known as the Bilderbergers. The technology came from back engineering alien-disc wreckage and at times with alien assistance."

I think we can begin to build points on a historical timeline from the very strong foundation of the 1956 Declassified Wright Patterson Electrogravitics paper to the present day Secret Space Fleet. One very important point has been presented by Senior Research Engineer Boyd Bushman who worked for Lockheed Martin, Texas Instruments and Hughes Aircraft.

In October of 2011 he provided evidence to investigators in an interview that by 1959 the U.S. government had already reverse engineered an extraterrestrial spacecraft using a nuclear reactor for propulsion! I mean this was three years after the Wright Patterson Electrogravitics paper was published. It should not be hard for the reader to begin to logically create a time line from 1956 to 1959 to the present super-secret space fleet.[42]

There has been speculation and some evidence that the Navy has operational control over the Secret Space Fleet, in a case of fact imitating Star Trek fiction. It is well know that the Navy pretty much has had a monopoly on engineering small compact nuclear reactor power plants for its ships and carriers in its large ocean going fleets. The Navy's organizational structure is well suited for operating large ocean going fleets. On the other hand, the Air Force has experience in the research and development, testing and flying advanced aerospace craft and expertise in aerospace tracking and base support in conjunction with Air Force Space Command.

One would assume that some kind of working arrangement has been worked out over the years between the Air Force and the Navy. As in the fiction movie Avatar, one would expect the Army and Marines to have operational control of ground operations on Secret colonies and bases on the Moon, Mars and even on other solar systems.

A second important point on the historical time line to a Secret Space Fleet and it's off world bases and colonies that use exotic electromagnetic propulsion systems with compact nuclear power plants. These power plants that produce huge amounts of electrical power, may have been responsible for the Piney Woods Incident, the Cash-Landrum UFO Case that took place in December of 1980. One can speculate from the revelations of Bob Lazar, now backed up to some extent by Boyd Bushman and some material in *UFO Crash at Aztec*, that alien power plants are not that easy to replicate, so these first craft used electromagnetic and electrogravitic off the shelf power plant technologies.

The Cash-Landrum case[43] has been well researched and has withstood the test of time, and seems to have involved a core meltdown in a super-secret exotic aerospace craft. It was surrounded by military helicopters and it severely irradiated the witnesses involved. The three witnesses sued the U.S. government for damages to their health and the case even went to a Congressional Hearing but the government would not admit responsibility for the incident.

If the reader would like to investigate further into the evidence for a Secret Space Program and Space Fleet here are some links to the very credible Richard Dolan's videos[44] and Dr Michael Salla's articles on Solar Warden- Part 1: Reagan records & Space Command antigravity fleet[45] Part 2: NASA Decline and the Antigravity Space Fleet.[46] Part 3: Star Trek vs. Solar Warden – The Real Starfleet.[47]

Here are some more links that can be useful for those interested in the Secret Space Program it's historical timeline and the technologies involved: Boyd Bushman, Senior Research Scientist with Lockheed Martin.[48] Bob Lazar Interview on UFO/ET Propulsion.[49] Col. Corso and the Truth About UFOs.[50] Sightings investigation of Nellis UFO.[51] Detailed Description of a Secret Space Craft.[52] Astronaut Buzz Adrin Recounts UFO.[53] Testimony of Astronaut Edgar Mitchell.[54] Astronaut Gordon Cooper on UFOs.[55]

An Alien Spaceship on the Moon
Written Interview With William Rutledge, An "Apollo 20" Astronaut

The article titled; *An Alien Spaceship On The Moon*[56] written by investigator Luca Scantamburlo discribes an alleged crash retrival on the moon with video images and stills of a mumified human extraterrestrial and images of a crashed spaceship on the moon. This is the sort of case that often falls through the cracks because there are so many people faking alien pictures nowdays.

This case stands out because it would not be easy to fake so much material including some very spectacular images of a very well preserved extraterrestrial human body recovered from a triangular crashed spacecraft.

Unfortunately I can't print all these images in this book so the reader must go to the Internet to review this imagery. This case seems to have stood the test of time and I can not find any substantial evidence on the Internet that proves this case to be a hoax. If the reader goes online to Luca's website they can see from this article that there is a lot of detail here provided by Rutledge. Rutledge certianly seems to know a lot about the alledged Apollo 19 and 20 covert moon missions.

I also have noted in reviewing Luca's site that others have come forward to confirm parts of his story including the commander of Apollo 19.[57] It's hard to believe that with all this evidence that this case has not gathered more interest in the UFO/ET community. The debunkers even took the trouble of debunking this case on Wikipedia simply claiming hoax with little real supporting evidence that it is a hoax.

If this case is not a hoax and is real and Rutledge is right that this mummified human ET body dubbed the Mona Lisa being very old, it suggests that the mega-human root races are very old. Previously I had thought millions of years, but if Rutledge is right about the age of this mummified body, then the age is a hard to believe one and a half billion years. (I discussed this issue with Luca and this could be a translation or a communication error.)

The evidence Luca provides at to these secret covert missions to the moon further substantuates all the other material I have throughout my book about the covert secret space program and it's time line. All this material shows that NASA and the military never really ended manned exporations as claimed, but continuted covertly activities in space and on other planetary bodies. The reader can study the complete Rutledge interview and the Commander interview online. Luca

Scantamburlo states in his introduction to the Rutledge interview:

William Rutledge (according to his story, a man of 76 years old who lives in Rwanda, former of Bell Laboratories and employed by USAF) is the name of the "deep throat" who, since April 2007, has been disclosing information and spreading a lot of video and photographic material on YouTube, about the presumed Apollo 20 space mission. His user name on YouTube is "retiredafb," and the most amazing footage he released so far is the presumed flyover of an ancient alien spaceship found on the backside of the Moon by the Apollo 15 crew."

Luca gets into a lot of technical detail in this interview to clear up some misconceptions and misunderstanding in relation to the evidence Rudledge has presented on the Internet. The following part of interview is what I found to be of particular interest.

16) L.S. Now we can discuss the ancient "alien spaceship" and "the City" on the far side of the Moon. Did you go inside the spaceship? How big was it and what did you find inside?
W.R. We went inside the big spaceship, also into a triangular one. The major parts of the exploration was; it was a mother ship, very old, who crossed the universe at least billions of years ago (1.5 estimated). There were many signs of biology inside, old remains of a vegetation in a "motor" section, special triangular rocks who emitted "tears" of a yellow liquid which has some special medical properties, and of course signs of extra solar creatures. We found remains of little bodies (10cm) living in a network of glass tubes all along the ship, but the major discovery was two bodies, one intact.

17) L.S. Did you visit "the City" on the Moon? Where was it? Did you understand if there was a connection with the Space ship? Are "the City" and "the Ship" still there?
W.R. The "City" was named on Earth and scheduled as station one, but it appeared to be a real space garbage, full of scrap, gold parts, only one construction seemed intact (we named it the

Cathedral). We made shots of pieces of metal, of every part wearing calligraphy, exposed to the sun. The "City" seem to be as old as the ship, but it is a very tiny part. On the rover video, the telephoto lens make the artifacts greater.

18) L.S. What about the "Mona Lisa EBE"? [the correct Italian name is "Mona Lisa"] What does she look like and where was she at that time, when you found out her on the Moon. Where do you think she is now?

W.R. Mona Lisa – I don't remember who named the girl, Leonov or me - was the intact EBE. Humanoid, female, 1.65 meter. Genitalized, haired, six fingers (we guess that mathematics are based on a dozen). Function; pilot, piloting device fixed to fingers and eyes, no clothes, we had to cut two cables connected to the nose. No nostril. Leonov unfixed the eyes device (you'll see that in the video). Concretions of blood or bio liquid erupted and froze from the mouth, nose, eyes and some parts of the body. Some parts of the body were in unusual good condition, (hair) and the skin was protected by a thin transparent protection layer.

As we told to mission control, condition seemed not dead not alive. We had no medical background or experience, but Leonov and I used a test, we fixed our bio equipment on the EBE, and telemetry received by surgeon (Mission Control meds) was positive. That's another story. Some parts could be unbelievable now, I prefer tell the whole story when other videos will be online. This experience has been filmed in the LM. We found a second body, destroyed, we brought the head on board. Color of the skin was blue gray, a pastel blue. Skin had some strange details above the eyes and the front, a strap around the head, wearing no inscription. The "cockpit" was full of calligraphy and formed of long semi hexagonal tubes. She is on Earth and she is not dead, but I prefer to post other videos before telling what happened after.

19) L.S. Were you able to understand the origin of the spacecraft and how old was it?

W.R. The age was estimated to 1.5 billion years. It was confirmed during exploration, we found ejections from the original crust, anorthosite, spirals in feldspathoids, coming from the impact which formed Izsak D; The density of meteor impacts on the ship validated the age, also little white impacts on the Monaco hill at the West of the ship.

In Luca's other interview with the Apollo 19 Commander, the alledged commander further elaborates on Rudledge's fantastic claims and evidence. Whats more here is further evidence of extraterrestrial warfare that I have reported elsewhere in my book.

10) L.S. What were your mission targets, as Apollo 19 crew.

moonwalker1966delta: Our main targets were one of the triangular object located south of the main mothership, the mothership herself and the moon base located SW of the mothership. Our landing site was the same of Apollo 20. Soviets launched the SL-12 2 months before our mission and Luna 21 landed on the west side of the crater. Apollo 20 used Lunokhod 2 as a radio beacon to land exactly on the second largest rockstair not far from Luna 21. Rutledge and Leonov made and extensive use of Lunokhod 2 due to it's highly sophisticated equipment necessary for this kind of mission not only the 4 panoramic telephotometers but also the X-ray scope combined with laser telemeter and the radiation detector to verify the possible radiations emitted by the ship and the base.

11) L.S. What can you tell me about the origin of the alien spacecrafts resting on the backside of the Moon: the cigar-shaped object and the two triangles? Is there any relationship among them? And can you give me once again – as you have already done in a private message - the lunar coordinates of the triangle objects, never revealed before?

moonwalker1966delta: The origin of the two objects the mothership and the alien base were the same. Same materials and same age. We think they have been shot down during a sort of "lunar Pearl Harbor." The base has been completely destroyed and the mothership and the 2 spacecraft shot down during and emergency take off. That is what William and Leonov thought too. As I previously answered in our private message the 2 objects are clearly visible in AS15-P-9625 and AS15-P-9630 in the upper side of the pic and just right of the mothership at coordinates 18.7S - 116.92E and 18.31S - 117.48E. You can notice they are absolutly identical in their triangular shape. If you use a software like NASA World Wind it could be easy to locate them and notice the green metallic brilliance of the first object."

Luca located yet a third whistleblower whose father was involved in these secret missions and who posted to a thread on Above Top Secret adding to the growing body of testimony and evidence in this case. This information and links are also part of the Apollo Commander article.

The project was initiated, by Nixon's orders, in late 1971. My father's work began on the project began in 1974. The actual mission took place in 1976. My father said that he underwent an intensive psychological exam before he was selected to join the program. He said he thought he was bought in mainly because he "could be trusted."

The actual mission consisted of 3 American astronauts whose names he would not mention. He said that these men had been trained for nearly 4 years specifically for this mission. He also said that in 1973 it was confirmed the object was in fact a derelict spacecraft. He reviewed this pictures personally when selected for the project.

The spacecraft was speculated to be roughly 1.5 billion years old, although he was not allowed access to that exact information. The ship was badly decayed from meteor impacts and the ancient crash. The ship was cigar shaped, and massive, the section was roughly 1 mile. Evidence suggested it been explored before us. No alien remains were found. 300kg of artifacts were stripped and brought back. My father described what he called "strange hieroglyphs and markings" covering what was assumed to be the the "cockpit" of the craft."

It's just amazing that this case with all its accumulated testimony and evidence has recieved so little attention by the UFO/ET community. This really looks like the real deal and fits in very well all the other evidence I have been presenting in this book. One really has to be in denial not to realize the importance of this kind of evidence. If Luca's book; Apollo 20-The Disclosure[58] is not smoking gun evidence, I don't know what is.

Special Forces Extraterrestrial 1971 Encounter in Cambodia

Peter A. Bostrom provides us with good case of military interaction with extraterrestrials on the battlefield. I also like this case because of the insight if gives to MJ 12 operations in field. I thought it was particularly interesting in that it is alledged that MJ 12 authorized the release of this information apparently as part of their acclimation program. Peter Bostrom said:

> Abstract: The following is word-for-word as transcribed from a tape interview by myself with a retired military "Special Forces" officer who served in Thailand during the Vietnam War. This is an account of a close encounter with several EBEs and their space vehicle.

Unlike other countless reports of similar "high strangeness" meetings with extraterrestrials this account is maybe even more interesting because it happened in "war time" surroundings in Cambodia, a country out-of-bounds for US troops at the time, plus there is mention of MJ12 as a government entity who was involved with the gathering of information about Unidentified Objects in the air space in and around Thailand and it shows how determined the government is to extract all information it can on the subject. Also there is mention of another strange encounter from the same general area.

I will use the name Joe in place of this gentleman's real name. I spoke with Joe off and on for several weeks. When he spoke about this encounter he never changed his story and I believe he wants to give the true account as he himself believed it happened. As my conversations continued with Joe he said he had a message that he could freely speak about the subject of his encounter with the extraterrestrials in Cambodia and anything else concerning the subject "since this information will be made public in the near future anyway," but he was not to specifically indicate the true reason why he was in Cambodia.

This "other officer" also talked about the UFO subject in general saying such things as the Roswell crash really happened and described precise methods of how people are taken to see the alien vehicle and bodies using high security procedures in transporting these people who need to go there for various reasons. He also talked about two different alien beings. One name he used was the "Grays" and the other was the "Nordics."

Transcribed Account

Joe: Basically I will describe what happened. In September 1971 I was stationed with the Army in Thailand. Originally this was a routine mission in Cambodia close to an area called Tonle Sap just south of Ankor Wat, where the temples are.

We had gone on a previous mission in answer to some problems and had gone back in on a search and destroy mission. This area we were mainly concerned about was insurgents from the Khmer Rouge - Pol Pot's people. They were really wreaking havoc at the time with the local indigenous personnel. We were after one group and when going through the jungle we heard some noises coming from a hidden area.

Bostrom: You heard a noise? Joe: We heard some noises that sounded like generators or machinery. Something with a hum. Bostrom: So that's what attracted you? Joe: Yes, we assumed they had some kind of refueling station or something out there. It's quite common for the Khmer Rouge and Phaphet Lao to use a high clearing in the jungle to make an artificial clearing for refueling helicopters, things like that. They didn't have too many. Most of them were Russian made - and they could refuel them - and we thought we really struck on a good one this time or thought they were building equipment buildings or bunkers or such.

When we came into the clearing we were quite surprised to find something quite unlike what I've ever seen before. At the time I held the rank of Lieutenant. We had with us approximately fourteen Special Forces, of our country, and several dozen Thai arranged with us. Bostrom: So you were in Special Forces?

Joe; Yes, I was originally with the 101st Airborne Special Tactical Unit. We were reassigned 506th Air Calvary sent to Thailand. They were with the auspices of a group we won't discuss for obvious reasons. During this time there had been several reports of some strange instances. We more or less "poo-pooed" them thinking they were people getting scared in combat. You have a few guys taking drugs, we didn't have anybody in our unit that was. You just don't really know. Things come out of the jungle. You see them flying through the trees and it looks quite different than it would in broad daylight in an open area.

We entered the clearing. It was almost spherical in shape suspended on four legs. The base of which it looked like it touched the ground. I couldn't really tell if it was actually on the ground or not and there were a number of - the best description I could say, were humanoids. It's difficult to remember for a couple of reasons that we'll get into a little later. There were at least as many of them as there were of us. Bostrom: How many do you think?

Joe: I would say there was anywhere between 16 to 21. There was quite a few. There wasn't just a handful of fellows out there in the jungle. Their appearance was not that of any human being I'd ever seen on earth. Skin was a grayish whitish color. They were wearing what appeared to be a one piece jump suit which was silver in color. Much like the metalized Mylar like a heat suit. It didn't appear to be a pressure suit of any kind. We found out later that it was quite a strong material. When we approached they really didn't notice us at first and when they did they turned toward us. Some of the fellows were carrying items; the only way I can describe it, are some type of instruments.

Didn't see any weapons anywhere. Made a quick judgment. It didn't look like any weapon I'd ever seen so I thought it could be safe. We had a young corporal with us. Well, this was his second time in combat and he didn't react very well. These, well, I'll call them aliens; one of the aliens turned toward him with something in his hand which he evidently thought was a weapon of some type and he felt threatened and let loose a short burst of fire from a Browning FNFAL which is literally a three way Winchester. It has a 150 grain slug; the same hitting power as the 30-0-6 out to 15 yards. About the shortest burst you could fire on full auto is somewhere between 8 and 12 rounds, which of a distance from 30 to 35 feet where it struck this fellow would devastate a normal human being. The only thing I can justify, we wear flak jackets most of the time.

The material, whatever it was, is of the same material as the "second chance" like we had which was a compact, lightweight bullet proof vest. I've been struck several times with slugs with those - rib cage broken, you get bruised very badly. You feel like you are going to die, but as a general rule, unless it's an armor piercing slug or some type of Teflon siding jacket, they don't penetrate. I've never seen one penetrate. I've seen 50 caliber shells go through but nothing much smaller than that. Nothing except for that high caliber and high velocity will pierce it. Occasionally a tracer will burn a pretty good size hole in it. When it struck this fellow he went down - dropped like a stone, like he was dead. We assumed he was dead.

Out of the group most of them were all approximately the same height. I would say some were five foot or less; maybe four foot eight inches - in that range. They were very, very small people. More like dwarfs in nature and perfectly proportioned. The arms didn't seem to be any longer than they should be, except for one fellow who was about five-six or five-seven.

He intervened at this point. I pushed the weapon down that George had in his hand. I thought, "God" this guy is going to kill us. At this point I was terror stricken. We didn't know who these guys were. Something like this happens - all the science fiction movies you've ever seen in your life run through your mind. You think "Oh my God" are they going to pull out ray guns? Are they going to atomize us, or are they going to turn us into rabbits or pigs or something like this? Bostrom: Did any of them ever say anything?

Joe: Never heard a single word. This fellow turned to me evidently knowing that I was platoon commander. He raised his hand with palm out and fingers up in just a peaceful gesture and stopped and walked over to George and struck him on the cheek and it wasn't a real heavy blow. It was something like you'd smack your child to get his attention, but the effect was devastating. George went down like a limp rag, just like an electric shock had gone through him.

The only thing I could figure is either this fellow is lots stronger than we can imagine he was or he did something else. You've seen blows even in martial arts that don't appear to be very heavy but have a devastating effect. He went down like a stone - just a limp rag. He recovered very quickly. About that time I was trying to pull him up, I didn't know what we were going to do at that point. I didn't want anybody else to fire because I figured if we open fire on these guys - we were dead. I was scared. I soiled my pants at that point, a nervous reaction. I didn't know quite what to do.

With the exception of George, we were all veterans of at least 20 to 15 fire fights. We were relatively well seasoned combat veterans. It could have been George's third time out, it must have been his first or second, I would say probably second and he was green and he panicked and I thought, well, he just paid the price for it. This fellow just killed him. He recovered. I tried to pull him up and turned around about the time the fellow being shot got up and brushed himself off - and I thought "on shit" these fellows are going to wipe us out. If an FNFAL didn't take him down in 8 to 12 shots that is one tough little hombre. The only thing I could figure is that the material is tough enough that it acted as a cushion just like a vest. The fellow was visibly shaken. He didn't seem to be in tip top shape but he obviously wasn't dead and there weren't any marks on him.

We spent many times picking slugs out of our flak jackets and they'd get too worn and we'd just replace it. It smarts. It will knock you out cold sometimes from the impact. It's like having a very large electric shock run through your body. What takes people out, knocks them out flat, and is not the actual impact of the bullet, but the nervous reaction of the impact, and it will literally lay you out flat before you hit the ground. Every muscle in your body goes rigid. So they have basically the same physiological reaction that we do.

When he turned to me and made a gesture to stop, I thought OK, then everything is going to be alright. George recovered and he turned around again and placed his palm up toward me again to stop, and I had a feeling that everything was OK. I had a very strong impression. I'm not going to say that it was some kind of telepathic message. It didn't really seem like anything like that.

It seemed like "Hey, it's cool, he panicked and I understand the situation."

At this point they packed up all their little instruments, packed themselves back into the craft and left almost soundlessly. There was a little noise. It sat there on the ground as what looked like a quadruped with four legs resting on the ground with pads on them retracted back into the body of the craft which was spheroid and then it just lifted straight up off the ground. I didn't see any visible means of propulsion. There was a little noise. It was hard to tell if it was just the wind blowing through there or what. It was just like an instantaneous burst of speed. Bostrom: What do you think the diameter was?

Joe: It's hard to judge because we were a little distance from it. I would say that it was at a bare minimum of 50 feet. It could have been as far across as 150 feet. It was very difficult to judge. It was a mirrored surface. So you're looking at something and the jungle is being reflected and it's really hard to judge the size. I know it was at least as tall as a five story building. What didn't make any sense is why it should be spheroid. Whatever propulsion system it required, I don't know. Perhaps it's some type of anti-gravity drive and you'd have to have everything centered. Bostrom: Was it round like a ball?

Joe: Round like a ball. Perfectly round as far as I could tell. There was one symbol on the side of what appeared to be, I would say, black paint. Either this, or there was just no coating on this area, of a simple symbol of an arc. Almost like a pyramid with a line drawn underneath it.

We returned to base. The Thais of course weren't going to say anything to anybody. They saw nothing. They heard nothing. They were just along for the ride, which was a typical reaction for the Thais. They didn't want to get involved. They were quite shaken by it as we were. It took us approximately three days to get back to the border. Bostrom: What did everybody talk about on the way back?

Joe: Absolutely nothing. We decided on the way back that nobody say anything. We didn't hear anything. We didn't know anything about it. We got back to the base and the first thing we did was head for a hot shower, because you had to pull all the lice off you and everything else and felt pretty damn dirty. Bostrom: The boy that got knocked down, was he alright?

Joe: He was alright at that point at that point he was fine. He seemed to be just fine. He was a corporal and went to his barracks. I was in officer's barracks. A fellow from the Provost Marshal's office came in and informed me that I had to report to the Captain's office immediately, I said, do I have time to rinse off? He said, just barely. He said put on some clothes and get over there. They want to talk to you right now. I asked him what it was about. He said, I don't know, they won't tell me, just get your tail over there, it's something very heavy. He said they were quite confused about something, I walked into the Captain's office. We were met by the captain, a couple of majors, a Colonel and some civilians. If you've ever worked with anybody with the "firm" they reek of it. You generally expect them in gray flannel suits and white socks, but these fellows just reeked of the "firm" and (name withheld) was in it. Bostrom: Joe: This gentleman rode with MJ 12 and (name withheld) was in it. Joe MJ, Majestic 12. Bostrom: MJ-12?

Joe: Right. The only way we ever heard him call it was MJ-12 or MJ. We knew he worked for that. We didn't know what the heck it was. The only thing we knew was that any enemy aircraft that was sighted had to be reported to him. Any photographs we took had to be given to him. They were overly concerned about enemy aircraft, unusual sightings, and things like that. Just anything out of the ordinary. So we dealt with him sometimes almost on a daily basis. He'd call us in occasionally to look at photographs and say, what is this? And we'd say that's a Russian gun ship; it has so much armament - OK that's what I want to know, thank you very much, discuss this with no one and have a nice day.

He was very single sided with information. We gave him everything. He told us nothing absolutely nothing. He was a cold blooded man. I don't think I ever saw the man sweat. Most of the time he wore a black suit or a dark gray flannel suit. When you are in Thailand and it's at that point in the year it's somewhere between 97 and 100 degrees, 100 to 110% relatively humidity, it's so hot you get heat that's like fog. And he was cold blooded. I've never seen another human being in my life like that. I don't think

I ever saw him sweat except for this incident. And he had a cold sweat going into this.

He ended up taking his jacket off. You never see him outside of a jacket. They sat us down and they grilled us for that day at least 3 1/2 to 4 hours. And they kept asking the same questions over and over. And I was trying to find out who it was that told them because when we got back together later nobody had said anything. So something, or somebody, snitched and said well you don't tell anybody you told. Bostrom: Someone would have had to run in immediately and tell them.

Joe: We hadn't been back more than an hour. We usually took a shower, got cleaned up and got a little rest before we were debriefed because that could sometimes take many hours. It was very interesting. They even sequestered us in our quarters. We were told not to have any outside activities at all and meals would be brought to us. We were not to talk to any unauthorized personnel which meant them or someone directly with authorization from the Provost Marshal's Office.

Then we spent the next 3 to 3 1/2 weeks talking to various people, some of which I don't know who in the heck they were. Several were psychologists. It was very obvious by the kind of questions we were being asked and they started dragging out the ink blots. If your familiar with the Military when they generally bring in the ink blots and try to make it sound like something of a sexual nature they leave you alone. They figure this guy's healthy, this guy's fine and get out of my office - you are alright. We went on with this for two or 2 1/2 weeks then they started using narcohypnosis. Bostrom: How did that operate?

Joe: Essentially they sit you in a chair, make sure your nice and comfy. Hook up the sphygmomanometer, blood pressure tape, and get you highly relaxed using soothing music sometimes, and give you an injection of a basically, what is called a hypnotic drug. There were drugs like Seconal, Scopolamine - the type that have a tendency to reducing what they call psychic resistance. You get your body as relaxed as possible and you lose your will. They actually hypnotize you at that point. It's a combination of drugs and hypnosis. It's my understanding we were trained in our training to go through tortures and things like that. There wasn't a one of us that couldn't pass a polygraph test and lie about his age, the color of his mother and the color of the sky.

They had us as well covered as they could in case we were captured we knew how to respond. The only thing I can say that occurred during that time was that in one way or another they altered our memories. Now, I do not know whether they.. We saw something else... or they gave us a different memory and that's what we ended up with or what we saw was much worse than occurred and I toned it down. I do know that every one of us still have occasional nightmares about it and we get flashes of things that are just an incredible blood-bath. George was reassigned from our unit after we had all cleared through medical and psychological.

I was called into the Captain's office, approximately what would have been 6 or 8 weeks after the incident to identify a body they told me was George. Now I'd seen the man on the base a few days before. The body they showed me was far, far decomposed. Even in the jungle where you have rapid decomposition.
Bostrom: But you couldn't positively identify the body? Joe: I couldn't identify it as George. The flesh was all liquefied.
Bostrom: So for all you could see it may have been someone else.

Joe: The only thing I can say is his tissue had seemed to suffer from some kind of extreme disruption - like every cell wall had been broken. Like you see with a cold sore. It's called lisodumine when the cells rupture and the virus comes out for some kind of bacteriological agent in it that affected it. I don't think it was the latter. I think whatever happened to him - whether they transferred him to show me the body and say that's George.
Bostrom: Why would they show you a body you couldn't identify?

Joe: The people we were dealing with were very, very careful about covering all avenues. They never left a thread hanging - and I don't know - I lost all track of it at that point. As far as I knew he was dead. Why, I was called in to identify the body and sign the papers. The only way I could identify him was his dog tags. The usual thing was that during combat, because of the nature of our unit. Dog tags were retrieved by a ranking officer and returned to you when you returned to base. We carried what was called T8407-?-T101 which was called a get-out-of-jail-free card.

It was a cardboard card with two sides and department logo on one side to say the individual was allowed to be carrying strange and unusual weapons, may or may not be in uniform and not to be detained for any reason whatsoever. If this card is found on a body it is to be burned with the body and reported to a telephone number state side and a group to contact and it went back to combat. Bostrom: Is that about all you can remember?

Joe: Well that's the problem. If we really sit down and try to pressure us through it, you get confused. I talked to a couple of fellows that were involved in it and they have the same kind of problem. Slowly but surely, things emerge and over the years more and more has come up. It was years before I ever had a desire at all to talk about it. Not because it was frightening because the "firm" told us not to or that they were going to place it under the National Security act, but because I absolutely had no desire whatsoever to talk about it.

Bostrom: Do you remember any other details such as how they entered the craft? Joe: It was like a section slid down. Like it just created itself on the side and slid down. Bostrom: Do you remember a ramp? Joe: It slid down and it tilted down to the ground had a stair on it and formed a ramp for them to walk right up with steps on it. Bostrom: Did it look like they were walking on steps?

Joe: It had steps on it because they were stepping and it wasn't like they shuffled on the ramp. Their gait was very smooth, almost unerring and they covered a lot of ground in a little bit of time. But the main problem is like I said, if we sit down and try to really go through the details and think hard about it I end up almost with an anxiety attack. Whatever it was that they did to bury those things is pretty permanent. Over the years, I still occasionally have nightmares about it. I'd wake up in a cold sweat and I'd remember for a while. It's frustrating. I find myself angry because I don't know what the heck they did to us. Bostrom: Do you know one or two of the people and can you get a hold of them today?

Joe: Yes, there's five or six I could get a hold of. Most of them just refuse to talk about it at all. Two of them I know still work for the "firm." They are active so they're not going to talk about it. Bill suffers from delayed stress syndrome and when he came home he was never the same. Bostrom: Has someone contacted you lately on this? Joe: I still have some friends with the "firm." I did some work for them after I was discharged from the service, one of them called me on a very friendly basis just as a friend. Bostrom: What is the "firm"?

Joe: When you hear people involved in security; I'll let you in a little secret here. They never call a certain agency of the government the company. They like to call it - it's referred to as the "firm." Again, what we were with was literally a front for that agency military part which we are not supposed to have one of... it had one. Recently there have been little leaks about that. I did find out that a few weeks after we had our incident there were at least two more.

One of which, some fellows were pinned down and two of those little fellows stepped out of the woods. One of them threw a small object out between them and the Phaphet Lao that had them pinned down. They described it as a darkness grenade instead of a smoke grenade. It put up enough of a partition of darkness that they were able to escape and they came back. Regardless of how tight security is on a base like that everybody more or less sleeps in the same bed. Many things get out. These guys came back and immediately came down - what the hell did they do to you guys when you saw that thing and they went through the same procedure.

Recently I was talking to a good friend of mine who was in Thailand with the Air Force and we were talking about it and laughing about the fellow from the "firm" calling me and he said what happened when I told him and he looked at me and said, "Oh, you boys!" because he'd heard about the incident and people took it either with great hilarity - it was the funniest thing they had ever heard, or quite a few people were scared and we never did find out what Uncle Sam had determined about it. I can well imagine what they determined about it. We were all on drugs or swamp gas but they never released that information to us. Bostrom: Did you hear of any other cases like that in the region?

Joe: There was quite a few. They were always seeing them. Even back in World War II in Burma. They had the Foo Fighters. Fellows kept seeing them follow along the aircraft. The only thing I can say is whoever or whatever these humanoids are is they are very interested in our work here. Bostrom: What did the guys that saw the smoke bomb say about the craft?

Joe: They didn't see a craft. All they saw was the fellows that we had seen - some of the smaller ones. Bostrom: They just appeared there? Joe: They heard a noise out in the jungle and these two fellows came in and they heard it over the gunfire so evidently whatever it was - was very, very loud. These fellows peeked out - looked around - looked at them and they see them clearly. They turned to each other and whatever discussion they had- one of them reached up and threw a small object and they said it was small enough - it couldn't be any smaller than a tennis ball and it went off with a loud pop. Not an explosion but a pop. It's just like dark gas. It came up like smoke does but it was darkness and they looked at each other and said "what the hell is this? And one of them said, "I don't care, let's get out of here." So they hightailed it out. It took the Phaphet Lao back far enough that they couldn't pursue them. They never seen anything like that and never did we. Bostrom: Did they take their clothes to check for residue?

Joe: They'd done that several times. They took our fatigues. Other than that, one of the most interesting things about this - our memories were never exactly the same. Whatever they did it altered our memories - affected it with great permanence, but there is no such thing as a total block. Those things come in surges. I know that up to that point in time, I've always been fascinated with the idea - had always want to believe in it, but never really saw enough that really made me believe that there was any such thing. Whoever, or whatever, I'm convinced that they're not the present populace of this earth? Bostrom: You don't care about my recording this? Joe: No, I have no problems with it at all. I'm convinced that they are not present in the populace of this earth.

Footnote: Joe has returned to active duty with the rank of Lieutenant Colonel.

Technological Singularity: Beyond the Event Horizon

While many may not realize it, humanity is a rapidly approaching what is being called a Technological Singularity[59][60] and I believe the Breakaway Society has already passed beyond that event horizon leading the way for the rest of society to follow. It is believed that at the technological singularity boundary the technological rules change just as drastically as the rules of physics change at the boundary of a black hole. It is at this Technological Singularity where we begin to rewrite our genome[61] and our external reality giving us superhuman powers and intelligence.[62] In a case of monkey see, monkey do, I believe we are copying this process from covert extraterrestrial contact.

A friend of mine at Open SETI suggested to me after reading my article on genome security that my next article should cover the man in the machine or the concept of human machine hybrids.[63]

We need to explore what will happen to us and what will we look like when we no longer interface with our computers through keyboard and mouse but through mind-machine interfaces.

The first step toward a man-machine hybrid, as suggested to me by whistle-blower Clifford Stone, is through a bio-suit loaded with microprocessors and sensors, while the second and final step is integration of these devices into our genetic structure. Col. Corso discusses in his book that ETs in their bio-suits essentially become integrated into the craft where they and the craft act as one. I think the main driver behind the approaching Technological Singularity is extraterrestrial contact.

While this contact is still being hidden from the public it is filtering out into the public domain accelerating our technological development in ways suggested by Col. Corso. This has happened before in our history with the covert release of newly discovered Chinese technology in the 12th and 13th centuries by the autocrats of the day, so as to preserve their control over the masses.

I think that many of these extraterrestrial races and civilizations now becoming known to us are already in this technological singularity domain, and by association we are ourselves drawn rapidly into the domain as well. Let's hope we can handle ourselves in a creative rather than a destructive fashion, becoming an asset rather than a liability in this domain. I think that this domain is what the Hopi and other Native Americans have foreseen as the Fifth World as described to them by the Sky People in their past.[64][65] I think that the extraterrestrials are shepherding us into this technological or evolutionary singularity for better or for worse, but once there, our future is for us to decide, if we will take responsibility for our thoughts and actions.

ETs Ignite a Modern Renaissance Similar to China in Europe 600 Years Ago

I am always interested in discovering historical material that helps to better understand this process of humanities integration into extraterrestrial realities and the nature of information locked up in the Breakaway Society. I stumbled across the Gavin Menzies[66] book '*1434*' in the course of my studies that provide quite a body of evidence suggesting that the European Renaissance was sparked by the overt and covert introduction of advanced Chinese science and technology. This technological transfer from the world's only real superpower of the period reached its zenith in 1434 when the Chinese fleet that had already explored and mapped the world in 1421 sailed to Italy.

I had read Gavin's first book '*1421*' years ago, but the evidence he had collected was a bit flimsy and a fishing expedition of sorts, but since then many more historical scholars have become involved all over the world and a huge body of evidence is building supporting his speculations and initial data. This is causing a complete rewrite of history for the 1300's and 1400's, even interesting the Smithsonian, and gives us a roadmap of the process by which contact with a more technologically developed civilization integrates into a lesser advanced hierarchical society on earth.

History seems to be once again repeating itself where global rulers are allowing scientific and technological knowledge from extraterrestrial contact to covertly leak out into the public domain for their own benefit, while at the same time suppressing other knowledge that would weaken their hold on power. This exact same process seems to have happened in Europe when the Chinese leaders make contact with European leaders, who severely distorted the historical record as to where these ideas and knowledge originated. "On the cover jacket Gavin says,

> "Florence and Venice of the early fifteenth century were hubs of world trade, attracting traders from across the globe. Based on years of research, this marvelous history argues that a Chinese fleet (official ambassadors of the emperor) arrived in Tuscany in 1434, where they were received by Pope Eugenius IV in Florence."
>
> "The delegation presented the influential pope with a wealth of Chinese learning from a diverse range of fields: art, geography (including world maps that were passed on to Christopher Columbus and Ferdinand Magellan), astronomy, mathematics, printing, architecture, steel manufacturing, military weaponry, and more. This vast treasure trove of knowledge spread across Europe, igniting the legendary inventiveness of the Renaissance, including the work of such geniuses as Da Vinci, Copernicus, Galileo and more."

This new knowledge uncovered by Gavin Menzies and others clearly shows that learned men with access did not make many of the discoveries attributed to them, but simply copied already existing technological and scientific ideas that had been in use and known in China for hundreds of years. A small part of the huge Chinese fleet sailed to Italy in huge ocean going ships armed with cannon, mortars, exploding bombs, flamethrowers etc. At this time the European navies were little more that sail and row galleys, armed with archers. One can imagine the shock to the European political and military authorities when they realized they were basically defenseless against such superior military technology.

Not only did this spark the Renaissance; it sparked an arms race to catch up militarily with the Chinese very similar to what we have today after the crashes of extraterrestrial spaceships in the 1930's and 1940's. The Chinese after bankrupting themselves building such a huge ocean going fleet along with other excesses fell rapidly into decline while the Europeans rapidly became the world's technological power. There are many lessons from the past that are as applicable today as 600 years ago.

I find it interesting that contact between both humans and extraterrestrials seems to have resulted in the genetic mixing of races. In the 1400's there was also a flourishing slave trade of Chinese slaves mostly young girls to Italy, as many as ten thousand a year. This resulted in a genetic mixing in Italy that reminds me of the forced genetic mixing going on between earth humans and certain races of aliens today in what I call the abductee alien slave trade. In both cases the autocratic authorities approved and facilitated such abhorrent forms of human trafficking.

I believe extraterrestrials have ignited a modern global renaissance in science and technology the likes of which has not been seen for 600 years. When the Chinese ignited the Renaissance, they were just as alien and technologically advanced in relation to the Europeans as extraterrestrials are to us today. European political, military and religious leaders acted is very similar ways to exploit the technologies involved while at the same time suppressing the real source of the information and other information that would weaken their hold on power.

In both cases the initial cultural shock was quickly replaced in the minds of the leaders with the emotions of fear and greed. In *1434* the military feared the advanced gunpowder weaponry and naval capabilities of the Chinese, this quickly sparked a rapid gunpowder arms race and naval build-up that resulted in the European voyages of discovery and colonization. In 1947 the discovery of extraterrestrial weapons and advanced ET space fleets resulted in a rapid space and arms race resulting in a multi trillion dollar secret space fleet. The greed side of the equation kicks in as economic power discovers how the new information could be exploited for the benefit of the ruling classes at the expense of the lower classes.

In both cases the famous learned men of their time became complicit in cooperating with the ruling classes to suppress certain knowledge and to fraudulently take credit for the inventions and scientific discovers that were not theirs. How this was done 600 years ago is explained in *1434* just as Col. Corso explained how it was done after 1947 in the book, The Day After Roswell.

For those who would study the evidence accumulated in the book 1434 and on the website, it is obvious that Leonardo Da Vinci, Santini, Taccola, Di Giorgio all took credit for inventions and scientific discoveries that were not their own. Just compare the similarity of the illustrations in chapter 16 of the book *1434*. Furthermore the laws of celestial mechanics credited to Copernicus, Kepler and Galileo were know by the Chinese and used to create a very accurate calendar in 1280 for Kublai Khan that was later adopted by the Europeans. This calendar required very complex astrological calculations of the earth's rotation, varying speeds around an elliptical orbit around the sun, etc. The Chinese had even noticed moons around Jupiter visible to the naked eye in certain locations in China in 364 B.C.

How can we account for such similar political reactions and responses by the authorities of both periods and their learned servants? I think the answer is inherent in autocratic rule that is driven in a large part by fear, deception and greed and is by nature insecure as leaders can fall from power just as quickly as they rise to power. Obviously any democratic or populist countermanding force has been far too weak in both cases to have any significant immediate check on autocratic power and societal exploitation of the technologies involved.

It remains to be seen if the situation will change over the longer term in regards to extraterrestrial knowledge due to democratic disclosure rumblings and extraterrestrial disclosure activities by the ET's themselves. If the Chinese source for this advanced scientific and technological knowledge in 1434 could be effectively covered up for 600 years, 60 years seems a very short time. But on the other hand, just as Chinese advances in printing technology helped to rapidly integrate Chinese advanced knowledge and fuel the Renaissance, so too the Internet seems to be not only uncovering old Chinese-European secrets but now ET secret classified knowledge is being uncovered and distributed to the public.

CHAPTER FOUR

THE WRIGHT-PATTERSON ELECTROGRAVITICS DOCUMENT

"While flying with several other USAF pilots over Germany in 1957, we sighted numerous radiant flying disks above us. We couldn't tell how high they were. We couldn't get anywhere near their altitude."

"While working with a camera crew supervising flight testing of advanced aircraft at Edwards Air Force Base, California, the camera crew filmed the landing of a strange disk object that flew in over their heads and landed on a dry lake nearby. As camera crewmen approached the saucer, it rose up above the area and flew off at a speed faster than any known aircraft."

"For many years I have lived with a secret, in a secrecy imposed on all specialists in astronautics. I can now reveal that every day, in the USA, our radar instruments capture objects of form and composition unknown to us. And there are thousands of witness reports and a quality of documents to prove this. But nobody wants to make them public. Why? Because authority is afraid that people may think of God knows what kind of horrible invaders. So the password still is: We have to avoid panic by all means." NASA Astronaut, L. Gordon Cooper.

"The power of the Team derives from its vast intragovernmental undercover infrastructure and its direct relationship with great private industries, mutual funds and investment houses, universities, and the news media, including foreign and domestic publishing houses... All true members of the Team remain in the power center whether in office with the incumbent administration or out of office with the hard-core set. They simply rotate to and from official jobs and the business world or the pleasant haven of academe." Colonel Fletcher Prouty

The following report is long and technical but it already shows how far advanced the field of electogravitics had become by 1956 before it completely disappeared from the public domain and into the hands of the cartel corporations listed in this document. The reader can see that this is quite in line with the advancements that have now led to the Secret Space Program that Ben Rich and other engineer whistle-blowers have been talking about in the public domain for years.

For some folks to say that there is no evidence for a very advanced secret space program that is nonsense. Please remember that this is a real document and not a leaked document, and its existence is not in question. This document clearly shows that a secret space program using electromagnetic and electrogravitic technologies is well advanced, and running parallel to rocket propulsion technologies.

By the 1960s, rocket propulsion is already obsolete and remains as only an expensive and dangerous propaganda cover program. This is the real reason that overt moon and planet exploration and mining were seemly cancelled, only to be continued in earnest covertly, a huge fraud perpetrated on the whole of humanity by the governments and corporations involved.

(For those lay people who are not interested in a rigorous detailed examination of electrogravitics and the early roots of the Secret Space Program, should skim or skip this and go on to the next Chapter) For those with a rigorous detailed mindset fasten your seat belt.

ELECTROGRAVITICS SYSTEMS

An examination of electrostatic motion, dynamic counterbary and barycentric control.

It has been accepted as axiomatic that the way to offset the effects of gravity is to use a lifting surface and considerable molecular energy to produce a continuously applied force that, for a limited period of time, can remain greater than the effects of gravitational attraction. The original invention of the glider and evolution of the briefly self-sustaining glider, at the turn of the century led to progressive advances in power and knowledge.

This has been directed to refining the classic Wright Brothers' approach. Aircraft design is still fundamentally as the Wrights adumbrated it, with wings, body, tails, moving or flapping controls, landing gear and so forth. The Wright biplane was a powered glider, and all subsequent aircraft, including the supersonic jets of the nineteen-fifties are also powered gliders. Only one fundamentally different flying principle has so far been adopted with varying degrees of success. It is the rotating wing aircraft that has led to the jet lifters and vertical pushers, coleopters, ducted fans and lift induction turbine propulsion systems.

But during these decades there was always the possibility of making efforts to discover the nature of gravity from cosmic or quantum theory, investigation and observation, with a view to discerning the physical properties of aviation's enemy.

It has seemed to Aviation Studies that for some time insufficient attention has been directed to this kind of research. If it were successful such developments would change the concept of sustentation, and confer upon a vehicle qualities that would now be regarded as the ultimate in aviation.

This report summarizes in simple form the work that has been done and is being done in the new field of electrogravitics. It also outlines the various possible lines of research into the nature and constituent matter of gravity, and how it has changed from Newton to Einstein to the modern Hlavaty concept of gravity as an electromagnetic force that may be controlled like a light wave.

The report also contains an outline of opinions on the feasibility of different electrogravitics systems and there is reference to some of the barycentric control and electrostatic rigs in operation.

Electrogravitics might be described as a synthesis of electrostatic energy used for propulsion - either vertical propulsion or horizontal or both - and gravitics, or dynamic counterbary, in which energy is also used to set up a local gravitational force independent of the Earth's.

Electrostatic energy for propulsion has been predicted as a possible means of propulsion in space when the thrust from a neutron motor or ion motor would be sufficient in a dragless environment to produce astronomical velocities. But the ion motor is not strictly a part of the science of electrogravitics, since barycentric control in an electrogravitics system is envisaged for a vehicle operating within the earth's environment and it is not seen initially for space application. Probably large scale space operations would have to await the full development of electrogravitics to enable large pieces of equipment to be moved out of the region of the earth's strongest gravity effects.

So, though electrostatic motors were thought of in 1925, electrogravitics had its birth after the War, when Townsend Brown sought to improve on the various proposals that then existed for electrostatic motors sufficiently to produce some visible manifestation of sustained motion. Whereas earlier electrostatic tests were essentially pure research, Brown's rigs were aimed from the outset at producing a flying article. As a private venture he produced evidence of motion using condensers in a couple of saucers suspended by arms rotating round a central tower with input running down the arms.

The massive-k situation was summarized subsequently in a report, Project Winter haven, in 1952. Using the data some conclusions were arrived at that might be expected from ten or more years of intensive development - similar to that, for instance, applied to the turbine engine. Using a number of assumptions as to the nature of gravity, the report postulated a saucer as the basis of a possible interceptor with Mach 3 capability. Creation of a local gravitational system would confer upon the fighter the sharp-edged changes of direction typical of motion in space.

The essence of electrogravitics thrust is the use of a very strong positive charge on one side of the vehicle and a negative on the other. The core of the motor is a condenser and the ability of the condenser to hold its charge (the k-number) is the yardstick of performance. With air as 1, current dielectrical materials can yield 6 and use of barium aluminate can raise this considerably, barium titanium oxide (a baked ceramic) can offer 6,000 and there is promise of 30,000, which would be sufficient for supersonic speed.

The original Brown rig produced 30 fps on a voltage of around 50,000 and a small amount of current in the milliamp range. There was no detailed explanation of gravity in Project Winter haven, but it was assumed that particle dualism in the subatomic structure of gravity would coincide in its effect with the issuing stream of electrons from the electrostatic energy source to produce counterbary. The Brown work probably remains a realistic approach to the practical realization of electrostatic propulsion and sustentation.

Whatever may be discovered by the Gravity Research Foundation of New Boston a complete understanding and synthetic reproduction of gravity is not essential for limited success. The electrogravitics saucer can perform the function of a classic lifting surface - it produces a pushing effect on the under surface and a suction effect on the upper, but, unlike the aerofoil, it does not require a flow of air to produce the effect. First attempts at electrogravitics are unlikely to produce counterbary, but may lead to development of an electrostatic VTOL vehicle.

Even in its developed form this might be an advance on the molecular heat engine in its capabilities. But hopes in the new science depend on an understanding of the close identity of electrostatic motivating forces with the source and matter of gravity. It is fortuitous that lift can be produced in the traditional fashion and if an understanding of gravity remains beyond full practical control, electrostatic lift might be an adjunct of some significance to modern thrust producers. Research into electrostatics could prove beneficial to turbine development, and heat engines in general, in view of the usable electron potential round the periphery of any flame. Materials for electrogravitics and especially the development of commercial quantities of high-k material is another dividend to be obtained from electrostatic research even if it produces no counterbary. This is a line of development that Aviation Studies, Gravity Research Group is following.

One of the interesting aspects of electrogravitics is that a breakthrough in almost any part of the broad front of general research on the intranuclear processes may be translated into a meaningful advance towards the feasibility of electrogravitics systems. This demands constant monitoring in the most likely areas of the physics of high energy sub-nuclear particles. It is difficult to be over-optimistic about the prospects of gaining so complete a grasp of gravity while the world's physicists are still engaged in a study of fundamental particles - that is to say those that cannot be broken down any more. Fundamental particles are still being discovered - the most recent was the Segre-Chamberlain-Wiegand attachment to the bevatron, which was used to isolate the missing anti-proton, which must - or should be presumed to - exist according to Dirac's theory of the electron.

Much of the accepted mathematics of particles would be wrong if the anti-proton was proved to be non-existent. Earlier Eddington has listed the fundamental particles as:- e. The charge of an electron. The mass of an electron. M. The mass of a proton. h. Planck's constant c. The velocity of light. G. The constant of gravitation, and λ. The cosmical constant.

It is generally held that no one of these can be inferred from the others. But electrons may well disappear from among the fundamental particles, though, as Russell says, it is likely that e and m will survive. The constants are much more established than the interpretation of them and are among the most solid of achievements in modern physics.

Gravity may be defined as a small scale departure from Euclidean space in the general theory of relativity. The gravitational constant is one of four dimensionless constants: first, the mass relation of the nucleon and electron. Second is $(e*e)/(h*c)$, third, the Compton wavelength of the proton, and fourth is the gravitational constant, which is the ratio of the electrostatic to the gravitational attraction between the electron and the proton.

One of the stumbling blocks in electrogravitics is the absence of any satisfactory theory linking these four dimensionless quantities. Of the four, moreover, gravity is decidedly the most complex, since any explanation would have to satisfy both cosmic and quantum relations more acceptably and intelligibly even than in the unified field theory. A gravitational constant of around 10.E-39 [equation form] has emerged from quantum research and this has been used as a tool for finding theories that could link the two relations. This work is now in full progress, and developments have to be watched for the aviation angle. Hitherto Dirac, Eddington, Jordan and others have produced differences in theory that are too wide to be accepted as consistent.

It means therefore that (i) without a cosmical basis, and (ii) with an imprecise quantum basis and (iii) a vague hypothesis on the interaction, much remains still to be discovered. Indeed some say that a single interacting theory to link up the dimensionless constants is one of three major unresolved basic problems of physics. The other two main problems are the extension of quantum theory and a more detailed knowledge of the fundamental particles.

All this is some distance from Newton, who saw gravity as a force acting on a body from a distance, leading to the tendency of bodies to accelerate towards each other. He allied this assumption with Euclidean geometry, and time was assumed as uniform and acted independently of space. Bodies and particles in space normally moved uniformly in straight lines according to Newton, and to account for the way they sometimes do not do so, he used the idea of a force of gravity acting at a distance, in which particles of matter cause in others an acceleration proportional to their mass, and inversely proportional to the square of the distance between them.

But Einstein showed how the principle of least action, or the so-called cosmic laziness means that particles, on the contrary, follow the easiest path along geodesic lines and as a result they get readily absorbed into space-time. So was born non-linear physics. The classic example of non-linear physics is the experiment in bombarding a screen with two slits. When both slits are open particles going through are not the sum of the two individually but follows a non-linear equation. This leads on to wave-particle dualism and that in turn to the Heisenberg uncertainty principle in which an increase in accuracy in measurement of one physical quantity means decreasing accuracy in measuring the other.

If time is measured accurately energy calculations will be in error; the more accurate the position of a particle is established the less certain the velocity will be; and so on. This basic principle of the acausality of microphysics affects the study of gravity in the special and general theories of relativity. Lack of pictorial image in the quantum physics of this interrelationship is a difficulty at the outset for those whose minds remain obstinately Euclidean.

In the special theory of relativity, space-time is seen only as an undefined interval which can be defined in any way that is convenient and the Newtonian idea of persistent particles in motion to explain gravity cannot be accepted. It must be seen rather as a synthesis of forces in a four dimensional continuum, three to establish the position and one the time. The general theory of relativity that followed a decade later was a geometrical explanation of gravitation in which bodies take the geodesic path through space-time. In turn this means that instead of the idea of force acting at a distance it is assumed that space, time, radiation and particles are linked and variations in them from gravity are due rather to the nature of space. Thus gravity of a body such as the earth instead of pulling objects towards it as Newton postulated, is adjusting the characteristics of space and, it may be inferred, the quantum mechanics of space in the vicinity of the gravitational force. Electrogravitics aims at correcting this adjustment to put matter, so to speak, 'at rest.'

One of the difficulties in 1954 and 1955 was to get aviation to take electrogravitics seriously. The name alone was enough to put people off. However, in the trade much progress has been made and now most major companies in the United States are interested in counterbary. Groups are being organized to study electrostatic and electromagnetic phenomena. Most of industry's leaders have made some reference to it. Douglas has now stated that it has counterbary on its work agenda but does not expect results yet awhile.

Hiller has referred to new forms of flying platform, Glenn Martin say gravity control could be achieved in six years, but they add that it would entail a Manhattan District type of effort to bring it about. Sikorsky, one of the pioneers, more or less agrees with the Douglas verdict and says that gravity is tangible and formidable, but there must be a physical carrier for this immense trans-spatial force. This implies that where a physical manifestation exists, a physical device can be developed for creating a similar force moving in the opposite direction to cancel it.

Clarke Electronics state they have a rig, and add that in their view the source of gravity's force will be understood sooner than some people think. General Electric is working on the use of electronic rigs designed to make adjustments to gravity - this line of attack has the advantage of using rigs already in existence for other defense work. Bell also has an experimental rig intended, as the company puts it, to cancel out gravity, and Lawrence Bell has said he is convinced that practical hardware will emerge from current programs. Grover Leoning is certain that what he referred to as an electro-magnetic contra-gravity mechanism will be developed for practical use.

Convair is extensively committed to the work with several rigs. Lear Inc., autopilot and electronic engineers have a division of the company working on gravity research and so also has the Sperry division of Sperry-Rand. This list embraces most of the U.S. aircraft industry. The remainder, Curtiss-Wright, Lockheed, Boeing and North American have not yet declared themselves, but all these four are known to be in various stages of study with and without rigs.

In addition, the Massachusetts Institute of Technology is working on gravity, the Gravity Research Foundation of New Boston; the Institute for Advanced Study at Princeton, the Caltech Radiation Laboratory, Princeton University and the University of North Carolina are all active in gravity. Glenn L. Martin is setting up a Research Institute for Advanced Study which has a small staff working on gravity research with the unified field theory and this group is committed to extensive programs of applied research. Many others are also known to be studying gravity. Some are known also to be planning a general expansion in this field, such as in the proposed Institute for Pure Physics at the University of North Carolina.

A certain amount of work is also going on in Europe. One of the French nationalized constructors and one company outside the nationalized elements have been making preliminary studies, and a little company money has in one case actually been committed. Some work is also going on in Britain where rigs are now in existence. Most of it is private venture work, such as that being done by Ed Hull a colleague of Townsend Brown who, as much as anybody, introduced Europe to electrogravitics. Aviation Studies' Gravity Research Group is doing some work, mainly on k studies, and is sponsoring dielectric investigations.

One Swedish company and two Canadian companies have been making studies, and quite recently the Germans have woken up to the possibilities. Several of the companies have started digging out some of the early German papers on wave physics. They are almost certain to plan a gravitics program. Curiously enough the Germans during the war paid no attention to electrogravitics. This is one line of advance that they did not pioneer in any way and it was basically a U.S. creation. Townsend Brown in electrogravitics is the equivalent of Frank Whittle in gas turbines.

This German overlooking of electrostatics is even more surprising when it is remembered how astonishingly advanced and prescient the Germans were in nuclear research. (The modern theory of making thermonuclear weapons without plutonium fission initiators returns to the original German idea that was dismissed, even ridiculed. The Germans never went very far with fission, indeed they doubted that this chain would ever be made to work. The German air industry, still in the embryo stage, has included electrogravitics among the subjects it intends to examine when establishing the policy that the individual companies will adopt after the present early stage of foreign license has enabled industry to get abreast of the other countries in aircraft development.

It is impossible to read through this summary of the widening efforts being made to understand the nature of matter of gravity without sharing the hope that many groups now have, of major theoretical breakthroughs occurring before very long. Experience in nucleonics has shown that when attempts to win knowledge on this scale are made, advances are soon seen. There are a number of elements in industry, and some managements, who see gravity as a problem for later generations. Many see nothing in it all and they may be right.

But as said earlier, if Dr Vaclav Hlavaty thinks gravity is potentially controllable that surely should be justification enough, and indeed inspiration, for physicists to apply their minds and for management to take a risk. Hlavaty is the only man who thinks he can see a way of doing the mathematics to demonstrate Einstein's unified field theory - something that Einstein himself said was beyond him. Relativity and the unified field theory go to the root of electrogravitics and the shifts in thinking, the hopes and fears, and a measure of progress is to be obtained only in the last resort from men of this stature.

Major theoretical breakthroughs to discover the sources of gravity will be made by the most advanced intellects using the most advanced research tools. Aviation's role is therefore to impress upon physicists of this caliber with the urgency of the matter and to aid them with statistical and peripheral investigations that will help to clarify the background to the central mathematical and physical puzzles. Aviation could also assist by recruiting some of these men as advisers.

Convair has taken the initiative with its recently established panel of advisers on nuclear projects, which include Dr Edward Teller of the University of California. At the same time much can be done in development of laboratory rigs, condenser research and dielectric development, which do not require anything like the same cerebral capacity to get results and make a practical contribution.

As gravity is likely to be linked with the new particles, only the highest powered particle accelerators are likely to be of use in further fundamental knowledge. The country with the biggest tools of this kind is in the best position to examine the characteristics of the particles and from those countries the greatest advances seem most likely.

Though the United States has the biggest of the bevatron - the Berkeley bevatron is 6.2 bev - the Russians have a 10 bev accelerator in construction which, when it is completed, will be the world's largest. At Brookhaven a 25 bev instrument is in development which, in turn, will be the biggest. Other countries without comparable facilities are of course at a great disadvantage from the outset in the contest to discover the explanation of gravity.

Electrogravitics, moreover, unfortunately competes with nuclear studies for its facilities. The clearest thinking brains are bound to be attracted to localities where the most extensive laboratory equipment exists. So, one way and another, results are most likely to come from the major countries with the biggest undertakings. Thus the nuclear facilities have a direct bearing on the scope for electrogravitics work.

The OEEC report in January made the following points: The U.S. has six to eight entirely different types of reactor in operation and many more under construction. Europe has now two different types in service. The U.S. has about 30 research reactors plus four in Britain, two in France. The U.S. has two nuclear-powered marine engines. Europe has none, but the U.K. is building one. Isotope separation plants for the enrichment of uranium in the U.S. are roughly 11 times larger than the European plant in Britain.

Europe's only heavy water plant (in Norway) produces somewhat less than one-twentieth of American output.

In 1955 the number of technicians employed in nuclear energy work in the U.S. was about 15,000; there are about 5,000 in Britain, 1,800 in France, and about 19,000 in the rest of Europe. But the working party says that pessimistic conclusions should not be drawn from these comparisons. European nuclear energy effort is unevenly divided at the moment, but some countries have notable achievements to their credit and important developments in prospect. The main reason for optimism is that, taken as a whole, "Europe's present nuclear effort falls very far short of its industrial potential."

Though gravity research, such as there has been of it, has been unclassified, new principles and information gained from the nuclear research facilities that have a vehicle application is expected to be withheld.

The heart of the problem to understanding gravity is likely to prove to be the way in which the very high energy sub-nuclear particles convert something, whatever it is, continuously and automatically into the tremendous nuclear and electromagnetic forces. Once this key is understood, attention can later be directed to finding laboratory means of duplicating the process and reversing its force lines in some local environment and returning the energy to itself to produce counterbary. Looking beyond it seems possible that gravitation will be shown to be a part of the universal electro-magnetic processes and controlled in the same way as a light wave or radio wave.

CONCLUSIONS

1. No attempts to control the magnitude or direction of the earth's gravitational force have yet been successful. But if the explanation of gravity is to be found in the as yet undetermined characteristics of the very high energy particles it is becoming increasingly possible with the bevatron to work with the constituent matter of gravity. It is therefore reasonable to expect that the new bevatron may, before long, be used to demonstrate limited gravitational control.

2. An understanding and identification of these particles is on the frontiers of human knowledge, and a full assessment of them is one of the major unresolved puzzles of the nucleus. An associated problem is to discover a theory to account for the cosmic and quantum relations of gravity, and a theory to link the gravitational constant with the other three dimensionless constants.

3. Though the obstacles to an adequate grasp of microphysics still seem formidable, the transportation rewards that could follow from electrogravitics are as high as can be envisaged. In a weightless environment, movement with sharp-edged changes of direction could offer unique maneuverability.

4. Determination of the environment of the anti-proton, discovery of the anti-neutron and closer examination of the other high energy particles are preliminaries to the hypothesis that gravity is one aspect of electromagnetism that may eventually be controlled like a wave. When the structure of the nucleus becomes clearer, the influence of the gravitational force upon the nucleus and the nature of its behavior in space will be more readily understood. This is a great advance on the Newtonian concept of gravity acting at a distance.

5. Aviation's role appears to be to establish facilities to handle many of the peripheral and statistical investigations to help fill in the background on electrostatics.

6. A distinction has to be made between electrostatic energy for propulsion and counterbary. Counterbary is the manipulation of gravitational force lines; barycentric control is the adjustment to such manipulative capability to produce a stable type of motion suitable for transportation.

7. Electrostatic energy sufficient to produce low speeds (a few thousand dynes, has already been demonstrated. Generation of a region of positive electrostatic energy on one side of a plate and neg-

ative on the other sets up the same lift or propulsion effect as the pressure and suction below and above a wing, except that in the case of electrostatic application no airflow is necessary.

8. Electrostatic energy sufficient to produce a Mach 3 fighter is possible with megavolt energies and a k of over 10,000.

9. k figures of 6,000 have been obtained from some ceramic materials and there are prospects of 30,000.

10. Apart from electrogravitics there are other rewards from investment in electrostatic equipment. Automation, autonetics and even turbine development use similar laboratory facilities.

11. Progress in electrogravitics probably awaits a new genius in physics who can find a single equation to tie up all the conflicting observations and theory on the structure and arrangement of forces and the part the high energy particles play in the nucleus. This can occur any time, and the chances are improved now that bev. energies are being obtained in controlled laboratory conditions.

ANTI-GRAVITATION RESEARCH

The basic research and technology behind electro-anti-gravitation is so much in its infancy that this is perhaps one field of development where not only the methods but the ideas are secret. Nothing therefore can be discussed freely at the moment. Very few papers on the subject have been prepared so far, and the only schemes that have seen the light of day are for pure research into rigs designed to make objects float around freely in a box.

There are various radio applications, and aviation medicine departments have been looking for something that will enable them to study the physiological effects on the digestion and organs of an environment without gravity. There are however long term aims of a more revolutionary nature that envisage equipment that can defeat gravity. Aviation Report - August 1954.

MANAGERIAL POLICY FOR ANTI-GRAVITICS

The prospect of engineers devising gravity-defeating equipment - or perhaps it should be described as the creation of pockets of weightless environments - does suggest that as a long term policy aircraft constructors will be required to place even more emphasis on electro-mechanical industrial plant, than is now required for the transition from manned to unmanned weapons. Anti-gravitics work is therefore likely to go to companies with the biggest electrical laboratories and facilities. It is also apparent that anti-gravitics, like other advanced sciences, will be initially sponsored for its weapon capabilities.

There are perhaps two broad ways of using the science - one is to postulate the design of advanced type projectiles on their best inherent capabilities, and the more critical parameters (that now constitutes the design limitation) can be eliminated by anti-gravitics. The other, which is a longer term plan, is to create an entirely new environment with devices operating entirely under an anti-gravity envelope.

THE GREATER THE EASIER

Propulsion and atomic energy Trends are similar in one respect: the more incredible the long term capabilities are, the easier it is to attain them. It is strange that the greatest of nature's secrets can be harnessed with decreasing industrial effort, but greatly increasing mental effort. The Americans went through the industrial torture to produce tritium for the first thermonuclear experiment, but later both they and the Russians were able to achieve much greater results with the help of lithium 6 hydride.

The same thing is happening in aviation propulsion: the nuclear fuels are promising to be tremendously powerful in their effect, but excessively complicated in their application, unless there can be some means of direct conversion as in the strontium 90 cell. But lying behind and beyond the nuclear fuels is the linking of electricity to gravity, which is an incomparably more powerful way of harnessing energy than the only method known to human intellect at present - electricity and magnetism. Perhaps the magic of barium aluminum oxide will perform the miracle in propulsion that lithium 6 hydride has done in the fusion weapon. Certainly it is a well-known material in dielectrics, but when one talks of massive-k, one means of course five figures.

At this early stage it is difficult to relate k to Mach numbers with any certainty, but realizable k can, with some kinds of arithmetic, produce astounding velocities. They are achievable, moreover, with decreasing complexity, indeed the ultimate becomes the easiest in terms of engineering, but the most hideous in terms of theory. Einstein's general theory of relativity is, naturally, and important factor, but some of the postulates appear to depend on the unified field theory, which cannot yet be physically checked because nobody knows how to do it. Einstein hopes to find a way of doing so before he dies.

GRAVITICS FORMULATIONS

All indications are that there has still been little cognizance of the potentialities of electrostatic propulsion and it will be a major undertaking to re-arrange aircraft plants to conduct large-scale research and development into novel forms of dielectric and to improve condenser efficiencies and to develop the novel type of materials used for fabrication of the primary structure. Some extremely ambitious theoretical programs have been submitted and work towards realization of a manned vehicle has begun.

On the evidence, there are far more definite indications that the incredible claims are realizable than there was, for instance, in supposing that uranium fission would result in a bomb. At least it is known, proof positive, that motion, using surprisingly low k, is possible. The fantastic control that again is feasible, has not yet been demonstrated, but there is no reason to suppose the arithmetic is faulty, especially as it has already led to a quite brisk example of actual propulsion.

That first movement was indeed an historic occasion, reminiscent of the momentous day at Chicago when the first pile went critical, and the phenomenon was scarcely less weird. It is difficult to imagine just where a well-organized examination into long term gravitics prospects would end. Though a circular platform is electrostatically convenient, it does not necessarily follow that the requirements of control by differential changes would be the same.

Perhaps the strangest part of this whole chapter is how the public managed to foresee the concept though not of course the theoretical principles that gave rise to it, before physical tests confirmed that the mathematics was right. It is interesting also that there is no point of contact between the conventional science of aviation and the New: it is a radical offshoot with no common principles.

Aerodynamics, structures, heat engines, flapping controls, and all the rest of aviation is part of what might be called the Wright Brothers era - even the Mach 2.5 thermal barrier piercers are still Wright Brothers concepts, in the sense that they fly and they stall, and they run out of fuel after a short while, and they defy the earth's pull for a short while.

Thus this century will be divided into two parts - almost to the day. The first half belonged to the Wright Brothers who foresaw nearly all the basic issues in which gravity was the bitter foe. In part of the second half gravity will be the great provider. Electrical energy, rather irrelevant for propulsion in the first half becomes a kind of catalyst to motion, in the second half of the century.

ELECTRO-GRAVITICS PARADOX

Realization of electro-static propulsion seems to depend on two theoretical twists and two practical ones. The two theoretical puzzles are: first, how to make a condenser the center of a propulsion system, and second is how to link the condenser system with the gravitational field. There is a third problem, but it is some way off yet, which is how to manipulate kva for control in all three axes as well as for propulsion and lift. The two practical tricks are first how, with say a Mach 3 weapon in mind, to handle 50,000 kva within the envelope of a thin pancake of 35 feet in diameter and second how to generate such power from within so small a space. The electrical power in a small aircraft is more than is a fair sized community the analogy being that a single rocket jet can provide as much power as can be obtained from the Hoover Dam.

It will naturally take as long to develop electro-static propulsion as it has taken to coax the enormous power outputs from heat engines. True there might be a flame in the electro-gravitic propulsion system, but it would not be a heat engine - the temperature of the flame would be incidental to the function of the chemical burning process.

The curious thing is that though electro-static propulsion is the antithesis of magnetism, Einstein's unified field theory is an attempt to link gravitation with electro-magnetism.

This all-embracing theory goes on logically from the general theory of relativity that gives an ingenious geometrical interpretation of the concept of force which is mathematically consistent with gravitation but fails in the case of electro-magnetism, while the special theory of relativity is concerned with the relationship between mass and energy.

The general theory of relativity fails to account for electro-magnetism because the forces are proportional to the charge and not to the mass. The unified field theory is one of a number of attempts that have been made to bridge this gap, but it is baffling to imagine how it could ever be observed. Einstein himself thinks it is virtually impossible. However Hlavaty claims now to have solved the equations by assuming that gravitation is a manifestation of electro-magnetism. This being so it is all the more incredible that electro-static - Though in a sense this is true, it is better expressed in the body of this report than it was here in 1954. Propulsion (with kva for convenience fed into the system and not self-generated) has actually been demonstrated.

It may be that to apply all this very abstruse physics to aviation it will be necessary to accept that the theory is more important than this or that interpretation of it. This is how the physical constants, which are now regarded as among the most solid of achievements in modern physics, have become workable, and accepted. Certainly all normal instincts would support the Einstein series of postulations, and if this is so it is a matter of conjecture where it will lead in the long term future of the electro-gravitic science.

ELECTRO-GRAVITIC PROPULSION SITUATION

Under the terms of Project Winter haven the proposals to develop electro-gravitics to the point of realizing a Mach 3 combat type disc were not far short of the extensive effort that was planned for the Manhattan District. Indeed the drive to develop the new prime mover is in some respects rather similar to the experiments that led to the release of nuclear energy in the sense that both involve fantastic mathematical capacity and both are sciences so new that other allied sciences cannot be of very much guide. In the past two years since the principle of motion by means of massive-k was first demonstrated on a test rig, progress has been slow.

But the indications are now that the Pentagon is ready to sponsor a range of devices help further knowledge. In effect the new family of TVs would be on the same tremendous scope that was envisaged by the X-1, 2, 3, 4 and 5 and D.558s that were all created for the purpose of destroying the sound barrier - which they effectively did, but it is a process that is taking ten solid years of hard work to complete. (Now after 7 years the X-2 has yet to start its tests and the X-3 is still in performance testing stage).

Tentative targets now being set anticipate that the first disc should be complete before 1960 and it would take the whole of the 'sixties to develop it properly, even though some combat things might be available ten years from now.

GRAVITICS STUDY WIDENING

The French are now understood to be pondering the most effective way of entering the field of electro-gravitic propulsion systems. But not least of the difficulties is to know just where to begin. There are practically no patents so far that throw very much light on the mathematics of the relation between electricity and gravity. There is, of course, a large number of patents on the general subject of motion and force, and some of these may prove to have some application. There is, however, a series of working postulations embodied in the original Project Winter haven, but no real attempt has been made in the working papers to go into the detailed engineering.

All that had actually been achieved up to just under a year ago was a series of fairly accurate extrapolations from the sketchy data that has so far been actually observed. The extrapolation of 50 mph to 1,800 mph, however, (which is what the present hopes and aspirations amount to) is bound to be a rather vague exercise. This explains American private views that nothing can be reasonably expected from the science yet awhile. Meanwhile, the NACA is active, and nearly all the Universities are doing work that borders close to what is involved here, and something fruitful is likely to turn up before very long.

GRAVITICS STEPS

Specification writers seem to be still rather stumped to know what to ask for in the very hazy science of electro-gravitic propelled vehicles. They are at present faced with having to plan the first family of things - first of these is the most realistic type of operational test rig, and second the first type of test vehicle. In turn this would lead to sponsoring of a combat disc. The preliminary test rigs which gave only feeble propulsion have been somewhat improved, but of course the speeds reached so far are only those more associated with what is attained on the roads rather than in the air. But propulsion is now known to be possible, so it is a matter of feeding enough KVA into condensers with better k figures. 50,000 is a magic figure for the combat saucer - it is this amount of KVA and this amount of k that can be translated into Mach 3 speeds. Meanwhile Glenn Martin now feels ready to say in public that they are examining the unified field theory to see what can be done.

It would probably be truer to say that Martin and other companies are now looking for men who can make some kind of sense out of Einstein's equations. There's nobody in the air industry at present with the faintest idea of what it is all about. Also, just as necessary, companies have somehow to find administrators who know enough of the mathematics to be able to guess what kind of industrial investment is likely to be necessary for the company to secure the most rewarding prime contracts in the new science.

This again is not so easy since much of the mathematics just cannot be translated into words. You either understand the figures, or you cannot ever have it explained to you. This is rather new because even things like indeterminacy in quantum mechanics can be more or less put into words. Perhaps the main thing for management to bear in mind in recruiting men is that essentially electro-gravitics is a branch of wave technology and much of it starts with Planck's dimensions of action, energy and time, and some of this is among the most firm and least controversial sections of modern atomic physics.

ELECTROGRAVITICS PUZZLE

Back in 1948 and 49, the public in the U.S. had a surprisingly clear idea of what a flying saucer should, or could, do. There has never at any time been any realistic explanation of what propulsion agency could make it do those things, but its ability to move within its own gravitation field was presupposed from its maneuverability. Yet all this was at least two years before electro-static energy was shown to produce propulsion. It is curious that the public were so ahead of the empiricists on this occasion, and there are two possible explanations. One is that optical illusions or atmospheric phenomena offered a preconceived idea of how the ultimate aviation device ought to work.

The other explanation might be that this was a recrudescence of Jung's theory of the Universal Mind which moves up and down in relation to the capabilities of the highest intellects and this may be a case of it reaching a very high peak of perception. But for the air industries to realize an electro-gravitic aircraft means a return to basic principles in nuclear physics, and a re-examination of much in wave technology that has hitherto been taken for granted. Anything that goes any way towards proving the unified field theory will have as great a bearing on electro-gravitics efforts as on the furtherance of nuclear power generally. But the aircraft industry might as well face up to the fact that priorities will in the end be competing with the existing nuclear science commitments. The fact that electro-gravitics has important applications other than for a weapon will however strengthen the case for governments to get in on the work going on.

MANAGEMENT NOTE FOR ELECTRO-GRAVITICS

The gas turbine engine produced two new companies in the U.S. engine field and they have, between them, at various times offered the traditional primes rather formidable competition. Indeed GE at this moment has, in the view of some, taken the Number Two position. In Britain no new firms managed to get a footing but one, Metro-Vick, might have done if it had put its whole energies into the business. It is on the whole unfortunate for Britain that no bright newcomer has been able to screw up competition in the engine field as English Electric have done in the airframe business. Unlike the turbine engine, electro-gravitics is not just a new propulsion system, it is a new mode of thought in aviation and communications, and it is something that may become all-embracing.

Theoretical studies of the science unfortunately have to extend right down to the mathematics of the meson and there is no escape from that. But the relevant facts wrung from the nature of the nuclear structure will have their impact on the propulsion system, the airframe and also its guidance. The airframe, as such, would not exist, and what is now a complicated stressed structure becomes some convenient form of hard envelope.

New companies therefore who would like to see themselves as major defense prime contractors in ten or fifteen years' time, are the ones most likely to stimulate development. Several typical companies in Britain and the U.S. come to mind - outfits like AiResearch, Raytheon, Plessey in England, Rotax and others. But the companies have to face a decade of costly research into theoretical physics and it means a great deal of trust. Companies are mostly overloaded already and they cannot afford it, but when they sit down and think about the matter they can scarcely avoid the conclusion that they cannot afford not to be in at the beginning.

ELECTRO-GRAVITICS BREAKTHROUGHS

Lawrence Bell said last week he thought that the tempo of development leading to the use of nuclear fuels and anti-gravitational vehicles (he meant presumably ones that create their own gravitational field independently of the Earth's) would accelerate. He added that the breakthroughs now feasible will advance their introduction ahead of the time it has taken to develop the turbojet to its present pitch. Beyond the thermal barrier was a radiation barrier, and he might have added ozone poisoning and meteorite hazards, and beyond that again a time barrier. Time however is not a single calculable entity and Einstein has taught that an absolute barrier to aviation is the environmental barrier in which there are physical limits to any kind of movement from one point in space-time continuum to another.

Bell (the company not the man) have a reputation as experimentalists and are not so earthy as some of the other U.S. companies; so while this first judgment on progress with electro-gravitics is interesting, further word is awaited from the other major elements of the air business. Most of the companies are now studying several forms of propulsion without heat engines though it is early days yet to determine which method will see the light of day first. Procurement will open out because the capabilities of such aircraft are immeasurably greater than those envisaged with any known form of engine.

THERMONUCLEAR-ELECTROGRAVITICS INTERACTION

The point has been made that the most likely way of achieving the comparatively low fusion heat needed - 1,000,000 degrees provided it can be sustained (which it cannot be in fission for more than a microsecond or two of time) - is by use of a linear accelerator. The concentration of energy that may be obtained when accelerators are rigged in certain ways make the production of very high temperatures feasible but whether they could be concentrated enough to avoid a thermal heat problem remains to be seen.

It has also been suggested that linear accelerators would be the way to develop the high electrical energies needed for creation of local gravitational systems. It is possible therefore to imagine that the central core of a future air vehicle might be a linear accelerator which would create a local weightless state by use of electrostatic energy and turn heat into energy without chemical processes for propulsion. Eventually - towards the end of this century - the linear accelerator itself would not be required and a ground generating plant would transmit the necessary energy for both purposes by wave propagation.

POINT ABOUT THERMONUCLEAR REACTION REACTORS

The 20 year estimate by the AEC last week that lies between present research frontiers and the fusion reactor probably refers to the time it will take to tap fusion heat. But it may be thought that rather than use the molecular and chemical processes of twisting heat into thrust it would be more appropriate to use the now heat source in conjunction with some form of nuclear thrust producer which would be in the form of electrostatic energy.

The first two Boeing nuclear jet prototypes now under way are being designed to take either molecular jets or nuclear jets in case the latter are held up for one reason or another. But the change from molecular to direct nuclear thrust production in conjunction with the thermonuclear reactor is likely to make the aircraft designed around the latter a totally different breed of cat. It is also expected to take longer than two decades, though younger executives in trade might expect to live to see a prototype.

ELECTROGRAVITICS FEASIBILITY

Opinion on the prospects of using electrostatic energy for propulsion, and eventually for creation of a local gravitational field isolated from the earths has naturally polarized into the two opposite extremes. There are those who say it is nonsense from start to finish, and those who are satisfied from performance already physically manifest that it is possible and will produce air vehicles with absolute capabilities and no moving parts. The feasibility of a Mach 3 fighter (the present aim in studies) is dependent on a rather large k extrapolation, considering the pair of saucers that have physically demonstrated the principle only an achieved a speed of some 30 fps.

But, and this is important, they have attained a working velocity using very inefficient (even by to-day's knowledge) form of condenser complex. These humble beginnings are surely as hopeful as Whittle's early postulations. It was, by the way, largely due to the early references in Aviation Report that work is gathering momentum in the U.S. Similar studies are beginning in France, and in England some men are on the job full time.

ELECTRO-GRAVITICS EFFORT WIDENING

Companies studying the implications of gravitics are said in a new statement, to include Glenn Martin, Convair, Sperry-Rand, Sikorsky, Bell, Lear Inc. and Clark Electronics. Other companies who have previously evinced interest include Lockheed Douglas and Hiller. The remainder are not disinterested, but have not given public support to the new science - which is widening all the time. The approach in the U.S. is in a sense more ambitious than might have been expected.

The logical approach, which has been suggested by Aviation Studies, is to concentrate on improving the output of electrostatic rigs in existence that are known to be able to provide thrust. The aim would be to concentrate on electrostatics for propulsion first and widen the practical engineering to include establishment of local gravity force lines, independent of those of the earth's, to provide unfettered vertical movement as and when the mathematics develops.

However, the U.S. approach is rather to put money into fundamental theoretical physics of gravitation in an effort first to create the local gravitation field. Working rigs would follow in the wake of the basic discoveries. Probably the correct course would be to sponsor both approaches, and it is now time that the military stepped in with big funds. The trouble about the idealistic approach to gravity is that the aircraft companies do not have the men to conduct such work. There is every expectation in any case that the companies likely to find the answers lay outside the aviation field. These would emerge as the masters of aviation in its broadest sense.

The feeling is therefore that a company like A. T. & T. is most likely to be first in this field. This giant company (unknown in the air and weapons field) has already revolutionized modern warfare with the development of the junction transistor and is expected to find the final answers to absolute vehicle levitation. This therefore is where the bulk of the sponsoring money should go.

CHAPTER FIVE

THE ALIEN RESOURCE CARTEL

"Lunch with 5 top space scientists... It was fascinating... Space truly is the last frontier and some of the developments there in astronomy etc. are like science fiction, except they are real... I learned that our shuttle capacity is such that we could orbit 300 people." President Reagan's diary for Tuesday, June 11, 1985.

"The world is governed by very different personages from what is imagined by those who are not behind the scenes." Benjamin Disraeli

"There are within our world perhaps only a dozen organizations which shape the courses of our various destinies as rigidly as the regularly constituted governments." President Roosevelt's son Elliot

Memorandum For General Twining, July 14, 1954 – Top Secret Restricted Information - Subject: NSC/MJ-12 Special Studies Project – The President has decided that the MJ-12 SSP briefing should take place during the already scheduled White House meeting of July 16, rather than following it as previously intended. More precise arrangements will be explained to you upon arrival. Please alter your plans accordingly. Your concurrence in the above change of arrangements is assumed. – Robert Cutler, Special Assistant to the President.

I believe that the single most important obstacle to UFO/ET disclosure are global entrenched business interests working in concert with global intelligence and military interests. Dwight D. Eisenhower called this kind of cooperation and collusion between global and national military and business interests the Military Industrial Complex. He warned in the 1950's that the MIC was a grave threat to constitutional government and democracy.

We believe that control over the UFO/ET cover-up and the exploitation of extraterrestrial technologies began in the hands of government and military officials through a working group called MJ 12.[67] According to whistle-blowers Ben Rich and Bill Uhouse, global entrenched business interests engineered a purge during the Nixon administration that gave these special corporate interests a multi-trillion dollar monopoly on the exploitation and insertion of alien resources into the aerospace industries and the public sector. Col Corso in his book; '*The Day After Roswell*,' describes in elaborate detail just how this introduction of exotic technologies was covertly inserted into aerospace and the public domain.

I have coined the name Alien Resource Cartel (ARC) to represent this corporate trust or monopoly as its real name has not yet been leaked to the public by whistle-blowers as was done with MJ 12. In fact the leaking of material on MJ 12 may well have served to distract public and business interest away from focus on the Corporate Cartel and its activities after the spinoff from MJ 12.

Naturally, the reader will ask, where is the evidence to support this speculation about an Alien Resource Cartel? I think the most important pieces of evidence comes from the testimony of Dr Ben Rich the past head to Lockheed's Skunk Works. Ben stated before his death.

> "There are 2 types of UFOs - the ones we build and ones 'they' build. We learned from both crash retrievals and actual "hand-me-downs." The Government knew and until 1969 took an active hand in the administration of that information. After a 1969 Nixon "purge", administration was handled by an international board of directors in the private sector."
>
> "It was Ben Rich's opinion that the public should not be told. He believed they could not handle the truth - ever. Only in the last months of his decline did he begin to feel that the "international corporate board of directors" dealing with the "Subject" could represent a bigger problem to citizens' personal freedoms under the United States Constitution than the presence of off-world visitors themselves.

Over the years the pieces keep falling into place. I hope the reader appreciates that it takes many years of hard study into UFO/ET in order to glean bits and pieces of real leaked information out of the huge body of UFO/ET information and disinformation. I have to put all these discreet pieces together properly to reconstruct the truth as to what is really going on. It's a very difficult and time consuming task.

The Admiral Wilson Incident was another important piece of information showing that corporations, not governments, were in control of these SAP's Special Access Programs[68] related to UFO/ET. The Admiral Wilson Incident[69] came about when in 1997 in a meeting with Dr Steven Greer and Dr Edgar Mitchell, Wilson was given codes to classified extraterrestrial related projects. Wilson then investigated and was met by a team of corporate lawyers who were obviously serving as gatekeepers to these classified ET projects. Wilson later denied this but Astronaut Edgar Mitchell later backed up Steven Greer.

As Greer informed a Portland, Ore., audience in 2001, Wilson said:

> "I am horrified that this is true. I have been in plenty of black projects, but when we tried to get into this one,' he was told, and I quote; Sir, you do not have a need to know. This to the head of intelligence Joint Staffs. You don't have a need to know. Neither did the CIA director and neither did the president."

The very well respected and credible UFO/ET investigator Richard Dolan contacted his sources and did some investigating of this case and concluded that this event happened as described by Greer.[70] Richard Dolan said:

> "I had known about this meeting before Greer published his account. The information came to me through another party. This other source, while not giving me Wilson's name, gave me some explicit information about the nature of the meeting (top level DOD official who met with Greer, then being denied access to black programs dealing with ET technology).
>
> As I understood it at the time, Greer and Edgar Mitchell met with Wilson in April 1997, and that Wilson took two months to continue looking into the matter. At that point, he reached the program but was denied access to it. My source indicated that the primary people who denied Wilson were not even DOD personnel, but rather private contractors, mainly attorneys. They told him that he did not have a need to know, and furthermore, that the only reason he got an audience from them was so they could determine how he learned about the program."

I had a chance to talk with an individual who claimed to have a piece of a crashed UFO. This individual recounted to me and others at an Atlanta meeting the following information. This individual had contacted Warner Robins Air Force Base and showed a piece of an alleged crashed extraterrestrial craft to very interested representatives of the military and civilian defense contractors on base. They were obviously working closely together. This personal experience got me to thinking more about how this working together between private enterprise and government could be organized at it relates to ET technology.

I think clues to which corporations might be involved can be found not only from whistle-blower testimony and leaked and declassified documents but also in the nature of the alien technology being exploited. It seems logical and reasonable to me that it would take a broad spectrum of expertise to understand and exploit such an exotic and complex technology as an extraterrestrial spacecraft.

I think that the multi-national corporations in the cartel can be categorized by the relation to the aspects of the spacecraft being exploited for commercial and defensive use. The limited evidence seems to suggest that American multi-national corporations dominate the Cartel but other international European companies may well be involved including those from Britain, Canada, France and Germany and Australia.

A spacecraft would imply the involvement of the major aerospace corporations. Lockheed Martin, which owns the Skunkworks that was once directed by Ben Rich, would top my list of defense contractors in this category. Ben Rich's testimony before his death seems to indicate Lockheed Marietta is very much involved. I would also look back into old declassified and leaked documents for clues to other aerospace corporation that might be involved or to past corporations that have been bought out by present day corporations. Dr Steven Greer has mentioned the names Lockheed Martin, SAIC, Boeing, Aesop Systems, EG&G.

The propulsion system of the spacecraft is based on electromagnetic and electrogravitic principles. General Electric would top my list in this category because its name is mentioned in the 1955 Wright Patterson declassified document on electrogravitics along with other major electronic companies of the period. Arch-debunker Phil Klass once worked for General Electric during this period in the 1950's. Many of these companies from the 1950's have either disappeared or have been merged into other companies but clues to the involvement of other present day corporations can be found here.

It has been widely reported that the composition of the spacecraft is made up of very strong, durable and so called "smart materials." Materials research has been dominated by petrochemical companies such as DuPont and Dow Chemical. I am told that the Corporation Monsanto shows up on historical UFO documents. I had a CIA source years ago that told me he saw a spacecraft in a DuPont Facility and one in a Dow Chemical facility. We could assume that these companies would be interested in suppressing any technologies that would depress petrochemical prices and a general global reliance on fossil fuels.

It takes highly developed computers and communication technologies to run and navigate a spacecraft. Computers are essential to the operation of spacecraft and the worldwide leader in computers is IBM. Corso mentions some early electronic and computer component makers like Bell Labs that were involved. Companies like Intel may have involved also later.

Spacecraft have been reported to have weapon systems and electronic warfare capabilities. Companies like Raytheon could be involved. I was also given detailed information years ago on the specs for very advanced exotic star wars weapons systems being developed by Philips Laboratories by inventor James Black.

A very important name surfaced into the UFO/ET literature recently, that of Baron Jesco von Puttkamer.[71] I think that this individual is critical to understanding the Alien Resource Cartel because after being brought over to the US by Operation Paperclip[72] and as a young man he quickly rose high in the ranks of NASA and seems to be a very high level bridge between official government bodies like NASA, the aerospace corporations and American and German Fascists.

I suspect that Puttkamer may possibly hold a very high level post in the International Board of Directors alluded to by Rich and Uhouse? Just look at the respect the classified world had for him as indicated by William Pawelec account of a secret meeting at Nellis AFB.

"The meeting was held in a heavily controlled room that was built like a Faraday cage making it impossible for communications to come in or out of the sealed room. "Briefcases, papers, pagers and any form of identification were not allowed at that meeting," Annie says. "Only the generals could be recognized by their uniforms. The tension was really high and Bill was surprised at how nervous the high-ranking generals were. He knew something BIG was up. "Bill saw a private jet escorted by two of our military jets land on the tarmac.

Surprisingly, this private jet rolled all the way to the building where the meeting was scheduled as the escort jets departed. "A very imposing man stepped out of the jet and entered the room. He was relatively tall, and wore a very expensive European suit. His shoes and briefcase were equally luxurious and there was an aide or bodyguard by his side. His demeanor was very aristocratic and he spoke with a High German accent. "The room was electrified with nervous tension as each person gave his status report and answered questions.

When everyone had spoken, the German man thanked them for their good work and simply left. He was never introduced nor identified in anyway. It is believed he was Baron Jesco von Puttkamer."

I decided to do some investigating into just who was this person and what role he could be playing in covert UFO/ET operations including NASA and SETI propaganda and cover-up operations. He even wrote a SETI article.[73]

I suspect the Baron's involvement is in propaganda as well as aerospace, because of his father's involvement in NAZI propaganda operations. He would have been useful in the further management of NASA-SETI's false narrative on ET contact. General Electric assisted Dornberger[74] who later worked for Bell Aircraft to get into Operation Paper Clip. Notice how these early founders of these Aerospace companies all had connections to each other, so what Bill Uhouse says begins to make sense, that it's all in the family.

Interestingly enough I found that General Electric was involved in bringing other Nazis over in Operation Paperclip. GE was a prominent general contractor for the early rocket programs and I suspect very involved in the super-secret electrogravitic and field propelled spacecraft program as well as public rocket programs.

I found some information on the Baron's father and mother.

> The Baron's father goes by the same name as he does as Jesco indicates the first born. Baron Jesco von Puttkamer Sr. was born in Grunewald (near Berlin); March 19, 1903 his rank/position with the Nazis was: Chief of Propaganda, he spent the years 1941-1947 in Shanghai China. He was sentenced to 30 years imprisonment in 1947 at Nuremburg.
>
> Baron Jesco von Puttkamer, a handsome, stocky man with a wide, toothy smile, was the only child of a Major-General and a half-Jewish mother who wrote erotic poetry and novels. Before joining the Nazi Party in 1932, Puttkamer, taking after his mother, wrote for family magazines and advertising agencies. In 1935, he worked under 'party philosopher' Alfred Rosenberg and rose to power as chief of propaganda in Shanghai where he tried to elicit understanding and sympathy for Hitler's Germany.
>
> He established his covert propaganda bureau in the penthouse suite of the Park Hotel and later in a villa next to the German church. Von Puttkamer was often seen traveling through town in a horse-drawn carriage with his Korean bodyguard by his side. At his trial, his attempt to portray himself as a reluctant bit player in the Nazi Party wasn't persuasive enough. American interrogators found him to be a "rabid Nazi," and he was given a 30-year sentence.

I think Operation Paperclip is a crucial link between American Nazi sympathizers and German Nazis. It is public knowledge that the Bush and Ford families had close ties to the Nazis. I found it interesting to run across this praise of Puttkamer by then President George Bush in the following article.[75]

"President George E. Bush congratulated Puttkamer in a message to the gala:

"Outstanding accomplishments are achieved through dedication, integrity and skill. Bush said. I appreciate all those who live by the principles of excellence. Your efforts contribute to the success of our Nation and reflect the true spirit of America"

The list of German Rocket scientists brought to the United States after the war from Germany is a very important window into exploring the fascist roots of America's military-industrial complex, and the Alien Resource Cartel.[76] Note the reference to the Baron being brought to the US in 1962. Check out all the American aerospace corporations that this German engineer[77] was involved in.

I would suspect there is also such a list of Nazi intelligence officials also brought over to build the United States Intelligence services.[78]

"When the JIOA formed to investigate the backgrounds and form dossiers on the Nazis, the Nazi Intelligence leader Reinhard Gehlen met with the CIA director Allen Dulles. Dulles and Gehlen hit it off immediately. Gehlen was a master spy for the Nazis and had infiltrated Russia with his vast Nazi Intelligence network. Dulles promised Gehlen that his Intelligence unit was safe in the CIA.

Apparently, Wev decided to sidestep the problem. Dulles had the scientists dossier's re-written to eliminate incriminating evidence. As promised, Allen Dulles delivered the Nazi Intelligence unit to the CIA, which later opened many umbrella projects stemming from Nazi mad research. (MK-ULTRA / ARTICHOKE, OPERATION MIDNIGHT CLIMAX)

Military Intelligence "cleansed" the files of Nazi references. By 1955, more than 760 German scientists had been granted citizenship in the U.S. and given prominent positions in the American scientific community. Many had been long-time members of the Nazi party and the Gestapo, had conducted experiments on humans at concentration camps, had used slave labor, and had committed other war crimes.

In a 1985 expose in the Bulletin of the Atomic Scientists Linda Hunt wrote that she had examined more than 130 reports on Project Paperclip subjects, and every one had been changed to eliminate the security threat classification.

President Truman, who had explicitly ordered no committed Nazis to be admitted under Project Paperclip, was evidently never aware that his directive had been violated. State Department archives and the memoirs of officials from that era confirm this. In fact, according to Clare Lasby's book Operation Paperclip, project officials "covered their designs with such secrecy that it bedeviled their own President; at Potsdam he denied their activities and undoubtedly enhanced Russian suspicion and distrust," quite possibly fuelling the Cold War even further."

So we can see that Dulles circumvented even the President of the United States order and in so doing began the creation of a shadow government unaccountable to legitimate government even to the President. The CIAs Dulles also seems to have been responsible for the wet memo also known as the burned document[79] to kill President Kennedy. Dr Michael Salla writes:[80]

"Earlier in this investigative series[81] I discussed the burned document and its genesis during the final months of Allen Dulles tenure as Director of the CIA. Dulles and other MJ-12 members were responding to Kennedy's initial effort on June 28, 1961 to be fully briefed on MJ-12 intelligence operations and UFOs. Kennedy, according to a leaked Top Secret Memorandum titled 'Review of MJ-12 Intelligence Operations,'[82] requested Dulles to give a brief summary.

In response and unknown to Kennedy, Dulles drafted a set of directives shortly before his November 1961 retirement. Dulles' draft document was addressed to another six members of MJ-12 requesting comments and their approval. It had clear instructions that under no circumstance would any U.S. President or his national security staff be briefed or given access to classified UFO files."

I hope the reader can understand how complicated it is to understand this fascist cancerous Breakaway Civilization with its associated Alien Resource Cartel. Many investigators both in the UFO/ET community and without are slowly pulling together the facts with the help of whistle blowing insiders who understand how dangerous the classified world has become to constitutional government and even earth human evolution. The global criminality and fraud is just staggering and very difficult for people to wrap their minds around.

CHAPTER SIX

THE TALL WHITES

As they were walking along and talking together, suddenly a chariot of fire and horses of fire appeared and separated the two of them, and Elijah went up to heaven in a whirlwind. Kings 2: 11

I looked, and I saw a windstorm coming out of the north; an immense cloud with flashing lightning and surrounded by brilliant light. The center of the fire looked like glowing metal, and in the fire was what looked like four living creatures. Ezekiel 1: 4

Then the Spirit lifted me up, and I heard behind me a loud rushing sound, May the glory of the Lord be praised in his dwelling place! The sound of the wings of the living creatures brushing against each other and the sound of the wheels beside them; a loud rushing sound. The Spirit lifted me up and took me away. Ezekiel 3: 12, 13, & 14

"I was furthermore a witness to an extraordinary phenomenon, here on this planet Earth. It happened a few months ago in Florida. There I saw with my own eyes a defined area of ground being consumed by flames, with four indentations left by a flying object which had descended in the middle of a field. Beings had left the craft (there were other traces to prove this). They seemed to have studied topography, they had collected soil samples and eventually, they returned to where they had come from, disappearing at enormous speed-I happen to know that authority did just about everything to keep this incident from the press and TV, in fear of a panicky reaction from the public" NASA Astronaut, L. Gordon Cooper.

I guess the best place to start as to an introduction to the extraterrestrial neighborhood, so to speak, would be with the Tall White extraterrestrials. I am willing to go out on a limb in support of this case because we have not only Charles Hall's detailed testimony in his four books and public interviews, but additional TW witnesses that confirm parts of Charles Hall's testimony. There is a key Open SETI article on Charles Hall and the Tall Whites. If you look to the right margin of this article there is a list of links to other Tall White Interviews and material. The material at Viewzone is also especially good and I have lifted some quotes from it for this chapter.

I feel comfortable with the awareness that the TW most likely exist as described by Charles Hall and other witnesses. I found this case so compelling that I travelled to Indian Springs and Nellis where I found an additional two witnesses, and while there Leslie Mitts found the Cherry Hinkle case in Las Vegas for me through the Internet. The only problem I have with the Charles Hall case at this point is that there was one heroic event in the four book series first published as fiction, that I personally could not confirm as true so far.

When I went to the only Ski Lodge in the Spring Mountains south of Nellis AFB , I could not see how the event happened as described that involved the TW deep space craft in Charles's books. There is a good view of a large part of Nellis from the upper parking lot and turnaround where Charles could have seen a large TW craft hovering and TW people exiting the craft to the ground. I just can't see how he could have seen them entering the ski lodge, because the lodge and the first parking lot are at an end of a narrow canyon where the line of sight is obstructed by trees.

I also talked to the past owner of the lodge who lives in Indian Springs whose family owned the lodge in the 1960's. He said to his knowledge there never was an evacuation of the lodge and a friend of his who worked at the lodge at the time agreed. But Marie Therese & Charles tell me, "As Charles states in book IV, everything is true, & happened to him. Regarding the ski lodge incident, Charles was able to drive anywhere he wanted. Viewing angles were more numerous than those you may have investigated. Charles had his theodolite. Also; it wasn't yet ski season; the number of people to be evacuated was very small; therefore, the closing would not have been a particularly memorable incident, even to the owner of the ski lodge."

Even though there is much information in the links I provide in this chapter, I suggest that the serious student of the TW purchase all four books. Especially the first three books, because even though the forth book does have some good extra material in it, a lot of the fourth book repeats material in prior books. Much of the detailed information on the TW is spread out through these four books in dramatic fashion in order to keep the reader hooked, interested and involved. I thought Charles did a good job in writing this alleged experience in fictional format.

What is important about taking the time to read the books, are that the books involve and convey to the reader very well, what it was like for Charles and others at a very exciting and frightening time in their early lives. A time when they were cast unknowingly by the military brass into the lion's den of mutual distrust and fear, felt by both the earth humans and the TW humans in the early stages of early 1960's extraterrestrial contact. Charles and the other airmen found themselves right smack in the middle with two clashing very feudal autocratic regimes that seem to have had little regard for the common individual.

The American military generals seem to have little regard for the rights and liberties of these ordinary enlisted men, who could be used in times of war as necessary disposable pawns, for what the generals perceived to be the greater good of society. The Tall White feudal caste society and their generals also seems to see little value in these enlisted men and treated them with distain and fear, almost as wild animals, which they were, under such extreme conditions.

The Tall Whites guards as described by Charles and others, appear to me much like the Samurai society of old feudalistic Japan where the serf were expected to honor and respect the elite Samurai, else the simplest infraction could lead to the loss of his or her head in several seconds. On the other hand the TW doctor and the teacher were very compassionate, loving and understanding, so we should not draw conclusions about individuals and society in such a small sample of the TW population. Some of the security people at Nellis are just as hard and tough as the TW security people, so should we as a society be judged by our security people, I think not.

As I read the books I came to understand why Charles became special to both sides in this conflict. Charles is a very religious Christian person and he took the abuse on both sides and just tried to do his job and maintain his sanity to the best of his ability as a range weatherman on Nellis AFB. The contact was so foreign and frightening that Charles was plunged into denial and came to accept for a long time that the TW were hallucinations of his own mind and treated them as such, much to the amusement of the TW and their children and even the American generals.

Clifford Stone, who is a lot like Charles, also is very religious and humble, but Clifford had the advantage of contact from an early age, claiming to me that this was one of the reasons he thinks he was picked by the military to be involved in crash retrievals. This even though he was a low ranking enlisted man as was Charles. In his early years Clifford was observed by and communicated with a military individual familiar with contact, and I assume it was this individual who steered Clifford into the contact programs because he was already acclimated to contact.

Clifford told me that some others who were not acclimated had freaked out and there even were suicides because of contact, as these individuals were thrown suddenly and without preparation into contact. So it makes perfect sense to me why Clifford, a low ranking enlisted man, was moved into the program even though he has been criticized by those unfamiliar with how this system works as was described by Bill Uhouse. It seems to have been the same with Charles who just happened to be able to adapt and stick it out, when others could not, gaining the respect and even love of the TW and maybe a few American generals as well.

Other enlisted men had been severely injured even killed by the TW, one who threw a stone into the sagebrush at what he thought was a coyote and was chased by a very angry TW mother threating his life if he was to ever show up there again. The stone broke the arm of her son, a very serious injury, because the TW are not as strong and sturdy as we are and that child had to be taken back to their world for treatment. Charles himself was almost accidently killed by a very frightened young TW woman being acclimated by the adult TW to Charles in preparation of future work with earth humans. Here is a quote from page 129 of Millennia Hospitality III;

> "My right leg had just come forward, my foot had just touched the ground in front of me when, once again, Pamela icked. Their nervous system, running two and a half times faster than ours, allowed her to point her white pencil at me and activate it before I could do much more than tighten my throat muscles and blink my eyes. Screaming at her father, she blurted out in a panicky manner, "He is out of control! See I told you, father! He

has broken out of the controls! See, I have to readjust them!" Then the teacher grabbed the pencil from Pamela's hand and forcefully exclaimed; "He meant no harm. He just could not hear your father! There was no reason to kill him!"

What happened was that Pamela was so panicked that she had inadvertently set the weapon on kill and Charles was soon lying on the ground bleeding to death. He survived by pressing his knuckles on his throat and was left to die for several hours while the TW and the military watched, but over time the bleeding stopped. Nobody could help him because even the TW were surprised when he did not die immediately, but once they realized he might not die, they would not allow him to be disturbed else the bleeding start up again. Charles managed to survive, but the TW got a real dressing down by the Generals and the TW accepted it, and later Pamela met Charles in the desert alone and defenseless, just as he had been before them.

George LoBuono sent me this Charles Hall quote that further illustrates the intense distrust and disrespect by the TW ruling class as to ordinary folks.

> "Worse yet was the behavior of a Tall White female who had gone to meet with a select (4) members of Congress, and was leaving, coming down the West steps of the Capitol." Hall said a CIA guard tried to help the Tall White female down the stairs, but the guard accidentally hurt the Tall White female, who threatened the CIA guard and he had to beg her to spare his life. Apparently, the female threatened to kill him with a pencil-like device, right there, on the stairs."

Charles also says in his books that when he was at Nellis the TW considered ordinary humans with contempt, one of the reasons for this was the way we treated our children. The TW are very loving and protective of their children and they spend much of their time teaching and playing with them out in the desert and the mountains. It would appear, thanks to other good people like Charles Hall, that these perceptions have begun to change maybe a notch or two. ☺

Over time Charles claims to have earned the love and respect of the generals and the TW, and to this day Charles is protected by treaty that no harm will come to him for speaking out as from this quote from a Hall interview by Karma One: Charles said;

" Remember, as I describe in "Millennia Hospitality" in the chapter entitled "The Happy Charade" the decision to send me, and no one else, out to the ranges, was made by a committee of individuals that included the Tall Whites as well as high ranking USAF Generals and other high ranking members of the U.S. Government. "

"The Tall Whites are very meticulous about keeping their agreements and expect the U.S. Government to be equally meticulous about keep its agreements as well. If I were victimized or threatened by anyone, The Tall Whites would interpret that to mean that the U.S. Government could not be trusted to keep its agreements. The consequences would be enormous. Remember also that I was a weather observer. I was an enlisted man. I was never shown any classified documents. I was never given any classified briefings. I was never a part of any classified program such as building secret aircraft. I never took any photographs. I did not bring any government property, anything material, any diary, or log book with me when I came off the ranges."

Charles has said. "It is my personal observation that their society has an organization very similar to our own American society, or to the societies in Western Europe." What really intrigues me is just how human the TW are as portrayed by Charles, even though their bodies are thin and frail by our standards, with the females only able to lift 30 pounds. Their movements are much quicker and they can run much faster than we. They also become very uncomfortable at less than 80 degrees and this is why they only venture out mostly in the Nevada summer in the desert and the very beautiful Spring Mountains; where they spend a lot of time, both families and children. They have glowing suits in which they can travel many miles that also levitate them up into trees where they play with their children.

I found confirmation of these glowing suits and levitation into the trees as described by Charles, from an individual that lives at Indian Springs. He was doing a garbage run late in the Spring Mountains south of Nellis and when coming back he noticed what he thought were military flares in the trees and on the ground far down below. Thinking that he would visit friends in the military he drove down and investigated to find only darkness and silence, he became very frightened and turned around and began praying to himself to get out of there all in one piece. I figure the TW had simply turned off their suits when they saw him coming and were still there just watching him with their usual curiosity as described by Charles throughout his books.

One can see from the material in Charles's books that the TW are very intelligent, emotional and curious feeling both love and anger much more intensely than we do. In spite of their fierce nature when angry or fearful, Charles does an excellent job of portraying them in a very human light as fellow humans who have all the individual characteristics as us, ranging from sadistic to very loving. Through his books I came to find myself appreciating, even loving, the TW as I love our own people. I think it really helps me that I grew up in the natural world and raised frightened and dangerous animals from a pet wild turkey and many types of birds, to dangerous rattlesnakes. Each animal has its own individual nature, as well as its collective characteristics to the species it belongs.

I have been impressed by the very human nature of the Tall Whites as reported by Charles in his books. In one case Charles claims he watched as a TW female on repeated occasions floated a little human girl out of her bedroom window to play with her little TW girl of about the same age. I was able to document while in Indian Springs, that Charles could have viewed the TW ship settle down at Wheeler Pass where there really are charcoal ovens from the 1800's, and float in their suits up and over the hills or small mountains just south of Indian Springs.

I heard this from the past owner of the Ski Lodge that these ovens really exist at Wheeler Pass in the Spring Mountains. Charles in his book claimed to watch from a vantage point that is now about where the Casino is in Indian Springs. I was told that one can really see Wheeler Pass from this point and the TW could have been seen floating in their glowing suits to the town from this point. Tom Fox reports a very similar experience.

Interestingly, it is possible that the past owner of the ski lodge is living in the very same house or one close by where Charles claims the little earth human girl was being floated out through the window. Unfortunately the family there at the time had moved and nobody knew where they are. I would assume the little girl at that time would well remember such an experience and if she could be found that would be powerful confirmation of this part of Charles's story.

In the book there is also a claim by Charles that a little TW girl got lost in the desert and that he helped to rescue her, further endearing himself to the TW and especially that little TW girl's mother and father. Interesting, this is not the only case to be found where ET children have been alleged to stray from their parents to get themselves in real or potential trouble as is illustrated by this case from South America. It's this kind of detail in Charles's material that is so unusual and compelling as to the detailed insight it gives us to the humanity of other type of human ET. The following ET incident was written by Jorge Martin and is in his book; 'Vieques: Caribbean UFO Cover-Up of the Third Kind.'

> "Mr. Anibal Perez from Vieques encountered a strange 'child' when he was 14 years old. This was in 1982 while he was enjoying a trip to Media Luna Beach, east of Sun Bay beach, on Vieques. He was with his nephew, who was 13 years old, and his

nephew's grandmother. The grandmother was the adult in charge of them. He still wonders about what happened that day.

Perez and his nephew were swimming in the sea and playing on the beach. It was a clear, sunny day. Suddenly, something emerged from the sea, approaching them from a distance. It was a child who was about their own age, 12 to 14 years. They all were in the water and the 'kid' approached them in a friendly demeanor, "trying to befriend them," and would not leave their side. Perez's nephew asked, "What is he doing following us all the time? Do you know him?"

Perez answered that he did not know the 'kid' and asked the boy who he was and what it was he wanted. "But he would not talk," he said,"...he kept emitting weird sounds similar to the ones dolphins make." That is when the boy swam away to deeper water and submerged, disappearing from sight. He emerged a few minutes later and came near the two boys again. The boys couldn't understand how the "kid" was able to stay under water as long as he did without drowning.

In the palm of his hand," Perez explained, "the boy had something that looked like sand granules, which he began picking at with his other hand and eating from it... and at the same time making gestures, offering some of the stuff to us. He wanted us to eat some of it." They refused to eat the material, but were amazed to see the strange boy eating the sand-like substance he had apparently brought up from the bottom.

The two boys were growing tired of the intruder's presence, and kept playing in the water close to the shore. The 'kid' kept following them everywhere they went. Annoyed, Perez's nephew threw water at him and the 'kid' did the same to him, imitating everything they did. The 'kid' swam back to the deep water and submerged once again. Moments later, he again emerged and approached them. This time he had seaweed in his hand, and was eating some of it. He made gestures for them to eat the seaweed, too, but once again was refused.

"We were amazed," stated XXX. 'He was eating seaweed from the deep, and something that looked like sand. Who was he? He would not talk. He only made some weird screeching sounds. An hour had already gone by since the 'kid' first appeared. There was no one else there. Only my nephew's grandmother and she was at a distance, up on the beach. We later told her about the kid, or whatever he was.

Why do you say 'Whatever he was?'" we asked? "Well, my nephew kept asking him who he was and what he wanted, but he wouldn't answer. He kept making those weird noises. We came out of the water for a while, and returned later. He clapped his hands, joyful that we returned.

We kept asking him questions, and he would only stare at us, making gestures... it looked as if he was concentrating, trying to understand what we were saying. After a while, he began to repeat the things we were saying in Spanish, but his voice had a screechy tone. My nephew was angry because he thought that the 'kid' was making fun of us. We spoke some foul words to him, and the 'kid' kept on repeating them.

He looked normal, like any kid. He was white, Caucasian, and about 4 feet 3 inches tall. He was slender and had dark brown eyes and hair. His hair was curled, but not much, and fell down to his neck. He had normal hands with five fingers. "He had a normal nose and a mouth with fine lips and teeth which we could see whenever he would repeat what we said or laugh when we laughed. His ears looked normal, too. He was only wearing pair of tight fitting, short, white pants. The pants material seemed normal, like textile.

The only two things that were odd about the 'kid' were his ability to stay under water for long periods of time, and the way he talked, making screeching sounds at first, and then speaking in broken Spanish with the same screechy voice. Anibal added, "My nephew pushed him, asking him who he was and what country he came from. He just stared at us for a moment as if thinking of what he was going to say, and then he said 'Sea...Bottom... Country.' He then pointed down to the deep with his finger.

He then moved away from us, looked at us and said; "Goodbye...humans." He made a gesture to us with his right hand and submerged again into the sea. We waited there for a while, expecting to see him come out again, but he did not resurface. That is when we were really shocked because, even though we were very young at the time, we were surprised by what he said. We understood what he meant by those words.

Even with his strange behavior, I believed that he was a normal kid, until he said those words, "sea...bottom...country." To me, he was telling us that he came from the sea. And when he said 'goodbye...humans,' we realized he was not normal at all. "Look, if there's life and intelligent beings on our planet, there could very well be life on other planets, too. Perhaps, everything we are seeing here around Vieques has to do with the fact that we are not alone in this universe... that other beings are visiting us. "There are also some legends about underwater cities. Was this child from one of them? To me, this incident remains a mystery."

While at Indian Springs I also met a woman from a ranch family that settled to the north of what is now Nellis back in the wagon train days. She claimed to be a TW abductee hybrid, and if true, this tends to confirm that the TW not only watched the wagon trains come to their land, but became involved with some of the first families to the area. She suggested I go and spend some time at her parent's ranch and that I would have a good chance to see evidence of the TW there.

In his book Charles said that he believed that the TW had been in the area since at least the time of when Madison was president because the TW known, as the teacher had mentioned Madison. She also said that she had sat on a ledge and watched the wagon trains roll into the area. Having such a long lifespan of 800 years it really must have been something to watch earth humanity evolving from horse and buggy to space travel in such a short period of time.

Charles Hall also talks about that at the time he was at Nellis and Indian Springs, the TW were getting interested in Vegas, and on R&R visits would go there. The women grew tired of the bland nurse's uniforms that the military were furnishing them and wanted modern clothes so they came to department stores in disguise with their guards to shop.

Charles has stated that the laws of economics apply across the universe just as do the laws of physics. The TW decided to exchange shuttle craft technology, but not deep space craft technology with the American military, in return for support for their base and to even have the military make shuttle craft for them. Charles claims to have been inside these craft and noticed corporate off the shelf stamps on the inside furnishings.

Charles claims the more important TW also liked to gamble in Vegas and came in surrounded by their TW guards. This part of the story has been confirmed by people like Tom Fox and Cherry Hinkle and an Internet investigator who believes he saw a TW in Laughlin NV. Tom has seen the TW out in the desert and in Vegas while Cherry apparently met one, thinking at the time that it was some kind of albino human. Here are their accounts. Tom Fox has written;

"It actually started back in the 60's I did a homework assignment were I clipped out a time magazine article entitled- Who were they? It showed a picture of the Talls all dressed-up having crashed an embassy ball! Yet, these ambassadors from N Spain were not invited, were trying to fit in. Hall tells me the issues of the magazine were recalled.

In the '80s at a used book store, I came across the lost book of the Talls, written by a NJ housewife who befriended military people, photos of Talls were used in book. I tried emailing many UFO-book-sources, to no avail. Charles Hall once owned the book yet it vanished. If anyone knows of this book please contact me. It's about 150 pages, dark front cover black & white photos.

It must have been confiscated. Then in '90 I came out of the bathroom of the Tropicana Casino late one night and noticed 4 Talls, one was climbing the stairs in a most peculiar manner. I later found it was due to not being used to earth gravity, thus a new arrival. I was dumbfounded. I felt guilty for staring as they turned to watch me.

Charles Hall informed me who they were. It was 15 years later that I heard the Charles Hall interview. He informed me that they play poker at nearby casinos. I went back and confirmed that those stairs led to the poker room! (The casino was remodeled but workers shared what it was like then. In 2005 I camped near their Indian Springs Base - scout craft came out one night, signaled my light, it went in reverse and hid in a cloud.

A few nights later one levitated nearby. A Tall guard descended down from the ridge. A few nights later one, appeared behind where I was camped. It was levitating and dancing about. I tried signaling; it would stop and would change its luminosity, then go back to various movements. I walked towards it, yet it was miles to the back and before long I couldn't see it anymore. One thing I didn't mention was that another light which looked like a being illuminated descended from the Wheeler Ridge area. This I believed to be a TW-guard."

Tom Fox quotes George LoBuono. "This was also confirmed to me directly by Charles Hall in person." This opens a window to insights as to the conflicts and interactions between different ET races.

George LoBuono said, "Airman Charles Hall suggests that Air Force generals thought the Tall Whites were near-enemies of the Greys. Hall: "I am quite certain that the Tall Whites and the Short Greys hate each other. I am quite certain that the Tall Whites would never permit the Short Greys to come anywhere near their base areas or near to their housing areas or anywhere that their children might be playing, etc." But what is Hall's basis for that assumption? I asked him, and he replied, "I was with the Tall Whites for over two years. Various remarks were made, and in particular, the Teacher (a Tall White) made the point quite clear to me." (Charles Hall, personal email to the author 3-13-09)."

From these accounts by other witnesses to the TW, one can see the similarities of TW behavior and activities described in much more detail in Charles's books. Cherry Hinkle also has an apparent TW encounter in Vegas as described and passed on to me by Leslie Mitts when I was still out west. I have a mobile laptop now with mobile access and could access the Internet even while in Indian Springs.

Cherry Hinkle said: "Yes, there have been a few rumors. The fact is that most all the casinos have underground tunnels, a few on the strip are supposed to be connected and end up in Nellis. I used to work in the Aladdin, and Desert Inn, and I know the tunnels under that casino ends up at Caesars Casino a huge underground area, hidden rooms, secret high roller rooms etc. I walked from Aladdin to Caesars underground, where I spotted a group of Airmen from Nellis, and an "albino" in an electric golf cart type car.

I was escorted out of the underground facility and warned not to be caught there again. I worked at Aladdin for a few years, and met either that same albino or one that looked like the first one, he enjoyed Keno games. His hair was so white it almost looked transparent, with very pale blue eyes, except his pupils looked pink not black like everybody else. I wouldn't be surprised to discover he was a Tall White.

I chatted with him same as with the others playing Keno, I recall he spoke English clearly, but with a tight lipped accent, similar to someone from a Scandinavian country. He drank something from his own beverage holder, like an opaque plastic container, with a straw. He didn't order from the cocktail waitress. We made eye contact when we spoke. His voice was soft and pleasant.

Yes, he stayed with Airmen, they didn't gamble, he did. They weren't friendly. I remember wondering if he was a scientist or a visiting dignitary, and the Airmen were guarding him. That was back in the middle 1970s, and I thought he was "just" an albino. It was a few years before I heard about the Tall Whites.

I can't even guess why he liked to gamble, but I remember that he liked 'way tickets' - very complex style of gambling. It is hard to win, but when you win - you win big. I like Keno too, I once placed a one dollar bet - 7 numbers, and two minutes later I watched as all seven numbers came up - I collected $14,000.00. Nice.

I'm sure I never touched the TW, or never photographed him. The only reason I remember is because I saw him in the tunnels, and was escorted out, only to later see him again gambling. I don't mean to be rude, but haven't seen too many albinos in my life, and I know meeting him and being inches away from him is something that I doubt too many other people would forget either."

What I found interesting in Cherry's account is that by the 1970's the TW were confortable enough to allow themselves to be guarded by Nellis employees. The encounters that Charles said he had in Vegas involved a dignitary surround by TW guards rather than Nellis guards. This is evidence of a developing relationship of trust between the TW and our military.

Charles says that the TW can live to be about 800 years old so this is no small matter to trust our military with their lives. I think I would be a lot more careful about my security if I knew I might live that long if I were especially careful.

We found that George Flier had a 1970s satellite photo of a TW ship[83] on his Fliers Files. The photo fits the description of the bus like ship described in detail in Charles second book. The picture was sent to Charles and was confirmed by him. This craft is described also in this Kevin Smith interview with Charles. George Flier is a very well respected Eastern Regional MUFON Director who claims to be a contactee who met and entered a human ET ship and was apparently sent on a mission to help the people of earth.

Radio talk show host, 'Sweeps' Fox, another TW witness in Ireland, at one time held a Top Secret security clearance while working in Saudi Arabia. He told me and in interviews that not only has he seen the TW going through his garbage on the street, but he and his family have seen the TW shuttle craft. Sweeps got very interested and involved in the TW material and broadcast it to the world, apparently getting the attention of the TW.

Charles Hall through his books and interviews has found additional witnesses to the TW, so to me this proves beyond a reasonable doubt that the TW exist, completely separate from Charles Hall's testimony. Because there is such a solid foundation backed up by my own personal investigations, I feel I can use this case to not only peer into the lives of the TW, but get a better perspective on other ET races as well.

I found the following quote by Charles especially useful as to the nature of extraterrestrial life on other worlds. Charles asked,

"Are there many planets like the Earth out in space? I asked." "Yes." she (The Teacher) responded. "There are quite a few. However, humans are the only people that we have seen who live so closely with their animals. For example, you feel comfortable milking cows, riding horses, and playing with dogs. Every one of those animals could kill you, but you naturally use your intelligence to determine how each of those animals is thinking. Then you naturally take control of them. Only humans do that. On most planets, once people become intelligent, they don't want to have anything to do with the animals that are much less intelligent than they are, so the kill them off. Also humans will eat almost anything. On all of the other planets the intelligent people will only eat plants. We, for example, only eat plants."

George LoBuono found another important case that he attributes to Richard Boylan that may involve more information about the TW if this is a TW case, but it could be some other type of human extraterrestrial as there are many types being reported.

"I connected the dots on this one. Col Major Wilson had begun his duties at the Papoose Lake installation, still not knowing what existed 30 stories farther down. He had been well indoctrinated in Top Secret work and knew all the consequences of keeping the nation's most guarded secrets. The past six years had been slow and boring, he recalls, and other than what he saw at Wright-Patterson AFB, he felt that he was in a vacuum going nowhere.

He was sitting in his office at S-4 mulling this over one morning, when a Lieutenant Colonel Bennet came in. He asked Wilson if he was busy, ("Like he gave a damn," Wilson recalls) and said; "Let's go." Wilson followed the Lieutenant Colonel, and they eventually wound up two stories down at the super-secret

"S-4" UFO technology area. As they came out on a landing there, Wilson saw eight different kinds of UFOs!

There were intellectual-looking people all over the area, whom he guessed were scientists. He glanced at Bennett, who cut off his implied question with a curt "Forget it." The Colonel and the Major went into a cubicle where there were about twenty officers and civilians sitting around. Wilson was startled, when a woman came in who was at least eight feet tall. There was not an ounce of excess fat on her body, he recalls. She wore a strange-looking jump suit, which had a * HI * pattern on the right side above the breast line. To this day, Wilson recollects the details of this striking encounter.

"The woman had finely-chiseled features. Her blonde hair cascaded neatly past her shoulders. Her eyes were the bluest blue I'd ever seen. Somehow she was different. Little did I know then, how different! She sat a large crystal on the table, and without warning, her fingers began to glow as she ran them over this crystal. A 3-D hologram began to form above it! I looked around the room and everyone's mouth was hanging open, and suddenly I noticed mine was, too. Little did I realize that at that moment my life would forever be changed? My past teachings slipped from me as I stared. My whole concept of life did a 180-degree turn, as I watched the Hologram, complete with sound, unfold the mysteries of the past and the present, and of other worlds."

Colonel Wilson related that among the scenes, which the female extraterrestrial's crystal hologram displayed for the assembled group, was the history of the Earth and of extraterrestrial involvement with it. That involvement included fashioning the consciousness of Jesus and sending him to live among Earthlings to point to a better way to understand life and to live. The extraterrestrial woman also showed the officers and scientists scenes from inhabited planets of other star systems. Wilson was transformed by this experience. When it was over, I knew that, whatever part I was to play in all of this, my life as I knew it had ended forever."

I have run across yet another case that could be a Tall White encounter on the Internet that did not turn out well for the Russians. This Russian case[84] in which divers were killed in a severe defensive reaction sounds a lot like the Tall Whites.

"Russia's Lake Baikal is the oldest and deepest lake on the planet at 25-30 million years old, and the second largest following the Caspian Sea. It has had its own share of water based UFO encounters. In 1982 Russian military divers were on a training mission in the Lake when they were confronted with a group of other beings. The alien divers were described as being humanoid but about nine feet (3 meters) tall, encased in tight silvery body suits with no apparent diving equipment other than spherical helmets. This was at the depth of 50 meters (over 160 feet). The Russian divers attempted to pursue the strange beings but ultimately gave up the attempt after three of their numbers were killed and the other four injured."

This following case[85] from Collin Andrews's website would seem to be very likely a TW case, especially indicated by how fast these people can run. I think Charles Hall said up to thirty mph. This case thus backs up another part of Charles's story.

"I received a call from a contact within Wiltshire Police constabulary. I have built-up a few friendly contacts due to my continual use of the Freedom of Information Act to extract information of UFO's, and this police sergeant is one of them. The contact, who doesn't want to be named, was driving past Silbury Hill early Monday morning (6th July 2009) when he saw three figures in the formation there. At first he thought they were forensic officers as they were dressed in white coveralls. He stopped his car and approached the field."

"The figures were all over 6ft and had blond hair. They seemed to be inspecting the crop. When he got to the edge of the field he heard what he believed to be a sound not dissimilar to static electricity. This crackling noise seemed to be running through the field and the crop was moving gently close to where the noise was moving. He felt the hair on his arms and back of his neck raise up. He shouted to the figures that at first ignored him, not glancing at him. When he tried to enter the field they looked up and began running."

"He said "They ran faster than any man I have ever seen. I'm no slouch but they were moving so fast. I looked away for a second and when I looked back they were gone. I then got scared. The noise was still around, but I got an uneasy feeling and headed for the car. For the rest of the day I had a pounding headache I couldn't shift."

Hopefully I have given the reader enough information here that they will investigate the Tall Whites in more depth. The reason I started with the TW chapter in this book is that the TW interactions are relatively straightforward and the intrusions on earth human freedoms and liberties nothing like that of some other races of ETs, especially the Greys, that I will get into in the next chapter. Another reason the TW case is simpler is that the TW space travel technology is not that advanced with the TW craft simply exceeding the speed of light to the point that it takes two or three weeks to reach earth. This requires forward operating bases as the TW ships travel between other worlds of interest to them. For them we seem to be simply a way station pit stop. ☺

Charles believes that the total TW at the Nellis base are only about 300 and the base is simply a stopover for maintenance and repair of their deep space craft traveling elsewhere in the galaxy. They are not warping space-time as the Greys and some other species are doing. Charles vigorously disputes this, but the evidence is overwhelming that this is so. I seem to remember that Clifford Stone said that an ET he has known since childhood told him it took about 3 of our hours to reach his home planet.

The treaties the TW have with the US military seem to revolve around TTPs (Technology Transfer Programs) where in return for sharing shuttle technologies their base is supplied by us. It's a simple matter of economics for them as the cost of shipping material to this base from elsewhere is high. The TW also get the benefit of not being harassed by our military as their base is protected within the boundaries of Nellis AFB.

So how is this relationship with the TW possibly developing? Perhaps a partial answer came from an offhand comment Charles made to me in the spring of 2011 when I interviewed him at his home in New Mexico. He said that the TW have several planets around other stars that are too chilly for them, but fine for us and told the generals that we could establish colonies there in return for supplying their bases on these planets around other stars.

Also in this regard Charles has said that the TW use Titanium or a Titanium alloy in the hulls of their deep space craft. It strikes me that this might be a very valuable commodity, not just for our Secret Space Fleet, but for trade with the Greys, TW and other ET races who might be helping us access this resource.

While writing this chapter I remembered two important articles, that together with some other testimony from whistleblowers about blotted out NASA imagery, that suggest a Top Secret classified Titanium mining operation and colony has been in operation since the 1960s on the moon. It is widely assumed that black operations are 50 years advanced over public knowledge so go figure! Did we ever stop making manned missions to the moon or like with electrogravitic technologies, it just went black and into the hands of the Globalist Feudalistic Elite's breakaway civilization?

There has been Internet speculation and testimony that this moon base is a joint Grey-Human operation, but I have yet to find much confirming testimony on this. I am working on it and hope to present more material in another chapter. I suspect that the TW might be involved as well as the Greys in such an operation, as their exotic shuttle technology could be used to transport heavy mining equipment, facilities and other supplies to a secret moon base and mining operation. The same for technology gained from the Greys as suggested by Bob Lazar and others.

Is NASA trying to tell us something in releasing the following information into the public domain now? And how long have they been sitting on this information? This article[86] and other articles say that the Moon is loaded with titanium ore with concentrations up to 18%. Discovery News says; "Lava flows that turned into rocks on the moon are enriched with titanium in concentrations far higher than what is found on Earth. The precious material could be used to construct equipment for lunar and other spacecraft." "Detailed maps from a robotic NASA science satellite circling the moon show deposits as rich as about 18 percent, planetary geologist Jeffrey Gillis-Davis, with the University of Hawaii, told Discovery News."

Another article titled; *'Titanium on The Moon: Resources to spark sew Space Race?'*[87] States; "Titanium has been discovered on the moon in abundance. Since it is a rare element on Earth, lighter and more durable than steel, could the demand for it possibly spark a renewed interest in getting to and even establishing bases on the moon?" Wow says I, just imagine that!

A further article[88] by *Discovery News* shows that Robert Bigelow understands how important the moon's resources are, but does not seem to realize that the US has already staked out a claim to the moon and can defend this claim against excursions by China.

It makes sense to me that maybe titanium is a very important trade item amongst space faring civilizations. It is an important material for exotic space craft construction, part of the same metal alloy, smart metal that is alleged to have been from Roswell and other ET crashes. Today it is manufactured and known as Nitinol. The following two excerpts are from the extremely detailed study and analysis that links the development of Nitinol with ET spacecraft crashes.[89]

> "In the months immediately following the Roswell crash, the Air Force contracted Battelle Memorial Institute to perform first-ever work on novel Titanium alloys. This included work on develop-

ment of Titanium and Nickel alloy- the basis for "memory metal" today, and similar to some of the debris reported at Roswell."

Four Wright-Patterson sponsored technical studies on 'memory metal' in later decades cited a 1949 Battelle report on Nickel and Titanium (NiTi) alloy. Nickel and Titanium are used to create 'Nitinol' the premiere 'memory metal' on the planet."

Perhaps the reader can see that with all the information surfacing on the Secret Space Fleet that treaties may have been signed and secret colonies and bases established, not only in our solar system, but on other star systems 50 years in advance of public understanding and government acknowledgement. I hope to get more into this in later Chapters, but for now it's something to think very seriously about.

So knowing what I already know about the Secret Space Fleet and the evidence for it that presented to the reader, this got me to thinking that it might be taking a lot of titanium to build this fleet's hulls. Perhaps as alleged, we never really stopped going to the Moon. It just went Classified and in the intervening 40+ years the US and its allies now have bases there mining Titanium possibly in a rumored joint Grey-Human project.

I also got to thinking that maybe ETs have been mining our Moon for a long time and this accounts for all the alleged alien structures and activities that are blurred out in NASA photographs. Already people have come forward and admitted that they had seen evidence that NASA was airbrushing out past and present activity. One wonders if all this sophisticated underground excavation of secret facilities extends to our moon as well. It would take some very large electrogravitic exotic spacecraft to move mining equipment to the moon, if it were disassembled and then reassembled on the moon. Maybe a craft like the one in this account would do the trick?

"A professional hiker 'witness' was deep in the Utah desert, 25 miles from the nearest road in a high inaccessible area. Suddenly, he saw an arrowhead-shaped craft 600 feet long appear and hover, a giant camouflaged sliding door opened in the desert floor, and the craft disappeared into what was a concealed underground base."

John Lear, son of the founder of the Lear Jet Corporation has a reputation for snooping into classified programs involving the breakaway society and aliens, but seems to present a mix of real and unreal information to the public. In the following account[90] he and other researchers are looking into stories of covert mining on the moon. Why would a security clearance be needed to know about mining equipment? ☺

"An insider I talked to in 1990 told me that he worked on a piece of mining equipment for the moon that was 30 stories tall. He told me that toward the end of the contract he rented an airplane and flew around it just to get an idea of its enormous size. So by accident Zorgon stumbled onto all of this mining information and it appears that a massive, well organized effort is under way to prepare to mine on the moon and mars.

We are considering that the possibility exists that they have decided to make the operation public. And rather than just say "We lied and Mercury, Gemini and Apollo were just window dressing," they are ramping up for public disclosure that will dovetail into what's already there in such a way that nobody will suspect we have been there for 45 years.

NOTE: When John called the gentleman, he got an answering machine and left a simple message... we would like to get some information on bucket wheel excavators... nothing more... nothing about the moon etc... When Dale returned the call his first question was "What's your clearance level?" Since Norcat is a government contractor I would imagine their caller ID is more than just a name and number. But in the conversation Dale did volunteer that Tim Muff is no longer with them and is now working at Lockheed Skunkworks... There was no real reason to tell us this, we never asked... It is bits and clues like this that tell us they are leaving us bread crumbs to follow..."

Readers of Col. Corso's book the Day After Roswell will recall that Corso talks a lot about Project Horizon in his book. In fact Corso reproduces the Project Horizon Report, A U.S. Army Study for the Establishment of Lunar Outpost 9 June 1959 in the Appendix of his book. It's my contention that this study was secretly implemented in the 1960's. I further believe that Corso devoted so much of his book to this because he was trying to hint that when he wrote his book that the Army already had a super-secret operational moon base in operation. On chapter one the introduction the manual states:

> "Horizon is the project whose objective is the establishment of a lunar outpost by the United States. This study was directed by letter dated 20 March 1959 from the Chief of R&D, Department of the Army, to the Chief of Ordnance. Responsibility for the preparation of the study was subsequently assigned to the Commanding General, Army Ordnance Missile Command. Elements of all Technical Services of the Army participated in the investigation. This report is a limited feasibility study which investigates the methods and means of accomplishing this objective and the purposes it will serve. It also considers the substantial political, scientific and security implications which the prompt establishment of a lunar outpost will have for the United States."
>
> "The extent to which future operations might be conducted in space, to include the land mass of the moon or perhaps other planets, is of such a magnitude as to almost defy the imagination. In both Congressional and military examination of the problem, it is generally agreed that the interactions of space and terrestrial war are so great as to generate radically new concepts."

It would appear that the globalists have been building their secret empire not only on earth but in space as well. Don't forget that image that surfaced from Google Earth of what appears to be a bio-station on Mars.[91] [92] The debunker propagandists, true to form, tried to explain it away as a cosmic ray when the discovery got into the mainstream news. It's obviously a detailed structure under magnification and not an image artifact.

CHAPTER SEVEN

THE GREYS

Grey Driven Advancements in Genetic engineering, Microbiology and Aerospace

"In our obsession with antagonisms of the moment, we often forget how much unites all the members of humanity. I occasionally think how quickly our differences, worldwide, would vanish if we were facing an alien threat from outside this world." President Ronald Reagan

"If I become President, I'll make every piece of information this country has about UFO sightings available to the public and scientists. I am convinced that UFOs exist because I have seen one." President Jimmy Carter

"In the firm belief that the American public deserves a better explanation than that thus far given by the Air Force, I strongly recommend that there be a committee investigation of the UFO phenomena. I think we owe it to the people to establish credibility regarding UFOs, and to produce the greatest possible enlightenment of the subject." President Gerald Ford

There is speculation that the alien species known as the Greys are perhaps just as diverse and spread across the universe as, are the human species. Therefore, it is important not to paint what appears to be a vast network of Grey species with the same brush. As with cosmic humans, it seems that the Greys run the gamut from being highly predatory using competitive win-lose tactics, to being cooperative and using win-win tactics.

Abduction investigators investigating Grey activity seem to fall into two very contradictory camps, those that see threat, like David Jacobs and those that see promise, like Steven Greer and Carol Rosin and John Mack. It's possible both sides are right and both sides are wrong, because of the diversity of individuals and groups of Greys. Understanding this diversity as with cosmic humans, is complicated by processes of artificial evolution.

Investigator and probable abductee George LoBuono got me interested in the idea of a Grey Collective and he had this to say.

> "Krapf is the first to outline a larger mega-population directly and in detail. It poses an overview of the Greys and the Roswell hybrids, also. We should expect to see some larger populations, given the age of the universe and the way that the Kepler satellite suggests an abundance of Earth-like planets."

"I'll state my experience with Verdants, again. Among aliens, telepathic and remote sensing is considered a reliable evidentiary basis for data and reporting. I've interacted and have criticized Verdants and their associated aliens for years- even my kids have probably been abducted, i.e. their stories of "dreams" about going up with aliens, after one of which I found a perfect, lentil-sized scoop mark taken out of my son's foot soles (it absolutely wasn't there before)."

"In years of interactions & rigorous remote probing and questioning of Verdants, it has been as is all such interaction. I see them, the inside of their craft (faintly) and I hear urgent, clear critiques of them by other aliens. I can say that I know the manner, character and behavior of some Verdants as well as I know that of some humans with whom I have been acquainted for years.

Even more so, actually, given that in such interactions you resonate into their minds, not just seeing them visually. Having interacted with them and some of their sub-populations, I have absolute zero doubt about their existence. Again, this is in a more alien-like context: where remote checking and detailed interactions are normal, every single day."

I don't like to use ethical and moral terms like good and evil anymore to compare different races of extraterrestrials, because what the fox may consider moral and ethical, the rabbit, the fox's prey might tend to disagree. I see morality and ethics as cohesive agreements that individuals or groups or even civilizations make between themselves, so as to be able to cooperate together and rise up to a higher level of fractal above those that don't.

Some investigators like George have come to call the agglomeration of Grey species, the Grey collective, a term for this very diverse group of individuals groups and civilizations. Likewise maybe we should call the agglomerate of galactic human species the galactic human collective. Some evidence seems to suggest that these two collectives and even other cosmic collectives may be colliding and competing, not only on earth, but on a much larger universal playing field.

I am suggesting that not only are competitive and cooperative struggles going on within collectives, but between different collectives themselves. I see all this as simply just an extension of what is happening in nature all around us, here on earth. Why should the evolutionary laws of nature not apply elsewhere? The laws of physics do not stop at the edge of space, so why should the laws of nature, politics, science and economics stop at the edge of space.

Charles Hall has told me that the TW are in a cold war with the Greys, disliking even hating the Greys, and a source known to Jeff Adams claiming to be the step-son of an Air Force general with close MJ 12 connection told Jeff this:

> "The Nordics and the Greys had an alliance which fell apart at this same time. The Nordics, who can be quite warlike when they want to be, opened up a can of whoopass on the Greys, and the war cost the Greys a lot of ground. The Greys were apparently using the Nordics for their own purposes, and the Nordics were not amused. The US/EU/UN still works with the Greys,[93] so we all know where this going to end."

I have heard similar stories of conflict between cosmic humans and Greys from my local contactee friends with one saying that he doubts that the Greys are going to leave us alone anytime soon. It's pretty obvious from abductee accounts like those of Jim Sparks, that the Greys think of us as property. In this quote from Jim's book on page 100 this point was made very clear.

> "They seemed to sense my rage, and they left me alone for a little bit. I was clear-headed but angry." "Then, instead of answering any questions, they made their presentation again, though this time in written form, in their language. I watched it and found that, again, I could comprehend it, and it all underlined their message: "We've been around for a while. We've been working on your personal family line. We know you well. Humans are ours."

Jeff Adams source gave more detail, but it's similar to what I have heard elsewhere on the number of ET races know to the government.

"To Jeff: Just got off with some friends in the know. Here is what they had to add. They also told me what to look for; (deleted for security reasons) there are 7 major and 57 minor alien races in our section of the universe. If we expand to include our galaxy, the number rises to 11 and 124. So much for the 'no life in the rest of the universe' theory!! LOL :)"

This leads me to believe that the really big picture in which we are intimately and subtly involved is a continuous struggle where the Greys are pressing and testing the defenses of the celestial human collective over wide portions of universal space. Because we are dealing with advanced sophisticated beings, the competitive struggles can be very subtle and range far beyond our normal perceptual awareness, even into our individual minds creating a cosmic mental battlefield.

It may be that competitive struggles start as inter-galactic psyops, a kind of advanced multidimensional chess game that may or may not degrade into open material conflict on many material worlds. An analogy would be that a family fight begins with name calling, disinformation, propaganda and lies, then may or may not degrade down into violent action.

The Greys seem to be fundamentally different than humans with some having atrophied digestive tracts as discussed in alleged military autopsy reports and may be absorbing nutrients through the skin rather than through a digestive tract. The skin may function like the inside of our digestive tracts, that's why some feel clammy and damp and smelly when touched.

There is some evidence and speculation that the mutilation of animals and even humans, where the bodies are drained of blood, that some kind of food mixture using blood, is being externally ingested into their bodies through the skin. Maybe there is something to the vampire myths after all. Most Greys interacting with abductees also seem to be lacking of feelings and deep emotions while surpassing us in intellectual abilities.

Accounts of an early meeting by extraterrestrial humans with earth humans have indicated that the Eisenhower Administration and his military generals were warned by these human ETs not to get involved with the Greys. Gerald Light was the first to report on Eisenhower meeting with extraterrestrials.

Gerald Light's letter is dated April 16, 1954 to Meade Layne, who was at the time director of Borderland Sciences Research. In the letter Light claimed he was part of a delegation of community leaders who met with extraterrestrials at Edwards Air Force Base.

"My dear friends: I have just returned from Muroc [Edwards Air Force Base]. The report is true -- devastatingly true! I made the journey in company with Franklin Allen of the Hearst papers and Edwin Nourse of Brookings Institute (Truman's erstwhile financial advisor) and Bishop MacIntyre of L.A. (confidential names for the present, please).

When we were allowed to enter the restricted section (after about six hours in which we were checked on every possible item, event, incident and aspect of our personal and public lives), I had the distinct feeling that the world had come to an end with fantastic realism. For I have never seen so many human beings in a state of complete collapse and confusion, as they realized that their own world had indeed ended with such finality as to beggar description.

The reality of the 'other plane' aeroforms is now and forever removed from the realms of speculation and made a rather painful part of the consciousness of every responsible scientific and political group.

During my two days' visit I saw <u>five separate and distinct types of aircraft</u> being studied and handled by our Air Force officials -- with the assistance and permission of the Etherians!

I have no words to express my reactions. It has finally happened. It is now a matter of history. President Eisenhower, as you may already know, was spirited over to Muroc one night during his visit to Palm Springs recently. And it is my conviction that he will ignore the terrific conflict between the various 'authorities' and go directly to the people via radio and television - if the impasse continues much longer.

From what I could gather, an official statement to the country is being prepared for delivery about the middle of May."

The truth seems to be very clear that some Greys are managing the earth human race, considering us their property. It's very clear in abductee accounts that we are expected to submit to them in every way. However from reports I have been seeing, resistance has been growing from many quarters both inside the breakaway civilization and outside in the public domain. The net result seems to be a state of insider cooperation based on human failings very well understood and useful to the Greys, and in other cases, resistance, outright hostility, fighting and shoot-downs. One Special Forces patch has "Tastes like Chicken" written around an image of a typical alien face with a red line across the face as well.

I have come to believe that incorporation into the Grey Collective or Mega-population is a far greater security threat to humanity than even overpopulation, war and environmental degradation combined. I believe the Globalist Elite are being secretly manipulated to support the Grey Agenda and we are gradually losing our precious human sovereignty and individual human rights to a Grey controlled Orwellian New World Order. UFO/ET secrecy plays right into the Grey Agenda because lack of awareness by the prey, is to the advantage of the predator.

What is also becoming clear is that it must take thousands perhaps even tens of thousands of Greys and their hybrids cooperating within the classified breakaway civilization to manage our rapidly growing population and rapid technological evolution. The evidence suggests that these operations are headquartered in underground mazes of tunnels, military bases even underground cities on earth and now perhaps even in joint mining operations on the Moon.

Reports and books by very credible investigators like Richard Sauder in his books on underground and underwater bases describes very well a little of the history behind the breakaway civilizations creation and move to extensive underground secret secure facilities. This began before the 1950's, when underground excavations and tunneling began in earnest, again seemingly in parallel with extraterrestrial contact. The following was written by Richard Sauder Ph.D.[94][95] and was adapted from his book *Underground Bases and Tunnels*.

"The nuclear subterrene (rhymes with 'submarine') was designed at the Los Alamos National Laboratory, in New Mexico. A number of patents were filed by scientists at Los Alamos, a few federal technical documents were written - and then the whole thing just sort of faded away. Or did it? Nuclear subterrenes work by melting their way through the rock and soil, actually vitrifying it as they go, and leaving a neat, solidly glass-lined tunnel behind them.

The heat is supplied by a compact nuclear reactor that circulates liquid lithium from the reactor core to the tunnel face, where it melts the rock. In the process of melting the rock the lithium loses some of its heat. It is then circulated back along the exterior of the tunneling machine to help cool the vitrified rock as the tunneling machine forces its way forward. The cooled lithium then circulates back to the reactor where the whole cycle starts over. In this way the nuclear subterrene slices through the rock like a nuclear powered, 2,000 degree Fahrenheit (1,100 Celsius) earthworm, boring its way deep underground.

The United States Atomic Energy Commission and the United States Energy Research and Development Administration took out Patents in the 1970s for nuclear subterrenes. The first patent, in 1972 went to the U.S. Atomic Energy Commission.

The nuclear subterrene has an advantage over mechanical TBMs in that it produces no muck that must be disposed of by conveyors, trains, trucks, etc. This greatly simplifies tunneling. If nuclear subterrenes actually exist (and I do not know if they do) their presence, and the tunnels they make, could be very hard to detect, for the simple reason that there would not be the tell-tale muck piles or tailings dumps that are associated with the conventional tunneling activities. The 1972 patent makes this clear. It states:

"Debris may be disposed of as melted rock both as a lining for the hole and as a dispersal in cracks produced in the surrounding rock. The rock-melting drill is of a shape and is propelled under sufficient pressure to produce and extend cracks in solid rock radially around the bore by means of hydrostatic pressure developed in the molten rock ahead of the advancing rock drill penetrator. All melt not used in glass-lining the bore is forced into the cracks where it freezes and remains...

"... Such a (vitreous) lining eliminates, in most cases, the expensive and cumbersome problem of debris elimination and at the same time achieves the advantage of a casing type of bore-hole liner." U.S. Patent No. 3,693,731 dated Sept. 26, 1972. There you have it; a tunneling machine that creates no muck, and leaves a smooth, vitreous (glassy) tunnel lining behind.

Another patent three years later was for: A tunneling machine for producing large tunnels in soft rock or wet clay, unconsolidated or boulder earth by simultaneously detaching the tunnel core by thermal melting a boundary kerf into the tunnel face and forming a supporting excavation wall liner by deflecting the molten materials against the excavation walls to provide, when solidified, a continuous wall supporting liner, and detaching the tunnel face circumscribed by the kerf with powered mechanical earth detachment means and in which the heat required for melting the kerf and liner material is provided by a compact nuclear reactor.

This 1975 patent further specifies that the machine is intended to excavate tunnels up to 12 meters in diameter or more. This means tunnels of 40 ft. or more in diameter. The kerf is the outside boundary of the tunnel wall that a boring machine gouges out as it bores through the ground or rock. So, in ordinary English, this machine will melt a circular boundary into the tunnel face. The melted rock will be forced to the outside of the tunnel by the tunnel machine, where it will form a hard, glassy tunnel lining (see the appropriate detail in the patent itself, as shown in Illustration 41). At the same time, mechanical tunnel boring equipment will grind up the rock and soil, detached by the melted kerf and pass it to the rear of the machine, for disposal by conveyor, slurry pipeline, etc.

And yet a third patent was issued to the United States Energy Research and Development Administration just 21 days later, on 27 May 1975 for a machine remarkably similar to the machine patented on 6 May 1975. The abstract describes: A tunneling machine for producing large tunnels in rock by progressive detachment of the tunnel core by thermal melting a boundary kerf into the tunnel face and simultaneously forming an initial tunnel wall support by deflecting the molten materials against the tunnel walls to provide, when solidified, a continuous liner; and fragmenting the tunnel core circumscribed by the kerf by thermal stress fracturing and in which the heat required for such operations is supplied by a compact nuclear reactor. This machine would also be capable of making a glass-lined tunnel of 40 ft. in diameter or more.

Perhaps some of my readers have heard the same rumors that I have heard swirling in the UFO literature and on the UFO grapevine. Stories of deep, secret, glass-walled tunnels excavated by laser powered tunneling machines. I do not know if these stories are true. If they are, however, it may be that the glass-walled tunnels are made by the nuclear subterrenes described in these patents. The careful reader will note that all of these patents were obtained by agencies of the United States government. Further, all but one of the inventors are from Los Alamos, New Mexico. Of course, Los Alamos National Lab is itself the subject of considerable rumors about underground tunnels and chambers, Little Greys or "EBEs", and various other covert goings-on.

A 1973 Los Alamos study entitled Systems and Cost analysis for a Nuclear Subterrene Tunneling Machine: A preliminary study, concluded that nuclear subterrene tunneling machines (NSTMs) would be very cost effective, compared to conventional TBMs. It stated: " Tunneling costs for NSTMs are very close to those for TBMs, if operating conditions for TBMs are favorable. However, for variable formations and unfavorable conditions such as soft, wet, boulder ground or very hard rock, the NSTMs are far more effective. Estimates of cost and percentage use of NSTMs to satisfy U.S. transportation tunnel demands indicate a potential cost savings of 850 million dollars (1969 dollars) throughout 1990.

An estimated NSTM prototype demonstration cost of $100 million over an eight-year period results in a favorable benefit-to-cost ratio of 8.5. Was the 1973 feasibility study only idle speculation, and is the astonishingly similar patent two years later only a wild coincidence? As many a frustrated inventor will tell you, the U.S. Patent Office only issues the paperwork when it's satisfied that the thing in question actually works!"

In 1975 the National Science Foundation commissioned another cost analysis of the nuclear subterrene. The A.A. Mathews Construction and Engineering Company of Rockville, Maryland produced a comprehensive report with two, separate, lengthy appendices, one 235 and the other 328 pages.

A.A. Mathews calculated costs for constructing three different sized tunnels in the Southern California area in 1974. The three tunnel diameters were: a) 3.05 meters (10 ft.) b) 4.73 meters (15.5 ft.) c) 6.25 meters (20.5 ft.)

Comparing the cost of using NSTMs to the cost of mechanical TBMs, A.A. Mathews determined: Savings of 12 percent for the 4.73 meter (15.5 ft.) tunnel and 6 percent for the 6.25 meter (20.5 foot) tunnel were found to be possible using the NSTM as compared to current methods. A penalty of 30 percent was found for the 3.05 meter (10 foot) tunnel using the NSTM. The cost advantage for the NSTM results from the combination of, (a) a capital rather than labor intensive system, (b) formation of both initial support and final lining in conjunction with the excavation process.

This report has a number of interesting features. It is noteworthy in the first place that the government commissioned such a lengthy and detailed analysis of the cost of operating a nuclear subterrenes. Just as intriguing is the fact that the study found that the tunnels in the 15 ft. to 20 ft. diameter range can be more economically excavated by NSTMs than by conventional TBMs.

Finally, the southern California location that was chosen for tunneling cost analysis is thought provoking. This is precisely one of the regions of the West where there is rumored to be a secret tunnel system. Did the A.A. Mathews study represent part of the planning for an actual covert tunneling project that was subsequently carried out, when it was determined that it was more cost effective to use NSTMs than mechanical TBMs? Whether or not nuclear subterrene tunneling machines have been used, or are being used, for subterranean tunneling is a question I cannot presently answer."

One really can't delve into this subject of the Greys without coming to the conclusion that the Greys seem to be operating out of subterranean bases now networked into United States subterranean facilities throughout the western United States, the Nation and across the globe. This vast system of excavated underground tunnels, bases, even cities, that are part of the secret infrastructure of the Breakaway Society, would seem to be 50 to a 100 years advanced from what is public, just as is with the Secret Space Program. This even while the United States government sticks to is false narrative story line indicated in the 2011 response[96] to Steve Bassett's White House petition.

"Phil Larson, who works on space policy and communications at the White House Office of Science & Technology Policy, wrote the White House response to the two petitions. The response was posted on the White House Web site. Here is a summary:

> "The U.S. government has no evidence that any life exists outside our planet, or that an extraterrestrial presence has contacted or engaged any member of the human race, Larson writes. In addition, there is no credible information to suggest that any evidence is being hidden from the public's eye."

This official lie which continues to reinforce the 70 year false narrative, is just a continuation of official American public propaganda policy even though countries around the globe are now releasing declassified documents proving otherwise. I guess if it still works, don't fix it. The Air Force got into trouble by trying to adjust their lies in regard to Roswell that began with Weather Balloon, and then Mogul Balloon then dummies dropped out of airplanes. When will it ever end?

There is little doubt in my mind that the Greys have advanced the aerospace and biotechnology of the US and its allies, far beyond what would have happened naturally. Even the TW and other races have seemed unwilling to give us deep space technology to travel to other solar systems. The Greys seem to see us a weak link in the cosmic human collective, and see it's to their advantage to give us this technology at the expense of the greater cosmic human collective.

The Glowing Raccoon

The following is evidence that the Greys are accelerating our biotechnological knowledge. Cases like this also show how this most prominent species of Grey, employs so many of the attributes of a predator, stealth, deception, perception management, false memories, false appearance, misdirection, illusions etc. A flood of abduction cases starting in the late 50s and early 60s presents a huge body of evidence in support of this perspective.

When we select out the probable psychological noise of false cases from what appear to be real cases, a picture emerges of a serious threat to earth human rights and liberties and our genome sovereignty. It's becoming obvious that we are not the top predators of the planet that we think we are, and have little genome security defenses, let alone space defenses against such a crafty and sophisticated predator essentially doing with us what it will. I must say that this position is still vigorously contested by some UFO/ET investigators especially those that claim positive experiences with certain types of Greys. A good example of Greys possibly accelerating biotechnology and genetic research can be found in the following case.[97]

On a Friday night in April 1983, Dr Kary Mullis,[98] a biochemist, was driving up to his cabin in Mendocino County in northern California. During that drive to his Anderson Valley cabin Mullis conceived one of the great discoveries of modern chemistry: the polymerase chain reaction (PCR), a surprisingly simple method for making unlimited copies of DNA, thereby revolutionizing biochemistry almost overnight. Dr Mullis described his discovery in Scientific American ('The Unusual Origin of the Polymerase Chain Reaction,' April, 1990). He was awarded the 1993 Nobel Prize in Chemistry for his discovery.

On another Friday night, during the summer of 1985, Dr Mullis drove up to his cabin. Arriving around midnight after driving for about three hours, Mullis dumped groceries he bought on the way, switched on the lights (powered by solar batteries) and headed, with flashlight in hand, to the outside toilet located about 50' west of the cabin. He never got there that night. Quoting from his 1998 book Dancing Naked in the Mine Field, Mullis encountered something extraordinarily weird on the way. "...at the far end of the path, under a fir tree, there was something glowing. I pointed my flashlight at it anyhow. It only made it whiter where the beam landed. It seemed to be a raccoon. I wasn't frightened. Later, I wondered if it could have been a hologram, projected from God knows where."

The raccoon spoke; "Good evening, doctor," it said. I said something back, I don't remember what, probably, "Hello." The next thing I remember, it was early in the morning. I was walking along a road uphill from my house.

Mullis had no idea how he got there but he was not wet from the extensive early morning dew. His flashlight was missing. He was never able to find it. He had no signs of injury or bruising. The lights of the cabin were still on, along with the groceries on the floor. Some six hours had gone by unaccounted for. Later in the day he found that an area of his property; "…the most beautiful part of my woods," had inexplicably become a place of dread. A year or so later Mullis exorcised this fear John Wayne-style by shooting the woods up. While his attempt at psychotherapy proved successful it did not help him find out what had happened that night in the summer of 1985. Mullis would become the only known Nobel Prize laureate to claim an experience of what might be an alien abduction.

He describes himself as "a generalist with a chemical prejudice." Others have described him as "Hunter Thompson meets Stephen Hawking" or "the world's most eccentric and outspoken

Nobel Prize-winning scientist." It is not easy to dispose of Mullis's experience as a drug or alcoholic hallucination. For one, he was not affected by either that midnight. Plus, he has not been the only one to have experienced strange events at the cabin.

His daughter, Louise, disappeared for about three hours after wandering down the same hill. She also reappeared on the same stretch of road. Her frantic fiancée was about to call the local sheriff. Mullis had told no one of his experience until his daughter called to tell him to buy Whitley Strieber's Communion. She was calling to also tell her father about her strange experience. By coincidence when she called, Mullis had already been drawn to the book and was up to the point where Strieber reports strange "owls" and little men entering his house.

In his own book Mullis concluded, "I wouldn't try to publish a scientific paper about these things, because I can't do any experiments. I can't make glowing raccoons appear. I can't buy them from a scientific supply house to study. I can't cause myself to be lost again for several hours. But I don't deny what happened. It's what science calls anecdotal, because it only happened in a way that you can't reproduce. But it happened."

Dr Mullis confirmed all this and more when spoken with recently. Another person encountered a "glowing raccoon" between the cabin and the toilet. This was a friend of Mullis who did not know of the "raccoon" story and was a first-time visitor, during a party at the cabin after the announcement of the Nobel Prize win in 1993. This man did not stick around and fled up the hill towards the house. On the way he encountered a small glowing man, which then suddenly enlarged into a full sized man who said something like, "I'll see you tomorrow." The man, who was not experiencing a drug or alcohol-induced hallucination left with a friend without informing anyone.

They returned to their hotel at a nearby town. That night the man inexplicably found himself outside in the hotel car park troubled and terrified by the impression he had somehow been back at the Mullis cabin. He and his friend returned the following night to the cabin. The celebratory party was carrying on from the previous night. As the man arrived he was shocked to see the "full-sized man" seen as an enlarging apparition the night before drive up in a car.

This was too much for the first time visitor. He left in a panic, holding Mullis somehow responsible for the previous night's events. Sometime later in tears he revealed the full story to Mullis, who identified the man his friend he had seen as his elderly neighbor. Mullis checked with his neighbor and sure enough he had come to the party on the second night, arriving to be seen by the terrified visitor. However he was certain he was not there on the first night, not in person and not lurking as a glowing raccoon or a small glowing man that enlarged into a vision of himself. There is more but that can perhaps wait for another more detailed telling.

Engineer Bill Uhouse

A pretty clear cut case of Greys accelerating our secret aerospace programs is that of Bill Uhouse. Bill is now dead, but there are video interviews and transcripts that tell his story of working with a Grey on flying disk simulators to train pilots to fly the donated and reverse engineered disks in the government's possession. His testimony is very compelling and puts another critical node on the timeline to today's Secret Space Program.

I am very impressed by how consistent the testimony of so many whistle-blowers is with the historical timeline to today's Secret Space Program. Bill Uhouse[99] released this statement to Steven Greer's Disclosure Project that summaries his very detailed story of Grey – Earth human cooperation in the field of aerospace. There are at least a couple of videos of Bill on the Internet.[100] [101] [102]

> "I spent 10 years in the Marine Corps, and four years working with the Air Force as a civilian doing experimental testing on aircraft since my Marine Corps days. I was a pilot in the service, and a fighter pilot; I fought in the latter part of WWII and the Korean War Conflict, I was discharged as a Captain in the Marine Corps.
>
> I didn't start working on flight simulators until about – well the year was 1954, in September. After I got out of the Marine Corps,

I took a job with the Air Force at Wright Patterson doing experimental flight-testing on various different modifications of aircraft.

While I was at Wright Patterson, I was approached by an individual who – and I'm not going to mention his name – [wanted] to determine if I wanted to work in an area on new creative devices. Okay? And, that was a flying disc simulator. What they had done: they had selected several of us, and they reassigned me to A-Link Aviation, which was a simulator manufacturer. At that time they were building what they called the C-11B, and F-102 simulator, B-47 simulator, and so forth. They wanted us to get experienced before we actually started work on the flying disc simulator, which I spent 30-some years working on.

I don't think any flying disc simulators went into operation until the early 1960s – around 1962 or 1963. The reason why I am saying this is because the simulator wasn't actually functional until around 1958. The simulator that they used was for the extraterrestrial craft they had, which is a 30-meter one that crashed in Kingman, Arizona, back in 1953 or 1952. That's the first one that they took out to the test flight.

This ET craft was a controlled craft that the aliens wanted to present to our government – the U.S.A. It landed about 15 miles from what used to be an army air base, which is now a defunct army base. But that particular craft, there were some problems with: number one – getting it on the flatbed to take it up to Area 51. They couldn't get it across the dam because of the road. It had to be barged across the Colorado River at the time, and then taken up Route 93 out to Area 51, which was just being constructed at the time. There were four aliens aboard that thing, and those aliens went to Los Alamos for testing.

They set up Los Alamos with a particular area for those guys, and they put certain people in there with them – people that were astrophysicists and general scientists – to ask them questions. The way the story was told to me was: there was only one Alien that would talk to any of these scientists that they put in the lab with them. The rest wouldn't talk to anybody, or even have a conversation with them. You know, first they thought it was all ESP or telepathy, but you know, most of that is kind of a joke to me, because they actually speak – maybe not like we do – but they actually speak and converse. But there was only one who would [at Los Alamos].

The difference between this disc, and other discs that they had looked at was that this one was a much simpler design. The disc simulator didn't have a reactor, [but] we had a space in it that looked like the reactor that wasn't the device we operated the simulator with. We operated it with six large capacitors that were charged with a million volts each, so there were six million volts in those capacitors. They were the largest capacitors ever built. These particular capacitors, they'd last for 30 minutes, so you could get in there and actually work the controls and do what you had to – to get the simulator, the disc to operate.

So, it wasn't that simple, because we only had 30 minutes. Okay? But, in the simulator you'll notice that there are no seat belts. Right? It was the same thing with the actual craft – no seat belts. You don't need seat belts, because when you fly one of these things upside down, there is no upside down like in a regular aircraft – you just don't feel it. There's a simple explanation for that: you have your own gravitational field right inside the craft, so if you are flying upside down – to you – you are right side up. I mean, it's just really simple, if people would look at it. I was inside the actual alien craft for a start-up.

There weren't any windows. The only way we had any visibility at all was done with cameras or video-type devices. [See the testimony of Mark McClandlish. SG] My specialty was the flight deck and the instruments on the flight deck. I knew about the gravitational field and what it took to get people trained.

Because the disc has its own gravitational field, you would be sick or disoriented for about two minutes after getting in, after it was cranked up. It takes a lot of time to become used to it. Because of the area and the smallness of it, just to raise your hand becomes complicated. You have to be trained – trained with your mind, to accept what you are going to actually feel and experience.

Just moving about is difficult, but after a while you get used to it and you do it – it's simple. You just have to know where everything is, and you [have] to understand what's going to happen to your body. It's no different than accepting the g-forces when you are flying an aircraft or coming out of a dive. It's a whole new ball game.

Each engineer that had anything to do with the design was part of the start-up crew. We would have to verify all the equipment that we put in – be sure it [worked] like it [was] supposed to, etc. I'm sure our crews have taken these craft out into space. I'm saying it probably took a while to train enough of the people, over a sufficient time period. The whole problem with the disc is that it is so exacting in its design and so forth. It can't be used like we use aircraft today, with dropping bombs and having machine guns in the wings.

The design is so exacting, that you can't add anything – it's got to be just right. There's a big problem in the design of where things are put. Say, where the center of the aircraft is, and that type of thing. Even the fact that we raised it three feet so the taller guys could get in – the actual ship was extended back to its original configuration, but it has to be raised.

We had meetings, and I ended up in a meeting with an alien. I called him J-ROD – of course, that's what they called him. I don't know if that was his real name or not, but that's the name the linguist gave him. I did draw a sketch, before I left, of him in a meeting. I provided it to some people and that was my impression of what I saw, an art picture of an alien that is working in cooperation with earth-people as told here."

Linda Howe, a credible and well respected UFO/ET investigator, got into this case early. As you see from this quote from one of her early articles, presents Bill Uhouse evidence that the Greys were cooperating extensively with the American military to accelerate the Secret Space Program and Space Fleet. Linda Howe states:

"On visits to the flight simulator, Bill Uhouse would occasionally see who acted as a technical adviser to the ultra-secret program that Bill worked on. It was J-Rod, a typical gray-colored EBE, hairless and without facial expressions. He had large, black wrap-around eyes or eye-lenses that are typical of these creatures. He is reported to be 200 years old, suffering from cell deterioration and still located at Papoose S-4, Area 51 in Nevada. But I can't confirm that."

During my investigations of the Secret Space Fleet code named Solar Warden, at least for that part of it operating in our solar system, I contacted and talked to UFO/ET investigator Wendelle Stevens not long before he died, about Solar Warden. Wendelle was very interested in Solar Warden and was doing his own investigations and we shared information.

Wendelle told me that he was told by his source or sources that past NSA director Admiral Bobby Inman's company SAIC[103] was making the flying disks on earth and then flying them up to the very large carrier craft in space. These would seem to be the very same disks that Bill Uhouse was involved with. UFO/ET investigator and activist Steven Greer at his disclosure project Internet site, mentions SAIC, a transnational group having access to covert programs dealing with ET related technology.

I hope the reader can appreciate how all these tiny bits of testimony, while not so significant individually, when put together methodically and in context, make for a very compelling case for the classified breakaway civilization. We can see how that civilization is being fostered and developed with the help of several alien races, especially the Greys.

Bobby Inman got a lot of attention in the UFO community years ago when Bob Oechsler secretly recorded a conversation where Inman confirmed his knowledge of extraterrestrials and their craft. The full transcript of the conversation can be found at this site.[104] This material also illustrates the revolving door between government and the private sector, the so called military-industrial complex. In the article written by Lee Nicholson, Nicholson says:

"We are proud to announce that former NASA mission specialist, Robotics expert, and maverick UFO investigator Bob

Oechsler has kindly consented to a series of interviews with us here at the Open Minds Forum. Bob's contributions during the early 1990's were unparalleled in many respects, not the least of which was his infamous recorded telephone conversation with former Director of the NSA and Deputy Director CIA, retired Admiral Bobby Ray Inman. It is our belief that much of the work that Bob did at that time remains equally important today."

If one reads the complete phone transcript, it is obvious that Inman is talking about extraterrestrial technology when he answers Oechsler's question;

"Do you anticipate that any of the recovered vehicles would ever become available for technological research outside of the military circles?" Inman; "Again, I honestly don't know. Ten years ago the answer would have been no. Whether as time has evolved they are beginning to become more open on it, there's a possibility."

Dan Sherman a NSA Intuitive Communicator for the Greys

Dan Sherman[104] claims that he was told by his NSA superiors that the Greys developed a program into which he was unwittingly inducted as a fetus in his mother's womb in 1963. His role was to become a NSA intuitive communicator to be used to maintain Grey communications after an anticipated future global catastrophic communications breakdown.

The Captain said; "In 1947, the US government made contact with an alien species. Today, we commonly refer to them as 'greys.' Because of this contact, we have learned many things. Some of the things we learned were good, and some not-so-good. And it's one of those not-so-good things that has ultimately brought you here, Sergeant Sherman."
"The captain went on; "The experiment that I'm referring to was, and still is, named 'Project Preserve Destiny.' It started in 1960 and was fully operational by 1963. It was a genetic management project with the sole purpose of cultivating human offspring so

that they would have the ability to communicate with the greys. Your mother was initially abducted in 1960 for tests, then again in 1963 for the actual genetic procedure while you were in the womb." "Compatibility?" "Yes. Actually, it's a long story. I'll try to explain as much as I can but there's much that I don't even know. In a nutshell, you've been given an interesting ability through what we call genetic management."

"I mentioned you have a unique ability; we call it 'intuitive communications.' It's an ability to communicate through the intuitive manipulation of your mind. There have been a handful of people since this ability was perfected that have utilized this skill within the military establishment. There are many others throughout the general world populace that currently have this ability, but until it is brought out by proper exercise methods it lays dormant."

"In January of 1963, the first successfully managed embryo was produced under PPD supervision. There were only a certain number of 'intcomm' capable personnel required; hence the genetic management phase of PPD was terminated in March of 1968."

I got interested in this old time tested Dan Sherman case, not only because it is an example of the Greys accelerating our technological development, but because NASA has been warning for years of a massive communication failures caused by severe solar flares that could be extremely catastrophic. For instance, a flare in 1859 fried telegraph wires, just imagine what could happen to our civilization today if an event like this were to occur.

Communication satellites could be not only destroyed in earth orbit, but the area around the earth would be off limits for satellites for years because of the radiation. Our whole civilization could be set back a decade or more if this were to happen now when we have ascended so far into the electronics age. No wonder the Greys would be concerned with maintaining communication with their earth human assets and network in such a situation

This is powerful confirmation of Dan Sherman's story. If telegraph wires got fried in 1859 just think what would happen to our civilization if this happens again as is likely. We seem to be woefully unprepared in spite of NASA warnings.[105] [106]

> "The prediction is based in part on a major solar storm in 1859 that caused telegraph wires to short out in the United States and Europe, igniting widespread fires. It was perhaps the worst in the past 200 years, according to the new study, and with the advent of modern power grids and satellites, much more is at risk. A contemporary repetition of the [1859] event would cause significantly more extensive (and possibly catastrophic) social and economic disruptions," the researchers conclude."
>
> "Impacts would be felt on interdependent infrastructures with, for example, potable water distribution affected within several hours; perishable foods and medications lost in 12-24 hours; immediate or eventual loss of heating/air conditioning, sewage disposal, phone service, transportation, fuel resupply and so on," the report states. Outages could take months to fix, the researchers say. Banks might close, and trade with other countries might halt. Emergency services would be strained, and command and control might be lost," write the researchers, led by Daniel Baker, director of the Laboratory for Atmospheric and Space Physics at the University of Colorado in Boulder."

Dan communicated with one Grey he called Spock and another he called Bones before he got out of the program.

> "Is this an unauthorized comm?" I asked. "There is no harm in communicating on this plane," he said nonchalantly. I was surprised by how effortlessly he had said that. Here I had been sweating out the fact that I might have been doing something wrong and he acted as if it was no big deal.
>
> "How come you are comm'ing so candidly on this plane and you don't during our normal comms?" I asked. "You have never given me reason," he replied. I stopped to think about this. It

was true. I hadn't attempted to ask any questions or to communicate anything except what pertained to our regular comms. I had always assumed we were not to discuss anything else. My impression of Spock was one of being official, with no room for emotion. Even as we now communicated on this other plane, I still felt a sense of rigidity.

Perhaps this was just how they were. Pressing forward with my curiosity, I asked whatever came to my mind first. Since I was thinking of how formal Spock sounded I continued with that line of thought. "Do you have feelings like humans?" I asked bluntly. "We are quite alike in our emotional makeup, 118," he said, referring to me as my PPD code number. "We react to our surroundings, just as you do, but are much less impacted by what we sense. In the absence of markedly increased stimuli, emotion is not readily useful."

"A million questions came to my mind. I managed to pick one and throw it out before I lost my new friend's attention span. "Why did you think it was unintentional when I first comm'ed with you on this plane?" "Until now, we thought it impossible for a water-human to sustain communication on this plane. But we are continually being surprised by other IC's abilities as well." 'Water-human' is the closest I can come to an accurate translation of how Spock referred to humans. Other alternatives would be perhaps 'water-vessel' or 'water-entity.'

I realized by now that I had stopped typing our comms into my reporting window as soon as we had jumped to this other plane. I wasn't sure if I was supposed to continue or not. "Am I supposed to report our comms while on this other plane?" I asked. Wanting the answer to be "no" so I could concentrate on what was being communicated. To my surprise Spock said; "No, that is not necessary. Our communications are only being monitored through your reports so as to calculate an accuracy factor. Your communicating on this plane was never anticipated and therefore will never be known unless you discuss it with your chain of command."

"Will anyone get upset if they find out I have communicated with you on this other level?" I asked. I was still slightly paranoid about what rule I might be breaking, if any. "I am unaware of your people's standards for this. However, we are not averse to communicating with water-humans on this plane. It is interesting to us that we are able to communicate with water-humans as it is, but communicating on this plane creates even more interest."

The Second Grey That Dan Communicated With Called Bones

"There is no harm in this communication," he said responding the same way Spock had months earlier. Not wanting to cover too much of the same ground as I did with Spock, I tried to think of other things to ask. Because of my own personal needs at the time, the most profound thing I could think of was, "Do you eliminate waste like we do?" I could swear that if they were capable of laughter, I could "hear" it in the background. I could sense a bubble in our communication like I had never experienced before. Was it laughter? I don't know, but it might have been. "Yes, 118, we have that need as well, but not in the same manner," he answered back without any embarrassment or any other emotions that we as humans would feel if asked the same question.

"Over the course of 10 months at PPD Base #2, I received over 75 comms from Bones. During that time we communicated on the higher plane on numerous occasions. What I learned from Bones during that time frame doesn't come back to me in a neatly packaged chronological order. I remember the things I learned from Bones more as a gradual progression of knowledge that built upon itself over time."

Dan Sherman in his book recounts a detailed conversation with Captain White on the NSA security mechanisms involved in keeping the alien programs outside the public domain, which I think the reader will find interesting.

"As I said yesterday, PPD had its beginnings in 1960. The personnel in charge of the project, at the time, tried to figure out a better way to keep the program from the eyes of the increasingly aware public. Brute force and manipulation was intimidating, but not an effective long term solution. In order to protect any future information leaks they instituted what they called the 'onion' effect."

I was slightly confused by this time, so I asked; "When you say brute force and manipulation, what do you mean exactly? In what context are you talking about?" "The personnel working with alien projects at the time were simply told not to tell any unauthorized person about anything they knew or they, a friend, or a family member would meet with an unfortunate situation. Of course, fear is a prime motivator, but not the most effective.

They still had people stealing documents with classified markings all over them as proof to others about what was going on. In order to hide information effectively back then, it took a great deal of resources and manpower to oversee everyone involved with alien programs. So when PPD was first formed, it was the model for the new onion effect. It was also around this time period that a new black project was just getting started so they decided to hide the newly formed PPD behind this new black project to keep curious Congressmen and other nosy officials away.

"How the onion effect works is similar to the actual layers of an onion. An onion has many different layers. So does the military. On the outside of the military onion, the side everyone can see is the 'unclassified' layer. This is the layer that is typically portrayed to the public and may or may not have any bearing on the true mission of the organization, base or installation. At most government locations, the unclassified publicized mission of the base is perfectly accurate, and there is truly nothing to hide. But this is not true of every location."

"The next layer we uncover on our way to the center of the onion is called the 'For Official Use Only' (FOUO) layer, or Level 5. FOUO is mostly a formal way of keeping what is essentially unclassified information from being disseminated indiscriminately. If several FOUO bits of information were to be pieced together to form a more classified picture, the release of that information could inadvertently be as damaging as the release of a higher level of classified information."

"The next layer on the classified journey is 'Secret,' or Level 4. The unauthorized release of Secret information and above has the potential of causing serious damage to national security. "The next layer is 'Top Secret' (TS), or Level 3. Within the TS category there are code words that compartmentalize the release of information even further. These code words are used to protect many missions, including the ones referred to as black missions.

"Black missions, which we call Level 2, are what the alien projects are effectively hidden behind. The existence of black missions is only known by a handful of Congressmen and the President. These black missions are the last line of defense for the alien projects. Wherever an alien project is located there must be a black mission to cover its existence from prying eyes. It creates a highly sophisticated shield designed to mask the grey project's existence from high level officials who have no need-to-know.

Otherwise, the alien project would eventually come under scrutiny by someone within official channels. As it stands under the current system, if a nosy Congressman starts looking where he has no need-to-know, he can be briefed on the black mission, be made to feel important and thereby squelching any further digging. It's an extremely effective method of hiding alien missions and is the reason they have been hidden so effectively for so long."

"Last, but not least, on the trip through the onion, we come to the alien missions or Level 1; referred to as 'grey,' 'grey matter' or 'slant missions.' The center of the onion always contains the alien project. Not even the commander of a site is normally aware of the alien project residing beneath his nose. "Anyone who is or has been part of an alien project is considered to be 'first level,' or Level 1 personnel. Personnel who serve in a support function to the first level are considered 'second level' and are unaware of the link between their jobs and the alien project they are covering for. They work with the cover or black missions. In addition, the existence of the entire level system is only known by first level people."

"It gets even more complicated. Within Level 1 there are separate and distinct categories called 'steps' which directly correspond with your need-to-know." As he was explaining this onion effect, I remember being fascinated by the ingenuity of the system. It was obviously very effective in preventing information from being revealed."

Captain White finished explaining the onion effect. "Any questions, Sergeant Sherman?" he asked. "Yes, Sir," I replied. "You allude to the fact that there is more than one alien mission - is this true?" "I only refer to there being more than one because I assume there are several. I am not personally aware of any others, but since we have been in contact with them since 1947, I can only assume there are now and have been others in the past."

Well so much for those uninformed skeptics that keep repeating over and over that the government can't keep secrets. Of course we have these leaks, but once out in the public domain they become mixed with copious amounts of disinformation now circulating throughout the Internet and the social networks. This mostly by just an uninformed public engaged in wild opinion and speculations even outright fraud, but accelerated to some extent by government psyops operations.

Unless a person has been in this field for a long time with a mind suited for intelligence gathering and analysis or has a road map such as this book to follow; it's almost a hopeless task to find the signal in the noise. What the reader is seeing is a benefit of my life's work in a nutshell, mostly directed to the younger generation that needs to hit the ground running in regards to these matters so as to get society back on a positive evolutionary track.

Lyn Buchanan Abduction Story

There are so many abduction cases that I try to pick ones that bring up multiple issues.[107]

> "For something less than nine years Lyn Buchanan was a remote viewer in the U.S. Government's Project STARGATE, and, during that time, he was training military and government Remote Viewers. Presently, he is executive director of Problems>Solutions>Innovations (for short PSI), originally a data analysis company, but after the CIA has in December of 1995, declassified information about remote viewing techniques, due to overwhelming demands for training and services, PSI now spends

more than 90% of its time involved in special type of remote viewing works called Controlled Remote Viewing, or CRV.

A continuing public service which is sponsored solely by Lyn Buchanan himself, and which uses the volunteer services of other remote viewers and his own graduated students, is "The Assigned Witness Program," that performs free CRV services for police and other public-sponsored investigative agencies. Mr. Buchanan is considered to be one of the best remote viewing trainers.

At age 12, he had experienced several events which could be only described as psychic. However, as he was growing up in East and Central Texas, which is often referred to as the "Bible Belt", such things were never admitted to happening to decent people. Throughout his childhood and adolescent years, this tendency of his was not suppressed. They went largely ignored and/or hidden.

Finishing high school, he went into the U.S. Army and served for 3 years as a computer systems technician, after which, as a civilian, he worked for about 5 years for the IBM Corporation in El Paso, Texas. Realizing that a lack of education holds people back in such corporations, he returned to East Texas to attend college. During his college years, his special capabilities all but atrophied, except for occasional uncontrolled events, when some emergency, tragedy, or anger brought long-forgotten subconscious talents to the surface.

Having obtained a Master's degree at Stephen F. Austin State University in Nacogdoches, Texas, he taught foreign languages in rural East Texas junior and senior high schools for several years. After 12 years he left the military. He returned to the U.S. Army and became a linguist within the US Intelligence and Security Command. His first "second" languages being German and Spanish, he spent the first year of his enlistment studying Russian at the Defense Language Institute in Monterey, California.

Afterwards he was stationed in Japan as a Russian linguist for four years, where he also gained a small proficiency in Japanese and Mongolian. For his last 12 years in service, he was the only Mongolian linguist in the US military. From Japan he returned to the Defense Language Institute for another year to attend their intermediate Russian course and was then assigned to a 4 year stint at the US Intelligence Field Station in Augsburg, Germany. Here, due to his extensive ability with computers, he was mostly used as a systems designer and programmer for the uncountable number of US and foreign-manufactured mainframe and mini-computers.

It was in Augsburg that his psycho kinetic ability resurfaced one fateful day in an event, parts of which are still fied. Shortly thereafter, Major General Albert Stubblebine, who was at that time Commander of the U.S. Intelligence and Security Command, decided to transfer him to the Washington, D.C. area, where he spent the last 9 years of his military service in a special assignment. There he studied the CRV protocols and methodologies which had been developed by Ingo Swan, Ph.D., the father of US remote viewing programs some years earlier. He quickly became proficient at using this technique.

After retirement from the U.S. Army in 1992, he settled down in Mechanicsville, Maryland, and began working as a computer consultant, mostly on governmental contracts. At the same time, he began building his own company, the PSI. Among the other assignments it is known that he has been requested by the US government to search for Osama Bin Laden. On 06.06.2000 Lyn Buchanan was interviewed by Jim Marrs, a renowned journalist and writer. For a long time sound files of this interview were available on Jim Marrs's site to anyone for free, as if Marrs and Buchanan wanted its contents to become known to as many people as possible. Then, one day, the files just disappeared. What follows is an accurate description of this interview. Wording used is mostly those Lyn Buchanan has used himself.

According to Lyn Buchanan, he was trained by the military to take his psychic abilities and his mind, and go out for controlled remote viewing, so he could view enemies, and other things that were going around. When some of the remote viewers were sent out to look for things pretty conventional, like nuclear sites or atomic submarines, or something like that, they encountered things they had not expected.

One time, at one meeting, while Ingo Swan was tracking a submarine he just happened to mention that there was a UFO overhead. Everyone around the table laughed, and Swan was told: "OK, well, track it for us to tell us what it is doing," and then they sent the word out about it with a request to have the radar readings. They never got feedback on that. The real purpose for that meeting was to see if they were going to get funded for another year. Immediately after their request got out they got funded.

During his interview Lyn Buchanan said that the first exposure to things alien he had was probably about 20-25 years before he got into the unit. It was a personal abduction experience. He does not usually talk about that very much. At that time he was a circuit riding preacher for a little Methodist church in east Texas.

One night he was getting ready to move out of the parsonage, they were moving to a new circuit of churches. His family had gone on and he was just there alone packing the last bit of stuff into the boxes. Suddenly, he had to lie down on the floor and he heard this thing coming down from the sky landing in the back of the house. He tried to get up to see what it was but he was frozen, he could not move. All he could think of was that a flying saucer had landed in the back yard.

He thought that he had proof because the weeds were high up there, as this was way-up in the middle of the country. He would take a picture tomorrow. He heard some people, it sounded like, coming through the weeds up to the house. The next thing he knew was that he was just walking through the house, and it was morning time. He could not figure where he was, or what he was doing. Finally he remembered that he was cleaning up and moving. So he loaded the last bit of stuff into the truck.

That started about 20 years of a compulsion that he had of thinking: "I have forgotten something." He would leave the house and he would have to come back 8-10 times sometimes to check the lights, make sure he had locked the doors, because he knew that he had forgotten something.

One Sunday afternoon, when he was in the US Army Remote Viewing unit for about 5 years, he and his wife were going somewhere and he had gone back, and back, and back, checking, and checking, and checking. Finally his wife stood in the front of him and said: "Well did you check the roof top? Did you check the back yard?" The minute she said "Did you check the back yard?" it all came flooding back to him, the whole abduction experience. It was just overpowering.

He had the benefit of having controlled remote viewing training, a large part of which is weeding-out thoughts and information. So he started running through the process of weeding-out false information of everything that he remembered. And there was quite bit of it. What he finally did remember and came up with some fair proof that night back in east Texas, the people had come into the house, and had evidently, taken him into the ship.

The next thing he remembered was he was sitting there in a row of seats, and that the seats were empty to his right, and that there was a window over there. To his left was this little old woman. He tried talking to her but she was like a zombie; she was scared to death. Then this real tall guy came walking by and he was not human. He was at least 6.5 to 7 feet tall and just built like a muscle builder. As he came walking by Lyn said: "Excuse me may I sit by the window?"

He turned and looked at Lyn and fear came over his face. He turned and actually ran out of the room they were in. Pretty soon he and two others like him came back and there was this little 'Grey' that was in the front of them. They were actually sort-of hiding behind the Grey. They were grouped together. They were going to keep the Grey between them and Lyn because they were evidently just scared to death of him. The Grey came up and started talking to him and tried to put him back under, but it did not work. So, finally the Grey said: "Look, we have work to do."

He brought Lyn up front where they were working, where they could keep an eye on him, so he could not get into trouble. He knelt down beside the Grey as he lifted the ship off (the ground) and they would set it down and this tall guy would go out, bring somebody else in and then he would lift-off, and set down somewhere else again. They would go out, bring some more people in.

Lyn was asking questions and the Grey was showing him how to control the control panel. He was basically answering every question Lyn ever had. They took a long journey that lasted about 30 minutes and the Grey let Lyn try to handle the control board. Lyn has very large hands. When Lyn asked to try it, the Grey said: "No, human hands are too small," at which Lyn lifted his hand to show him that he has large hands. The Grey and Lyn's hands were the same size although the Grey was 3.5 feet tall. Finally the Grey let Buchanan fly the thing with very close

238

supervision. It was like holding a kid in your lap and letting it steer the car. They got where they were going and it was not Earth. It was a very dark place. It was day time because the sun was out and it was very warm, but it was very dark as in the middle of night. There were two other ships there.

The Grey let Lyn go back with the other people and they finally got out and formed the line along the path that went along the hillside. As they walked along, a Grey came up and grabbed him out of the line and said: "I have somebody you want to talk to" and sat him down on the hillside. Lyn just sat there, played with grass and looked around. The grass was solid black which sort of surprised him. He still does not know why this stuck out so vividly in his mind.

The other people went on that pathway to the pavilion on top of the hill and there were screams, belly laughs. Just a mixture of the belly laughs and horrid screams the whole time they were up there.

Pretty soon another Grey came up and asked him to hold up his hand. When Lyn did the Grey placed his hand against Lyn's and they had a long conversation. It took Lyn the longest time to figure out after he had remembered all this, what they talked about, but basically the Grey said they needed pilots and offered him a job. On this Lyn said: "Yes, but I will have to go back and get my family." Grey said: "No families, we are at war" at that Lyn replied that without his family he won't do it. The Grey did not say with whom they were at war with.

After this the Grey went away: first the Grey, then the pilot, sat down beside him to wait for the other people come down from the hill. They talked for a while. Lyn remembers he wanted to ask him what was going on up there but he did not want to get involved in it. He was trying to ignore it as much as possible.

Instead he asked him what they were doing there and the Grey said that they were a small contingency of only three ships and that different units have different purposes. Their purpose was a medical one. What they were doing was they were abducting people. They come in contact with a lot of diseases as they go from planet to planet. The Grey said that humans are, basically, antibody factories. So they were implanting their diseased tissues into humans and then picking them up again later on, and getting their antibody samples so they can create medicines and antidotes for their own people.

Lyn asked about the implants. The Grey answered, with a chuckle, that the implant is not the thing humans are finding, which is just a little tip off the instrument. He said that the implant is, actually, the piece of flesh around it. The actual cells of tissue that is right adjacent to that is what they have implanted. From what Lyn has figured out later if they would take the tissue around those things they are calling implants they would, probably, find out that they have a different DNA in it.

Meanwhile, people started piling back down from the hill and Lyn got back in line with them and the pilot got busy with his business. They were standing at the bottom of the ship waiting to go back in. The Grey came over and pulled Lyn out of the line again and said that it will be a while so they stood there and talked. Lyn remembers asking him: "Please let me remember all of this" and the Grey replied: "Well, you won't."

The next thing he remembered was waking up, wandering around the house not knowing who he was or what he was doing, and it was the next day. When he remembered all this he went back to the unit and told them about the experience he had. A person reported him back up to the chain of command. The following week he was at DIA on the seventh floor, going to see the director, and these two men in completely black suits, looking like Jehovah's Witnesses without their Watch Towers were there. He had worked with them before, so he knew who they were. They are professional interrogators. They stepped out into the hallway and funneled him off into a conference room and started asking him about his experience.

There are always two of them and one sits over to the side while the other one interviews you. The one that sits off to the side is quite often not a professional interrogator. Quite often he is a person from the unit who needs the interrogation done. He is a local expert. That was evidently the case. Lyn had thought immediately that they were checking to see if he had gone zy. They were not. They were extremely interested in the control panel and how it worked. One of the tricks they use is to ask the same question in about five different ways over a period of time to see if you trip yourself up. So the second time when he asked

Lyn how to work the control panel, Lyn re-explained, but the guy over to his left side slapped his knee with his hand and said: "So, that's it."

That guy is supposed to sit there and shut up so Lyn knew immediately that he was not a trained interrogator. This had to be some guy who had one of these things and did not know how to fly it. The interrogator sitting in front of Lyn did not make any facial changes at all, but his ears got beet-red. Within like 10 seconds the interview was over and they were gone. Then later at work a buddy told him that maybe all this was not imagination.

Later on he was out on a special mission that they went on every now and then. Lyn was at the location and met a guy that he has known way years before in the military. They got to talking and after asking his friend what he is doing he was answered with question about what his clearance was. Lyn answered and his friend said: "Oh well, we will just call in and get the permission for you to come in and see what I am doing."

They called, checked-up his clearance, it was OK, and his friend took him into the facility where he worked. Here they had several debris-field type things, like those hangars where they sort out the plane crashes. Evidently what they had was that a fighter plane had collided with a UFO and they had the debris field reconstructed in there. All you could see was pieces of junk, scrap metal and all.

They were walking along and his friend was telling him about how they reconstruct the collision from this debris. His friend had not mentioned UFOs so far when he bumped into one of the control panels and Lyn blurred out: "Oh, this is out of the UFO, isn't it?" All of a sudden a Colonel came rushing over and gave them the bums rush out of there and threatened Lyn with death or worse if he talked about it or revealed the location or anything like that.

For Lyn this was feed-back because he actually saw that one of the control panels was right there. So the US government has some of this equipment, in scrap form at least. Many of the people in the Unit have had some kind of UFO experiences. Lyn Buchanan retired from the Army after he had fully completed his term. "

William Pawelec Encounters Alien Craft at Tonopah

I find the following account of William Pawelec extremely credible. It shows what happens to a person and his friends when they get too close to the truth of the Breakaway Civilization. Notice that implants figure into the Grey agenda very prominently and David Rockefeller even told his friend Aaron Russo that the Globalist Elite's ultimate goal was to chip the earth human population.[108] Rockefeller also told Russo that there would be an event that would further consolidate globalist power before 9/11. The following article was written by Mary Joyce Annie DeRiso with husband William Pawelec.[109]

William (Bill) Pawelec had a long career working on top secret security projects around the world. In 2000, he shared some of those secrets in a video interview[110] for Dr Steven Greer's 'Disclosure Project.'

There was one stipulation; the video could not be released until after Pawelec's death. Though Pawelec died in 2007, it was three years before his wife, Annie DeRiso, found a letter among her husband's papers from Greer and learned about the video interview and her husband's stipulation. When she contacted Greer, he sent her a copy of the interview. After watching it, she gave him permission to release it to the public.

It went viral in December 2010 but there are even more secrets to be told and Annie shares some of those in this article. Pawelec saw alien craft at secret underground facility "Seeing an alien craft changes your life forever, as it did for my husband," says Annie. "Even while he was still in the Air Force, he joined APRO (Aerial Phenomena Research Organization) and began his quest to find out what they are, where they are from and what the extraterrestrials want here on Earth. It became a lifelong mission and led him into many mind expanding discoveries. Unfortunately, the discoveries shuddered his soul. "Even though Bill had seen a craft in the skies," she explains, "what he saw in the secret facility beneath the Tonopah Test Range in Nevada left no doubt in his mind that beings from other worlds are here on Earth.

"Because of his profession, Bill knew all the buzz words to get someone's attention which often led higher ranking individuals to tell him 'secrets' above his clearance level," she says. "During one of those conversations, he was taken to a building at Tonopah where a large section of the floor is actually an elevator that goes down many floors. I don't remember how far down they went, but Bill was taken to an area where they were reverse engineering a typical saucer shaped alien craft. This is what he is talking about when at about seven minutes into the Disclosure Project video he kind of laughs and says Our guys used to chuckle about the model not being quite right.

The craft Bill saw being worked on was later made into a plastic model by the Testors model kit company and is known as 'Area S4 UFO Revealed.' This craft is also commonly known as 'The Sport Model' and is based on Bob Lazar's description. Lazar worked on his craft at Area 51 but Bill saw his craft at Tonopah." Testor's model kit "Area S4 UFO Revealed" is similar to the alien craft William Pawelec saw at the secret facility deep below the Tonopah Testing Range in Nevada. Pawelec tried to stop nefarious plans for injectable chips "Bill was a security consultant for alphabet soup organizations like the CIA, FBI and NSA,"

Annie continues. "He also worked for those in Washington D.C. who are known as the 'Beltway Bandits.' "He was tops in his field and worked on keyless card entry systems, security systems for Air Force One and American embassies, including the now infamous Moscow Embassy where the Russians had listening devices hidden in the walls so they could easily spy on international diplomats. "Bill and his friends also were involved with the development of the RFID chip. When they learned about the nefarious plans for its use, 'The Powers That Be' stole the technology. Two of those friends were assassinated and Bill's own death remains suspicious."

It should be explained that a RFID chip is a tiny radio-frequency identification chip that is small enough to inject into animals and humans for monitoring purposes. Pawelec speaks about this in his video interview with Greer. There is a link to the video at the end of this article. Pawelec shaken to core at secret meeting "Another project Bill worked on was at Area 51," Annie continues. "It was his job to upgrade the perimeter security systems for Area 51 and it was his idea to install cameras in fake rocks. It was during this time that he learned about the Tonopah base which is more remote and inaccessible than Area 51. It also was where Bill's rose-colored patriotic glasses began to cloud over.

Satellite view of the Tonopah Test Range area "His disenchantment began when he was called to give what he thought was going to be a regular project status report at Tonopah. The meeting was held in a heavily controlled room that was built like a Faraday cage making it impossible for communications to come in or out of the sealed room. "Briefcases, papers, pagers and any form of identification were not allowed at that meeting," Annie says. "Only the generals could be recognized by their uniforms.

The tension was really high and Bill was surprised at how nervous the high-ranking generals were. He knew something BIG was up. "Bill saw a private jet escorted by two of our military jets land on the tarmac. Surprisingly, this private jet rolled all the way to the building where the meeting was scheduled as the escort jets departed. "A very imposing man stepped out of the jet and entered the room. He was relatively tall, and wore a very expensive European suit. His shoes and briefcase were equally luxurious and there was an aide or bodyguard by his side. His demeanor was very aristocratic and he spoke with a High German accent. "The room was electrified with nervous tension as each person gave his status report and answered questions.

When everyone had spoken, the German man thanked them for their good work and simply left. He was never introduced nor identified in anyway. It is believed he was Baron Jesco von Puttkamer, one of the Germans who came to the United States with Werner von Braun. "Whatever happened that day convinced Bill that the United States, and probably the whole world, was being controlled by Europeans," says Annie, "but exactly who 'they' were was the big question. It drove Bill and his friends on a quest to find out what was really going on.

After that, he frequently quoted his friend Jim Marrs who often says, 'The Nazis may have lost the battles but they won the war.' "The men also wanted to discover the true alien agenda and the reasons they were interacting with humans," Annie continues. "They concluded that while there are many benevolent extraterrestrials, the negative or dark ETs were using the Nazis, the Illuminati and the Bilderbergers as pawns in their plan to take over Earth and claim it as their own.

They learned that a parallel battle for Earth has been going on in space for thousands of years. "Bill and his friends wanted the people of the world to know all this but it took Bill four years of telling "them" what they wanted to hear before he could slip from their control and begin to live a somewhat normal life. "He still wasn't talking publicly about all of this until we met,"

Annie explains, "And he came to know that all of my friends were also in the UFO arena. About the same time, Bill's cancer started to grow and he began talking about what he knew. By the way, two of his close friends are professional remote viewers and see Bill's death as being highly suspicious. "All this leaves me and Bill's friends wondering WHAT ARE "THEY" NOT LYING TO US ABOUT?"

Mr. William Pawelec was a U.S. Air Force computer operations and programming specialist with numerous credentials in security technologies and access control systems. He gave this interview with Dr Greer prior to the 2001 National Press Club Disclosure event and asked that it not be released until after his death. We recently found out that Mr. William Pawelec passed away on May 22, 2007 and we received permission to release it in December 2010.

Alien Tissue and Fluid Samples: Preliminary Report

While the Greys usually come out on top when they interact with humans, that is not always the case. This article written by the very credible Retired Air Force Captain Robert Collins, illustrates this point. Bob like ex-CIA Derrel Sims allegedly have found themselves in the thick of things resisting the Greys attacks on the earth human genome and earth human individuals.

I do find it interesting that Bob Collins and Rick Doty were both involved in the disinformation operation against Bennewitz when working for AFOSI. Once retired, Bob has been a staunch and tireless advocate for UFO/ET disclosure. In his book, Exempt From Disclosure, Bob disclosed the core story about a U.S. Government team sent to the Eben planet called Serpo. A firestorm erupted from this claim and a disinformation operation ensued, run by a team of disinformation specialists who created false Serpo stories to wash out the core story.

I watched this counter-intelligence operation develop on the Internet, but Bob just cowered down like the old crusty Badger that he is, and took the abuse. It's ironic that once involved in AFOSI disinformation operations himself, he ended up on the side of the public having to contend with a disinformation operation run against him. So the reader can see how large and complex these Grey issues are, and how hard the government is working to keep the public confused and ignorant.

Among the numerous false whistle-blowers, contactees and abductees building fraudulent false narratives confusing the issues, there really are honest dedicated whistle-blowers, contactees and abductees coming forward to tell the truth. It's really a tough job to sort it all out and I too have been taken in by seemingly sincere frauds and deluded individuals, but just have to try to do the best I can to get the overall picture out into the public domain. The following article is written by Robert M. Collins USAF Retired and analyzed by W.C. Levengood[111] and Ammanda N. Nimke 2009.

> Prologue: Given the threats, we decided to go forward with this material. However, the latest word from John Edmonds (09-27-011) is that the threats and warnings are still coming. Samples purported to be alien extraterrestrial tissue and fluid samples were shipped from a ranch near Phoenix, Arizona where bizarre incidents have taken place over many weeks, months and years, culminating in a number of extraterrestrial entities being stabbed, wounded or killed in the ranch house by its owner, John Edmonds, who wrote:
> "...wiped up the blood/Fluid and tissue of the Grey I nearly split in two parts with an exceptionally well sharpened Samurai sword, after hand to hand combat with these little parasites. We have

plenty of evidence to prove it, gathered over many years." See, "John Edmonds elaborates," at bottom of page. This gave plenty of fluid and tissue samples to work with." In summary: Blood found? The sample appears to be pure hemoglobin like that found at the Cattle Mutilation sites with what appears to be segment rods in the blood, never seen anything like it.

Skin? Looks like segmented grass except it's not grass Levengood said, see attachment 2. Details/data and analysis: Numerous samples have been collected under correct forensic technique by several skilled investigators and were sent to independent labs of high regard. All came back with the same result that the proteins in the samples could not be identified as anything they had seen before either plant or animal or human.

One lab did add that the samples sent to them did match the samples they had tested over the last 30 years of fluid specimens they had tested from various cattle mutilations across the South West US. They believed that there was a 100% compatibility that the two were from the same creature(s). Finally a smoking Gun that absolutely links cattle mutilations to alien life forms. One scientist was extremely elated by the discovery!

The important significance of these fluid matches is that according to W.C. Levengood, the fact that they matched so well was proof that indeed they were both extraterrestrial as the samples match nothing from the animal or plant kingdoms on Earth. However, as said above, the samples match the samples from mutilated cattle sites, and that would in Levengood's words show a correlation between aliens, cattle mutilations, and the obvious hostile intent of the Grey Aliens. "You have the smoking gun. This is proof of alien life visiting Earth and links the phenomenon together positively!" These were Levengood's words!

Robert Bigelow and his agency spent close to a month studying the ranch and the events here and my wife and I underwent extensive interviewing, videotaping, and analysis by ex FBI and CIA investigators. Everyone involved has had a consensus that the events here are real, accurate in nature, and have not been publicly released due to my desire to avoid a deluge of publicity which will neither further the investigation nor heighten the hard science approach to an unexplained phenomena that deserves the respect of remaining a discussion between professionals.

Further details/data W.C. Levengood 06-30-011: He said he is not going to write a report at this time, however, recent phone conversations suggest he may never write a report, but he was very excited about the samples sent which contained tiny segmented fibers. These were not cloth. This is what was in the photomicrographs he sent. Levengood explained blood as we know it does not contain segmented fibers. This made the sample highly unusual. He also explained normal antibodies that are positive or negative determine the type of blood which is something totally different. It is very peculiar because "the cell parts look like joint grass, but are not grass."

He has not written a report as stated above, but he did mail the photomicrographs, which photographs are taken through a microscope, attachment 2. Levengood said the material did not look like human skin. "It was weird," he said. When asked why he didn't send the tissue out for DNA testing, he said there wasn't enough material and it was very expensive and to do so.

John Edmonds elaborates: Let me be absolutely clear for the record on the samples of Alien DNA collected from our ranch in regards to the death of a Grey I killed was in self-defense, after repeated home invasions by similar creatures over a period of many years. The assaults by these creatures were responded to in the most violent behavior I could respond with because of weekly and some times daily confrontations during which our home, ranch, horses and dogs were killed.

Our bedroom as well as our own bodies were assaulted leaving bleeding holes from syringe like wounds. Large bruises on both me and my wife in the inner thigh, lower stomach, and upper shoulder areas have occurred on many occasions. As a result my wife and I both have contracted diseases. My wife has a thyroid condition and I have type II diabetes. Neither of us have a personal history nor a family history of these diseases.

The events coincide with the onset of these diseases. Is it related? We believe it could be as we have no contributing behavior from a lifestyle point of view that likely caused it. We are not drinkers, people who use drugs, we watch our diets closely, and we are both very physically active. We have no reason to believe the fact we are both ill from these conditions has anything to do with our behavior."

The collection process of the fluid samples was done immediately after the incident where the fluid from the Grey Alien was I believed killed or at least mortally wounded, was done using the best forensic technique I could muster and was sent to W.C. Levengood in Michigan for analysis. He responded to me by phone conversation that it matched the many samples of blood and tissue he had collected over a thirty year span with regard to the many cattle mutilations he had studied.

He is the individual who repeatedly stated that "We Had The Smoking Gun" He went on to state we were the first to tie the cattle mutilations and the occurrence of alien life directly together with specific verifiable and documented proof. He was very excited about this fact and said he would continue to explore the subject more. He requested additional samples. I sent W.C. Levengood a second sample and included a piece of actual tissue left on the sword blade at the time of the incident that had been in cold storage in a container to preserve it.

He later reported he used this to vivisection samples and send them to other professionals for further study to verify his findings. Approximately two months later I had an additional phone call with Levengood and he said that he had received confirmation of the information he had already discussed with me and that his other associates from Michigan state and the University of Michigan were also amazed by the evidence and couldn't identify what or where the samples came from since they didn't match any plant or animal species they had any knowledge of and couldn't identify the sample origin. They were both perplexed and amazed by this development.

At the time Levengood stated he would prepare a report for world release to the press and I told him to please proceed, but to release it only to me and not the general public through the news media. I wanted to be able to control the release of this information and wanted to get suggestions on the most professional and scientific method for doing such. It was my hope do so and would be in the best interests of both myself, my wife, and Levengood to avoid any negative side effects from what I perceived would be quite a bit of attention and the perception it could have a negative impact on our lives.

As it turned out, I had nothing to worry about because Levengood stopped communicating with me and no longer expressed any interest in the subject. Repeated efforts to obtain the report nor any follow up from him at all were futile. Derrel Sims and I had several phone conversations after he was recommended to me, and he and Ron Regehr visited our ranch for nearly a week last summer.

   During that time Derrel collected numerous dried residual samples from the same area left behind after the numerous violent encounters I have had with the Greys in our master bedroom, master bathroom, halls and walls from various locations in our home. Please understand the fluids left behind are clear in nature and slightly oily. They are easy to see on a surface like a glass door, a white drywall type wall, but very difficult to see against a natural exposed brick wall. We have many such walls in our home.

   Derrel using a special light was able to detect many stains left behind that are apparently impossible to detect using only the naked eye. He scraped these stains off the surfaces he detected the samples on and reported to me they would be sent to experts he had available to him for analysis. He took comprehensive testimony from me, my wife, and observed photos and video collected at this ranch related to this phenomenon.

   With regard to subsequent follow up: The samples collected by Derrel Sims: Unknown. He has recently stated to me he has made preliminary analysis, but to complete the study it will require expensive lab analysis that may exceed $12000 in costs. I suggested he appear with me on Coast to Coast and report his findings and that we request a fund to be established so that interested contributors could fund the research through Pay Pal contributions set up for that express purpose. The request was declined. Coast to Coast contacted me and I referred them to Derrel. I have no understanding of why he has declined this interview since he and I have already done the show together on this subject one year before.

   So to wrap this up, I believe this is an important story that has important scientific as well as societal implications. I have done the best I can to report the events as they occurred. I used my best intentions to collect the samples and forward them to people who expressed great desire to follow up and provide expert witness testimony and scientific analysis of them. Beyond the control of the collection and distribution to these individuals I have had no control over what occurred.

    I have always tried to answer any and all questions about the information truthfully to the best of my ability. I have no answers beyond what I have reported as to the current status or disposition of what is happening in regard to the samples or any information about them. We continue to live at the same address where the events occurred as reported and we continue to experience many strange events. These events are no longer reported by me as I see no purpose in continuing to do so. No positive result has occurred by my previous reporting. I will continue to make a record of the events as they occur. John Edmonds.

CHAPTER EIGHT

THE CELESTIAL HUMAN MEGA-POPULATION

Then God said; "Let us make man in our image, in our likeness." Genesis 1:26

The sons of God saw that the daughters of men were beautiful, and they married any of them they chose. Genesis 6:2

The Nephilim were on the earth in those days – and also afterward – when the sons of God went to the daughters of men and had children by them. Genesis 6:4

The Lord appeared to Abraham near the great trees of Mamre while he was sitting at the entrance to his tent in the heat of the day. Abraham looked up and saw three men standing nearby. When he saw them, he hurried from the entrance to his tent to meet them and bowed low to the ground. He said, "If I have found favor in your eyes, my lord, do not pass your servant by." Genesis 18:1

The two angels arrived at Sodom in the evening, and Lot was sitting in the gateway of the city. When he saw them, he got up to meet them and bowed down with his face to the ground. "My lords," he said, "please turn aside to your servant's house. You can wash your feet and spend the night and then go on your way early in the morning." Genesis 19:

Then King Nebuchadnezzar leaped to his feet in amazement and asked his advisers; "Wasn't it three men that we tied up and threw into the fire?" They replied; Certainly, O king." He said, "Look! I see four men walking around in the fire, unbound and unharmed, and the forth looks like a son of the gods." Daniel 3: 24, 25

I think I should warn the reader if they have not already learned the lesson the hard way, that the chances are very high that when they begin investigating extraterrestrial human contact cases, they will be duped and defrauded by a noisy swarm of false contactees and whistle-blowers and their deluded promoters seeking attention. It's become the rage in UFO/ET circles on the Internet since its creation, to create false narratives of contact for a number of reasons or a combination thereof. For this reason I have tried to focus in this book on cases of contact that have not become part of UFO/ET popular culture past and present.

Some people just want attention and feel important, some are mentally ill, others want to sell their false narratives built upon information they have acquired in the UFO/ET community as a book or movie script. Other people have psychological Messiah Complexes and advertise for cult followers, some are cult followers looking for a Messiah, some are even skeptics feeling superior and important out to hoax the believers for being so gullible.

It seems like just about every major star or constellation has some contactee claiming to be in contact with celestial beings originating from this or that star or constellation. Some cases may be true, but a lot of it is pure BS, and it's only going to get worse as more and more of the uninformed general public gets interested in Exopolitics.

From what I have been able to tell with, over 40 years of study, is that extraterrestrial humans, if they are ethically advanced, communicate with people who are working very hard to move human evolution forward, or if less ethically advanced with people that they are monitoring, studying or experimenting upon. In both cases these contactees are usually very reluctant to become public, either because it will affect their credibility in everyday life, or because they fear the secret government involved in these matters.

If anybody with an open mind has any doubt about there being a vast cosmic mega-population of humans and humanoids with many species coming to earth and interacting with us and our environs, they have to go no further than the compilations of humanoid contact cases. Albert Rosales alone has compiled over 4000 humanoid cases since the 1940s and 291 humanoid cases for 1954 alone. Good grief!!!! Here are the first 20 cases out of the 291 for 1954, just to give the reader an idea of the scope of the evidence if they are unable to access this link. Albert Rosales states;

"1954 Humanoid Reports.[112] The focus is France. The unprecedented and until possibly 1973, unduplicated wave of humanoid reports took place throughout France and some parts of Italy. Other reports came in from England, US, Germany, Canada & other European countries but at a much lesser extent. Towards the end of the year the focus seemed to shift to Venezuela & Brazil. Whatever the case, it was indeed a memorable year. Following is a list of known Humanoid reports for the year 1954.

01: Location: Near Cincinnati Ohio. Date: 1954. Time: Unknown - A reported landing of a silvery disc from which a tall human like occupant resembling the "Adamski" type beings, with long blond hair and wearing a sky blue coverall emerged. He reportedly walked to a nearby stream and obtained some water; he then went back into the object and took off. No other information. HC addition # 1008 Source: Michael D Swords, IUR Vol. 18 #5, quoting Hunt-Williamson Files, Type: B

02: Location: Tenterden Kent England. Date: 1954. Time: Unknown - The witness was alone in her house when she encountered, standing in the passage on the landing in front of her, a man over six-foot tall. He wore a metallic blue siren type suit that was glimmering. She stood looking at the entity and he looked at her without a word being spoken. The entity had a very high forehead, a slit for a mouth, large eyes, and high cheekbones. He also had a large pointed chin and his eyes were deep blue in color. He wore a very tight fitting helmet made out of a translucent material; his skin appeared to be pink. After a brief moment he suddenly vanished in plain sight. HC addition # 412 Source: Norman Oliver, UFO Magazine Vol. 11 #5. Type: E

03: Location: Nord (Northern) France (exact location not given). Date: 1954. Time: Unknown - An anonymous witness reported seeing a disc-shaped object land and a small man come out of it. He was entirely covered in a dark tight-fitting diving suit, which did not allow distinguishing none of his features. The little man then communicated in French with the witness saying the following absurd sentences: "Intelligence is prohibited to the constipated and cancer comes from a tooth ache" The little man then walked back into the disc, which then took off and disappeared. HC addendum Source: Eric Zurcher quoting Aime Michel Type: B

04: Location: Near Minyushino, Yaroslavl region, Russia. Date: 1954. Time: Unknown - A local resident reported seeing a flying object shaped like a "box or basket" flying towards the village of Staroye Merzleyevo. The object flew at a low altitude and emitted a muffled humming sound. The object then touched and tree and landed and two strange "men" of unusual appearance then exited the object. Both men seemed occupied in performing several tasks around the environs.

After a few moments the two strangers returned to the object which then lifted up again and flew away. Local villagers, though simple people, noticed that the strange device was neither an airplane or a helicopter or an air balloon with basket, it was something they had not heard or seen before. HC addendum

Source: Vadim A. Chernobrov; "Encyclopedia of UFO visit" Moscow 2008 quoting Valeriy Kukushkin. Type: B

05: Location: Near Rushden England. Date: 1954. Time: Afternoon - An eight-year old boy was digging in his garden when he saw a strange oval shaped "cloud" and heard a voice giving him instructions. Apparently he has been involved in other encounters. No other information. HC addition # 3884 Source: Northamptonshire UFO Research Club. Type: F

06: Location: Queensland Australia, exact location not given. Date: 1954. Time: Afternoon - In an isolated farm area a man named Harry saw a being step out from behind a tree. The being wore a maroon tight fitting body suit with a broad belt. The entity was described as tall with long golden hair. No other information. HC addition # 2671 Source: Keith Basterfield Type: E

07: Location: South Pasadena California. Date: 1954. Time: Afternoon - The witness was out cutting wood in his yard when he saw a disc shaped object descend and hover about 20 feet from the ground. Three man-like figures descended to the ground by means of a ladder. The men approached the witness and attempted to communicate by using sign language. The witness reported that the three men apparently did not have any mouths, or were wearing some type of half faceplate or mask. HC addition # 1861 Source: George Hunt Williamson, Other Tongues Other Flesh. Type: B

08: Location: Pantelleria, Sicily, Italy. Date: 1954. Time: Afternoon - A 14-year old boy, Giuseppe Gabriele was exploring the island on his motor scooter and was rounding a bend on the path when he saw four small human-like figures standing next to a landed disc-shaped craft, afraid, he rode away from the area and did not investigate. HC addendum Source: Antonio Blanco "Catalogo degli avvistamenti della Regione Sicilia." Type: C

09: Location: Bankstown New South Wales Australia. Date: 1954. Time: Just after dark - Two persons working late at the local airport observed what resembled a disc shaped object hovering above the control tower. Several lighted portholes could be seen and dark figures could be seen moving inside. The object changed colors then shot up into the air at great speed. HC addition # 1302 Source: Keith Basterfield. Type: A

10: Location: Chelsea England. Date: 1954. Time: Evening - Air Marshal Sir Peter Horsley reported that a certain General Martin invited him to the apartment of a Mrs. Markham. There he met an apparent extraterrestrial of humanoid appearance, pale, with penetrating eyes and not totally human, which called himself "Mr. Janus." Fixing the Marshal with a steely gaze, the "alien" talked for hours about traveling in space and time. On a return visit, Horsley found the apartment empty. HC addition # 3023 Source: UFO-Mind. Type: E

11: Location: Near Madras, India. Date: 1954. Time: Evening - In a small village a disc-shaped object was seen landing on a field. Several human-like occupants exited the object and they approached a local woman and communicated with her and also walked to nearby several homes and communicated with its occupants. No other information. HC addendum Source: Denys Breysse Project Becassine. Type: E

12: Location: Wright City, Missouri. Date: 1954. Time: Evening - The witnesses were driving home on a gravel road heading east when one of them looked out the window and noticed something flying over them and observing them. It was just high enough that the driver could not see it. The witness could see human-like persons walking around inside the object which was lit up. They wore some type of uniform like clothing. There was no sound or exterior lights and the object was going roughly the same speed of that of the car. The car drove for about a mile or two and then turned left into an area that had a lot of trees and lost sight of the object. Type: A

13: Location: Near Terra Alta West Virginia. Date: 1954. Time: Night - The young witness was coming back from a visit to the outhouse when the family dog began whining and looking up to a nearby hill. The witness looked up and saw a large flat object with three yellow-lighted windows, hovering low above the hill. The object was emitting a humming noise. Suddenly a human face appeared on one of the windows and apparently looked at the witness. The object then moved slowly away and disappeared over the hill. HC addition # 1953 Source: Bob Teets, West Virginia UFOs, Close Encounters in the Mountain State Type: A

14: Location: Near Lancaster New York. Date: 1954. Time: Night - A couple living in a farm had been seeing mysterious maneuvering lights over the area for several nights in a row, then one night as they were watching television in their living room a foggy white beam of light shot through one of the windows. They then noticed, looking in the window the face of a man who appeared to be of a dark complexion.

He was estimated to have been only about four-foot tall, judging by the height of the window. The beam of light seemed to emanate from the entity's face. The witnesses approached the window several times but each time they did the face would disappear. HC addition # 1864 Source: George Hunt Williamson, Other Tongues Other Flesh. Type: E

15: Location: Saratov region, Russia. Date: 1954. Time: Unknown - Several (at least 2) UFOs were detected visually and on radars by the Soviet military. Objects flew over the secret missile and radar sites located in Saratov and Volgograd regions near the river Volga and towards the launch missile positions of "Kapustin Yar" state central test range # 4, one of the first Soviet missile test ranges.

According to military opinion; "The flight appeared to be for reconnaissance purposes." Three or four Mig-15 aircraft were immediately scrambled from Volsk airbase NE of Saratov with orders to force the UFOs to land. After several aggressive attempts to compel the UFOs to land, the Migs opened fire. Immediately after that the radio communication with the all the Migs was interrupted and the Migs did not return to their base. A search and rescue operation brought no results. No wreckage was found. The pilots were reported missing.

Apparently the Migs were either totally destroyed or abducted by the UFOs. A state commission was created to investigate the case. A member of the commission, a Mr. Popov emphasized the similarity between the incident near Moscow in 1938 and this new case. A classified report was submitted to the special military Soviet archive on UFOs which was created in 1955 almost a year after the incident. The Soviet Ministry of Defense kept a special archive on UFOs inside an underground bunker in a military garrison named Beryezovka-2 on Krasnyi Kut range in the Saratov region. The archive existed from 1955 to 1991. The archive was reportedly destroyed by orders from Moscow in 1991. HC Addendum Source: Egveniy Valmer, retired officer in "Forth dimension and NLO" #5-1999 and Victor A. Zdorov. Type: G?

16: Location: Osceola, Iowa. Date: 1954. Time: 2330 - Michael Kelly, a young pre-school child at the time remembered finding himself one late evening surrounded by "boy-scouts" escorting him to a field near his home. They were about his size in height and were wearing some kind of uniform. The witness still thinking they were "scouts" asked the little men why were they not wearing hats or caps and one of them responded that they didn't wear hats.

Once in the field he found himself in a circle of beaming lights that appeared solid in nature. He looked directly above him and saw a large disc-shaped object hovering silently overhead. The object had colorful lights on its outer rim. He asked the "scouts" what the object was and they told him it was a "helicopter." He answered that it didn't look like a helicopter and after that his mind went blank. The witness has been possibly involved in other strange events. Type: C or G?

17: Location: Near March Field California. Date: Early 1954. Time: Unknown - Several witnesses were passing by the airfield in a vehicle when they observed a shiny disc shaped craft resting on the ground. In order to get a closer look they exited their vehicle and approached the object. The craft was smooth and silvery and there appeared to be no one around the object. The witnesses then decided to get even closer to the object when suddenly a man appeared and stepped in front of them.

He raised his arm and threw what appeared to be a fireball at them. The fireball passed by them and struck their vehicle. The witnesses immediately fled the area, driving to the nearest police station. The being was described as tall, man like and wearing some sort of half mask on his face, apparently metallic. The fireball reportedly dented the side of the vehicle and burned the paint. HC addition # 1860 Source: George Hunt Williamson, Other Tongues Other Flesh. Type: C

18: Location: Near Acapulco Mexico. Date: January 1954. Time: 0200A - While driving the winding roads that separate Mexico City from Acapulco, Armando Zurbaran only concern was arriving at the Pacific port city before sunrise, in order to meet a business partner. At some point during the drive, he was overcome by an almost hypnotic state of lethargy, which caused him to pull over. Not far ahead on the road, he was able to see a number of men clad in overalls with wide belts gathered around a strange, brilliantly lit object.

Before he realized, and having no idea how it happened, he was walking toward the object, escorted by the longhaired men. A slight buzzing sound filled his ears as he entered the saucer. Zurbaran was going down in history as his country's first Contactee (how about Salvador Villanueva in 1953?) and this was his first question to the ship's captain, "Why had he been chose for this honor?" "You are neither the first nor last earthman to be chosen for testing" his host replied; "Our task, slow though it may seem, is designed to persuade.

We choose the likeliest, most malleable persons for contact, so that they might better transmit our messages." Zurbaran was then treated to a review of the smallest details of his life on a screen within the vehicle's wall and a tour of the ship's interior, guided by one of the fair, longhaired crewmen (reminiscent of Adamski's visitors) who answered each of the puzzled human's questions in detail. The space travellers, he learned, employed a gravity repulsion system to cover the distance between their home world and Earth, scanning the space ahead of them with a radar-like device to dispel any objects that may lie in their path.

Unlike other contactee stories of the time, Zurbaran's visitors did not claim to originate from any planet in the Solar System, nor did they mention their planet of origin by name. The craft, he learned, had taken off while he was unaware and was now in space. Zurbaran peeked out a porthole, hoping for a glimpse of the world seen from above, but could only see a greyish mist until at a distance of 40,000 km, the ship's captain pointed out the planet to him through another porthole. Excited by the vista, the human asked the captain if he could perhaps be taken to visit their world, but his request was turned down.

He was told that perhaps someday such an invitation would be tendered, at the right moment. Zurbaran was able to sleep a normal sleep and eat with the UFO's crew. His description of taking a shower in space is particularly memorable, "I shall never be able to forget it. That bathroom was a new and unimaginable experience for me. Standing upright, facing an angle of the wall filled with tiny holes, I was covered in warm air, and as it grew stronger, it became transformed into damp air, impregnating my skin like a warm, wet breeze. When I was completely drenched, I was offered a sort of liquid soap, which I rubbed all over myself, from head to toe.

Standing once more before the warm air sprinklers, I felt the soap begin to evaporate and my skin become completely clean. The air then ceased to be damp, turning dry and warm instead of becoming colder until agreeably cool." Breakfast in orbit around the planet consisted of fruit juices tasting imperceptibly of mangoes or other tropical fruits. The ship's captain advised him that to his people, milk was a principal source of nourishment, but that they did not get it from cows but from a mixture of terrestrial and marine plant life.

Zurbaran ate grilled meat, butter and cheese in the vehicle's mess-room. He was told that the provisions were transported aboard the craft via telepathy (?). Unknown to Zurbaran, thousands of miles away, in the Pyrenees between Spain and France, Jaime Bordas a resident of the village of Castell, was engaged in a strange experience with a six-foot tall, overall wearing humanoid with long blond hair. The otherworldly being would only drink milk as its sole nourishment. (1951).

After the meal, the captain proceeded to regale Zurbaran with his world's philosophy, religion and history, children and the elderly received special consideration, and there was equality between the occupations. The average life span was 250 years, and collaboration had replaced competition in the area of commerce a utopia made possible by a being they termed, "The Master" or "Beloved Number Nine" who was at the heart of their religion, and who had ruled them for a span of three thousand earth years.

The spaceship returned Zurbaran to his car by the roadside. Confused but excited by his experience, he continued the balance of his drive to Acapulco, learning upon his arrival that it had only taken him an hour and a half to complete a six-hour journey. He did not see the space-people who had befriended him and offered him hospitality again for 15 years, until one night in January 1969 near the outskirts of Mexico City; he gave a ride to a young hitchhiker who turned out to be one the crewmen aboard the UFO that night 15 years in the past. HC addition # 1715 Source: Scott Corrales, Samizdat 1993 Year One Type: G

19: Location: Los Toldos, Salta, Argentina. Date: January 1954. Time: Late night - 25-year old Martin Antiman (now a local Indian "Cacique" 'chieftain') was in his room alone when he suddenly heard a very high pitched sound. At the same time a type of "magnetic" force somehow introduced him into a type cabin or "elevator" which had appeared in the room. Immediately after the cabin or elevator departed at fantastic speed and everything became very silent around him. The door suddenly opened and he stepped out finding himself in a sort of mountainous valley very desolate in appearance. He walked about 100 meters and saw several men carrying large bags on their shoulders.

He yelled and whistled at the men in order to communicate with them, but these seemed to ignore him. He then heard a voice in his mind that told him that the men did not answered him because "they had no brains" and could not hear the voice of the "creator." The voice then told him that he must tell all he could about this "vision." Soon he was introduced inside the cabin or elevator like object. Moments later the door opened and he found himself back in his room. He never spoke to anyone about this incident for at least 20 years. Type: G?

20: Location: Ostia, Rome, Italy. Date: January 14 1954. Time: 0130am - A young student, Miss E. D. Bonacini, was returning home with her boyfriend when both of them observed a rectangular red light in the sky. Looking at it again quickly, they saw that the light had changed its shape, becoming a kind of "upside down parachute" that was moving toward them. After 90 seconds, it was very close, nearly overhead, hovering at a height comparable with that of a three or four story building.

The object resembled a half sphere with a small protuberance in its lower section and a very bright area midsection, fading away toward its outer perimeter. The object was "as wide as the road," i.e. approximately 18 meters in width. The two witnesses watched from a hidden position for about nine minutes. They had the feeling that "somebody" was observing them from inside of the object. Then, they decided to run away. As they did, the object tilted 45 degrees, attaining a vertical orientation and departing quickly in the direction of Fiumicino. The craft slowed down after some kilometers and became lost from view following another 90 seconds or so. As it departed, the object displayed all the colors of the rainbow. HC addendum Source: Maurizio Verga "When Saucers Came to Earth." Type: F?

Even with just a small random sample of 20 out of 4000 the diversity of humanities interaction with the ET human megapopulation is just amazing. I can see I have to take the time to explore these humanoid cases in more detail. Some humanoid cases are very detailed and involve large numbers of people such as the Father Gill case of 1959.[113] For more detail on this very well documented case go to this link.[114]

Date: June 26, 1959 Location: Papua New Guinea - William B. Gill, an Anglican priest with a mission in Bosinai, Papua New Guinea, observed craft-like UFOs one with Humanoid figures on top -- on two consecutive evenings, June 26-27, 1959. About twenty-five natives, including teachers and medical technicians, also observed the phenomena. They "signaled" the humanoids and received an apparent response. This was one of sixty UFO sightings within a few weeks in the New Guinea area.

Okay, so let's bear down on some specific, credible, detailed, extraterrestrial cases shall we. Major George Filer Eastern Director of MUFON is one such very credible contactee who only now, as an old man, told of his contact with human extraterrestrials as a boy in an interview[115] with exopolitics investigator Neil Gould.

"In a relaxing moment Major Filer discloses for the first time that he and a childhood friend had consenting encounters with human looking ETs and had actually boarded their spacecraft where they were mentored by highly evolved beings with respect to human behavior, nuclear issues and man's inhumanity towards man. Major Filer admits that these encounters were the impetus behind his tireless work, keeping around 8000 people informed on UFO sightings worldwide through his Fliers Files."

Georges contact with human extraterrestrials is not unique among investigators and whistle-blowers. When I interviewed Clifford Stone in Roswell in the spring of 2011, he told me that one time when some evil men in the military were really coming down hard on him for speaking out, a human extraterrestrial met with him. This human extraterrestrial, that looks almost exactly like us, told Clifford that if he would just stick it out things would get better and they did. So we see that investigator and contactee George Filer is not alone in being mentored by human extraterrestrials.

The MUFON leadership has generally fallen into disrespect and is under siege from public and the rank and file for being little more than a civilian intelligence gathering and perception management asset for the intelligence community.[116] One of the exceptions is George Filer who still maintains great respect in the UFO/ET community for his integrity and credibility and ardent pro-disclosure activities that include the weekly publication of his Filers Files. George now has around 10,000 email subscribers and God know how many other people are following his weekly publication on his web page and elsewhere. As far as I am concerned he is MUFON's best.[117]

George would naturally have a great interest in extraterrestrial humans because of his early personal experiences with ETs that look so much like us that they can mingle with us at will. Because these ET humans are so similar in physical form, we might assume that they are further examples of a universal collective or mega-population of extraterrestrials that are the most closely related to us.

George researched and wrote the following very interesting article[118] and published it in his Filers Files. I think the reader can begin to see from exopolitical writings like this, that the exopolitical impacts upon earth human society have been and are profound both culturally and genetically. Earth humanity seems to be entangled, interconnected and embedded in this universal human mega-population or collective in so many ways, regardless if we are aware of it or not.

Are Homo Sapiens Part Alien?

My theory is that alien visitors have helped the development of humans. We humans and the world's ancient monuments are evidence for this theory. Genetic evidence indicates when humans left Africa all known people on Earth had dark skin, dark eyes and dark hair. Michael Holick, a professor Boston University School of Medicine who indicates when our ancestors left Africa they adjusted their skin tone to allow in more sunlight to get more Vitamin D. Essentially, from two million years ago to less than 100,000 years ago, the ancestors of all people alive were from Africa.

Genetic evidence indicates that light-skin-related mutations arose recently, and spread fast through Europe and Asia. The theory suggests that the reduction of game meat, fish, and some plants from the diet resulted in skin turning clear many thousands of years after settlement in Europe and Asia. This theory is supported by a study into the SLC24A5 gene which found that the allele associated with light skin in Europe may have originated as recently as 6,000–10,000 years ago.

According to scientists a whole series of fortunate mutations explains white skin, blue and green eyes and blonde hair. I have personally seen alien visitors and chased their extraterrestrial craft, so my experiences have provided insight into the likely actual situation.

A team of daring Chinese researchers, digging into the ancient mysteries of the origin of their country, has come to the inescapable conclusion that an interstellar, supreme alien race used much of the northern and western Chinese regions as massive Earth bases. Hundreds of strange pyramids cover parts of China and former Tibet. The data has been kept secret mainly because the alien race was blonde, blue eyed, with white skin. It seems logical that this alien race mated with the humans on Earth at that time. The ancient Chinese writings reveal this theme. Thanks to Gordon James Gianninoto

Nine university scientists gaped upwards at the gigantic, prehistoric pyramid that they determine was built some 10,000 years ago. One such base may be the astonishing pyramid structure that sits near the apex of Mount Baigong in the western province of Qinghai, the Xian yang pyramid. The Chinese pyramids look similar to those in Egypt, Mexico, Peru and on Mars. According to ancient Chinese legend, over one hundred pyramids discovered in China are the legacy of blue eyed blonde aliens.

Scientist Dr Carl Sagan in his book, "Intelligent Life in the Universe" indicated Earth had likely been visited by extraterrestrials numerous times. He states; "Sumer was an early, perhaps the first civilization. The contemporary sense on the planet Earth. It was founded in the fourth millennium B.C. or earlier. We don't know where the Sumerians came from. I feel that if the Sumerian civilization is depicted by the descendants of the Sumerians themselves to be of non-human origin, the relevant legends should be examined carefully."

He goes on to ask; "What might an advanced extraterrestrial civilization want from us?" He answered his own question by stating; "One of the primary motivations for the exploration of the New World was to convert the inhabitants to Christianity peacefully if possible forcefully if necessary. Can we exclude the possibility of an extraterrestrial evangelism?"

Evangelism essentially is a method of bringing a belief system to others," The Webster's New Twentieth Century Dictionary states, Evangelize is to preach the gospel, from 'Greek Eu; good and Angelos; a messenger, to instruct in the gospel, to preach the Gospel, also to convert to Christianity. The sacred writings of most religions clearly claim that Angels or extraterrestrials brought their religious beliefs to Earth. Sumerian brick tablets found all over what is today is Iraq; also tell the story of extraterrestrial visitors and how they brought civilization to Sumer. They explain the visitors taught them to build Ziggurats.

Kenneth Larson writes, "The reason why I found it so interesting concerning your reported ancient Chinese pyramid layouts in your website at and my strong interest in the ancient Great Pyramid complex near Cairo, Egypt is that there seems to be a basic mathematical-engineering design pattern to the pyramid layouts on the Earth's surface." My research books and drawings try to show how the entire Earth exhibits intelligent mathematical design patterns and grid patterns, and the designs relate to key UFO sightings and the primary American West design patterns and layouts, etc.

One key site is the Great Salt Lake, Utah, settled first by Mormons on July 24, 1847, with related key UFO report sites. Joseph Smith said, "The Earth obeys the laws of a celestial kingdom and the glory of God is intelligence. Hence, the celestial kingdom laws seem to be designs and grid patterns as well as scientific and mathematical precepts and designs based on the pi value."

Egyptian pyramids were supposedly built by Egyptians in about 3000 BC, as attempt to imitate the stars in the Belt of Orion. They were not exactly at the correct angle to match up with the pyramids unless the location of the stars is traced back to the belt when it was exactly aligned with the pyramids in 10,500 BC. Allegedly no civilized humans were living on the earth at that time.

The Great Pyramid is so huge and so perfect it is unlikely we could construct it today using the same specifications. Each giant Stone ranges from 1 to 20 tons in weight, and the Great Pyramid was built with well over 100,000 stones. But the Egyptians had no machinery, engines, helicopters, or construction equipment, so it is doubtful they could have built without technological help.

The stones came from quarries 500 miles away. Just cutting the stones is extremely difficult, getting them to the building site is a monumental task and how did they place 20 ton stones perfectly hundreds of feet high. The top of the pyramid is 481 feet high. A ramp would require as much material as the pyramid.

If the pyramid stones were cut it into foot square blocks, they would reach two thirds of the way around the world. The Great Pyramid lies on 31 degrees north by 31 degrees west. The pyramid is the center of all of the land mass of the whole earth! I examined the interior of the Great Pyramid and there was no writing or hieroglyphics and it seemed more like a power station than a tomb.

Sitting next to the Great Pyramid is the Sphinx with the body of a lion with a human head. At one time the Sphinx likely had a lions head that was perfectly proportioned for the head of a lion, not the human head. This human head looks tiny sitting on top of the lion body and was likely carved out of lion's head. The Sphinx was also built in 10,500 BC, probably to celebrate the constellation of Leo the Lion rising directly behind the sun. When I visited the Sphinx, it was obvious there are signs of water erosion all over the Sphinx again going back to the same time period. The Egyptians kept very careful historical records but there are no records of them building the Great Giza Pyramid.

Ancient Egyptian scriptures reveal the Tep Zepi, or the First Time when the "gods came from the sky" came down to Earth and raised the land from mud and water. Ptah (Gods of Heaven came to Earth from the Celestial Disk) installed as Egypt's first Divine Ruler his own son RA.

They flew with flying "boats" and brought laws and wisdom to man through a royal line of pharaohs. It is likely that a very advanced alien race came down and altered our genetic pool. Most ancient writings repeat the same theme that gods or extraterrestrial visitors came to make humans in their image. Professor Paul Davies, from the Australian Center for Astrobiology at Macquarie University in Sydney, believes a cosmic greeting card could have been left in every human cell. The coded message would only be discovered once the human race had the technology to read and understand it.

According to the Wikipedia, the free encyclopedia the peoples of the Caucasus Mountains in Russia refer to "Caucasian." The term Caucasian race has been used to denote the general physical type of some or all of the populations of Europe, North Africa, the Horn of Africa, Western Asia (Middle East), Central Asia and South Asia. Historically, the term has been used to describe the entire population of these regions, without regard necessarily to skin tone.

For 20,000 years during this closing ice age - called the Upper Paleolithic period - a term referring only to the type of culture that existed amongst these early Homo sapiens - our ancestors, the White race's ancestors, lived as hunter gatherers in Europe. Their physical remains and artifacts from this time are plentiful - and what is really amazing is how far spread out they were. This first race of people with whom we can claim a genetic affinity, were what is called the proto Nordic racial type with tall, light hair and eyes.

In certain isolated areas in Europe you can still find perfect living examples of this racial type, and they differ only slightly in height from modern day Nordics. This great proto Nordic race lived in a broad band spanning from Spain right across Europe all the way to central Asia and even to the Pacific Rim, where skeletal remains have been found as well. In Siberia and Asia they were eventually absorbed by the Mongoloid races and the same happened in the Pacific Rim - for example the Ainu people of Japan - that society's highest class - are very clearly crosses of Mongoloids and Whites. They differ substantially from the rest of the Japanese population

The first great White Egyptian civilization was in fact predated by about some 3000 years by the great Sumerian civilization - another population whose racial makeup was predominantly Mediterranean with Nordic ruling elite. This civilization, founded between the two great rivers, the Tigris and the Euphrates, even built pyramids - called Ziggurats - of their own long before the Egyptians apparently stole the idea from them. By this time the modern day Nordic racial type had fully developed, and it may come as news to some of you that original large Nordic concentrations were not in fact in Scandinavia, but in modern day Ukraine and South Eastern Russia (hence Whites are mistakenly called Caucasians - after the Causacas Mountains).

The town of Kiev, was for example one of the biggest Nordic cities, dating from about 7000 years ago, and had a population of 20,000 - huge by standards of the time. These Nordics slowly crept westward, invading and re-invading Western Europe for a period of nearly 6000 years, finally resulting in the establishment of a new Nordic heartland in Northern Europe.

These original Nordic tribes had stone buildings and worked bronze and copper. How much of this metal working skill was passed south to the Middle Eastern civilizations remains a matter of debate. However, what is for sure is that successive waves of Nordic tribes started invading central and Southern Europe in earnest about 6400 years ago, and caused the Mediterranean civilizations (the "Old European" civilizations) to topple. Nordic tribes occupied large regions of Turkey, Crete, Greece and Southern Europe and Italy. The invading Nordics did not kill the largely Mediterranean populations of these areas - obviously feeling some type of racial kinship, but instead just ruled over them.

Some Nordic tribes migrated into the Far East - as far as China, where some Nordic remains have been found in burial chambers. These Nordic tribes also invaded Egypt, but were in turn occupied by a Semitic invasion - the Hyksos, who we only expelled after 100 years of their rule. In the Arctic, the Inuit never developed light skin, although most Asians do have light skin. It is generally thought the light skin is the result of mutations.

According to Faye Flam staff writer at the Philadelphia Inquirer, Penn State professor of Biological Anthropology, Mark Shriver and colleagues isolated a genetic mutation that contributed to European's having white skin, a mutation that in zebra fish leads to the absence of the characteristic stripes. Mark Shriver indicates; there is apparently a ten percent of human genetic variation between Scandinavian versus West African races. Although we are similar there are obviously differences in skin color, hair and often eye color. There are also differences in illnesses among races. African-Americans have more diabetes, prostate cancer, and hypertension, while whites have more dementia and osteoporosis. I encourage these experts to look at the evidence for alien visitation, because it solves many scientific anomalies.

I realize this has been kept secret at the highest levels of government. Prince Philip and various high ranking personnel have revealed the well-kept secret. The discovery of DNA, (deoxyribonucleic acid) with all its implications of a very complicated genetic code creates additional evidence for intelligent design rather than theoretical evolution.

The DNA helix must have a planner, a designer. You are thousands of times more complex than even the most sophisticated computer who needed a designer and engineers to build. Even then you also have the spark of life needed to grow and reproduce! A well-known DNA scientist keeps encouraging me, who can't talk openly states, "The three most interesting genetic anomalies are Rah-factor, HIV, and delta-CCR5. Apes and primitives are Rah plus (+,+), while whites and Asians are close to 25% Rh minus (-,-), just as if our ancestor were blonde alien (-,-) mixed with local (+,+) by Mendelian statistics. A slight selection against pregnancy by (-,-) women lowers that to 20%.

If we had defective HIV in our bodies, we would get antisense resistance to modern HIV. Yet many chimps contain defective HIV, while we do not, at least until 1955 when it was transferred from monkeys to man. If we come from apes, why don't we see ancient HIV in our genome?"

The most interesting mutation is for HIV-resistance, found by looking for homosexuals without AIDS. They were all found in Scandinavia as "delta-32 CCR5." How to select for resistance to a virus which was not in man before 1955? Some people have shown that it might protect against smallpox or myxo, but why not in India or China where smallpox is rife? Why isn't it in apes, given the millions of years that an identical gene in apes was exposed to viruses?

The reason is because both chromosomal copies must be deleted at once to give resistance, by a double-hit which is almost impossible randomly. Now we see that delta-32 CCR5 is found with a very recent origin in Finland-Mordovia, spread weakly to northern Russia and northern Europe, but not southern Europe, Africa, Asia, or elsewhere.

Also the Ashkenazi Jews have many strange genes. The most obvious source of this mutation would be those tall blond visitors, who may have crossed with local women a few thousand years ago. Their progeny would go on to raise our scientific level over 5000 years. You can easily access recent information by searching for keywords on Medline / Pubmed at NCBI, say "Rh factor" or "delta-CCR5" crossed with other terms for specificity!

I feel the ancient sacred Sumerian, Chinese, Indian, Jewish writings are correct when they tell us that extraterrestrials (the sons of God mated with the daughters of men, they were fair, and they took them wives of all which they chose, Genesis 6.

The Khoury ET Human Encounter Case

The following 1992 case provides additional basis to the argument George Flier and other researchers are making suggesting that human extraterrestrials continue to impact humanity in a broad and invasive fashion. [119] I would call the following an abduction case, rather than a contactee case, because the male recipient Mr. Khoury a security guard, who passed a polygraph test, alleges that sexual relations were without his permission and against his will, imposed upon him while in an induced state of unconsciousness by an attractive tall blond extraterrestrial human female. A second extraterrestrial human apparently was watching and was being instructed or instructing, leading one to speculate that this case is one of many. As one can see something went wrong for the extraterrestrials in this ET experiment as the abductee broke through the mental restraints.

This earth human woke up during the sexual encounter and broke free from the induced mental state, forcing both ET human females to leave after he bit the nipple in a defensive reaction against the female having sexual relations with him. This case is significant because DNA evidence of a rare nature was recovered. The abductee recovered two pubic hairs left behind by the ET human female that was then sent for DNA analysis.

"...the world's first PCR (polymerase Chain Reaction) DNA profiling of a biological material implicated in an alien abduction experience. The analysis confirmed the hair came from someone who was biologically close to normal genetic, but of an unusual racial type - a rare Chinese Mongoloid - one of the rarest human lineages known, that lies further from the human mainstream than any other except African pygmies and aboriginals.

There was a strange anomaly of it being blonde to clear instead of black, as would be expected from the Asian type mitochondrial DNA. The study concluded, "The most probable donor of the hair must therefore be as (Khoury) claims: a tall blonde female who does not need much color in her hair or skin as a form of protection against the sun, perhaps because she doesn't require it."

Such ET cases where there is forensic evidence and lie detector tests for the contactee and abductees provide powerful evidence that some contactee and abductee experiences are real, and gives important insight into the agendas and motives of the extraterrestrials involved. The interests are not just genetic of course, but our genetics and genome do appear to be of great interest to other ET races including the human ones connected to us genetically and culturally, as George Filer has pointed out.

George has already stated that these tall blond Caucasian peoples once lived in China as is evidenced by around 500 mummies recovered. These mummies are really spectacular and well preserved as can be seen in this video.[120] Like in other parts of the world some seem to be royalty in order to get this kind of preservation treatment. Apparently, the information that goes with the mummies, is that these people were believed at the time to be sun gods who had descended from the sky and ruled over the people. Notice the swastika on the metal plate in the video,[121] were the Germans in the 1920's and 1930's on to something that got perverted and corrupted by the times?

Another case I would like to present is that while there is so many references to the Annunaki in ancient texts, it's hard to find any good cases of them active today. For this reason one should be careful about the Michael Lee Hill's Annunaki case because of the lack of collaborating cases. I have communicated quite a bit with Michael and he does seem sincere and truthful in his account.

Their does seem to be collaborating evidence in the sightings and video over Lake Erie that have garnered mass media attention and the connection to the Boyd Bushman interview. It would seem to indicate that even while there may be few Annunaki on the earth today, they are nevertheless collaborating with our government according to this case to suppress and regulate the ET information being released to the public.[122] For some Lake Erie UFO footage supporting the case click on this footnote.[123] Michael Hill replied on Facebook message:

"Ed, during that first meeting with "Them" which I believe now to be the Marduk led remnants, the Boyd Bushman subject was brought out first, and it was not done in a gentle way, Their Fangs came out if you know what I mean. This leader figure told me he worked for a group of people who decided what will be released, that he was an actual family member of the J. Allen Hynek Family and this family was still in control of what is released, and the Boyd Bushman info was not on the list, he asked me how this Boyd info came to be released.

I told him I willed it into manifestation and I thought it was BS that this info was being withheld from humanity. Well they found me hard to scare and the Leader Anunnaki figure stated, Michael, 'We need to know what you know," and they brought these wands that have what looked like a bright purple LED at the end of this, and it seemed almost to be kind of like a laser pointer. He pointed it directly at my 3rd eye.

Well this 'Mind Probing' changed the whole course of this unfolding meeting. The meeting went from interrogating me over the Boyd Bushman info to all of a sudden this leader figure becoming very excited, stating, "Oh My God, you are one of us! How did you come to be here?" We have been waiting for you to have a council meeting; we can do that right now if you please? I said regarding what? They said it would not be long until there would be another planet visible in our skies and they wanted to talk about what effect we believed this and the Anunnaki revealing themselves would have on humanity?"

"I was told that this being I was sitting before was a "King" of the Anunnaki. An actual name of this man was never given, but after all that went down; my own guess is Marduk of The Anunnaki. He went on to tell me that he was what is known as the Anunnaki, and that I am also a part of this Anunnaki family and it was a great synchronicity that I was "LED" there because now a meeting could commence between us all, over a "change in Anunnaki leadership" and there would be a new time arriving for mankind and a new "Game plan" needed to be discussed. They told me the truth of the situation was that another member of the Anunnaki and I had incarnated into this lifetime as a humans in every way, to be here for these changes.

The Anunnaki Loki then intervened and said I have spoken with Michael already and he believes as I that humanity is ready for open contact and that Humanity should have the chance to evolve into a Galactic society, they are ready. I then spoke up and backed up why I believe the masses are ready for first contact. I told them the exact same thing I have communicated to you already, that I believe that without the bondage that has kept the human race in survival mode, that humanity would & could reach its true potential. Loki & I teamed up on the "Give Humanity a chance to show their stuff, we are ready" bandwagon.

This male on the Bed (Marduk) said, well, it must be time! If that is what you feel, let's do it, let's make it so, I then said...."When?" He said Obviously BEFORE 2012, he answered in a tone like he was annoyed by the question :-) The next morning I awoke and got out of my tent and poured some water over my head and at that exact moment, I noticed a male and female walking by my tent on the dirt road and I instantly know that was the Anunnaki leader male I seen the previous night only now he looked very Human and he then looked me in the eye and said: "Good Morning Commander Michael!"

He now had a human appearance but you could still see the same sculpted facial features but they were subdued and he also had radiant blue eyes. We spent much of the next day together. He offered to make me dinner, the meal was really good, lamb with Okra and a curry sauce. We talked. I asked him what should be done about the "Boyd Bushman" info being revealed in mine & Sereda's film.

He said, "Now that they know you are one of us they will not be able to touch you, so don't worry about it." So to say they are part of the group withholding this information is correct, but they have also now backed the release of the Bushman info and revealing themselves to humanity, which is happening as we speak.

I was once told there was a meeting of galactic leaders as to why the Earth should be helped or not. There were a lot of quick judgments as to leaving the Earth and its inhabitants to their fates of doom and destruction. But there were also those who wanted to help and they couldn't just come here to do it themselves the way they were because it would violate free will... so there was a test given even to the Anunnaki. To be born here on Earth as humans, to be in THEIR shoes so to speak and if they gave in and were corrupted, the earth shall be left to its destruction.

If they could keep the light and awaken within this nightmare as humans, they can change things and bring about the golden age so no free will would be breached because it would all be done from within enemy territory, from behind enemy lines! This planet is not to fail for it would affect all else, because everything is connected."

Michael Hill found this interesting article from 1958 relating to the Anunnaki, in *Flying Saucer Review*. Gordon Creighton was a diplomat, publisher of *Flying Saucer Review*, and one of the most knowledgeable UFO/ET investigators of his time. I have no idea where Gordon found this alleged Anunnaki message,[124]

An actual message from the Anunnaki - MANKIND IN AMNESIA (Flying Saucer Review Magazine November-December 1958) Exhibit 19, Brinsley Le Poer Trench (Flying Saucer Review Magazine November-December 1958)

"We are already here, among you. Some of us have always been here, with you, yet apart from, watching, and occasionally guiding you whenever the opportunity arose. Now, however, our numbers have been increased in preparation for a further step in the development of your planet: a step of which you are not yet aware... We have been confused with the gods of many world-religions, although we are not gods, but your fellow creatures, as you will learn directly before many more years have passed.

You will find records of our presence in the mysterious symbols of ancient Egypt, where we made ourselves known in order to accomplish certain ends. Our principal symbol appears in the religious art of your present civilization and occupies a position of importance upon the great seal of your country (The United States of America). It has been preserved in certain secret societies founded originally to keep alive the knowledge of our existence and our intentions toward mankind."

"We have left you certain landmarks, placed carefully in different parts of the globe, but most prominently in Egypt where we established our headquarters upon the occasion of our last overt, or, as you would say, public appearance. At that time the foundations of your present civilization were 'laid in the earth' and the most ancient of your known landmarks established by means that would appear as miraculous to you now as they did to the pre-Egyptians, so many thousands of years ago. Since that time the whole art of building, in stone, has become symbolic, too many of you, of the work in hand—the building of the human race towards its perfection."

"Your ancestors knew us in those days as preceptors and as friends.. Now, through your own efforts, you have almost reached, in your majority, a new step on the long ladder of your liberation. You have been constantly aided by our watchful 'inspiration,' and hindered only by the difficulties natural to your processes of physical and moral development... "

"You have lately achieved the means of destroying yourselves. Do not be hasty in your self-congratulation. Yours is not the first civilization to have achieved—and used—such means. Yours will not be the first civilization to be offered the means of preventing that destruction and proceeding, in the full glory of its accumulated knowledge, to establish an era of enlightenment upon the earth." "However, if you do accept the means offered you, and if you establish such a 'millennium' upon the basis of your present accomplishments, yours will be the first civilization to do so.

Always before, the knowledge, the techniques, the instructions, have become the possessions of a chosen few: A few chose themselves by their own open-minded and clear-sighted realization of 'the shape of things to come.' They endeavored to pass on their knowledge in the best possible form, and by the most enduring means as their command.

In a sense they succeeded, but in another sense their failure equaled their success. Human acceptance is, to a very large extent, measurable by human experience. Succeeding generations, who never knew our actual presence, translated the teachings of their elders in the terms of their own experience. For instance, a cross-sectional drawing, much simplified and stylized by many copyings, of one of our traveling machines became the 'Eye of Horus," and then other eyes of other gods. Finally, the ancient symbol that was once an accurate representation of an important mechanical device has been given surprising connotations by the modern priesthood of psychology."

"The important fact is, however, that we are here, among you, and that you, as a world-race, will know it before very much longer! The time is almost ripe but, as with all ripening things, the process may not be hurried artificially without danger of damaging the fruit. There is a right time for every action, and the right time for our revelation of ourselves to your era is approaching."

"Some of you have seen our 'advanced guard' already. You have met us often in the streets of your cities, and you have not noticed us. But when we flash through your skies in the ancient traditional vehicles you are amazed, and those of you who open your mouths and tell of what you have seen are accounted dupes and fools. Actually you are prophets, seers in the true sense of the word.

You in Kansas and Oklahoma, you in Oregon and in California, and Idaho, you know what you have seen: do not be dismayed by meteorologists. Their business is the weather. One of you says, 'I saw a torpedo-shaped object.' Others report, 'disc-like objects,' some of you say 'spherical objects,' or 'platter-like objects.' You are all reporting correctly and accurately what you saw, and in most cases you are describing the same sort of vehicle."

"...Now that the art of manufacturing plastic materials has reached a certain perfection among you, perhaps you can imagine a material, almost transparent to the rays of ordinary visible light, yet strong enough to endure the stresses of extremely rapid flight. Look again at the great nebulae, and think of the construction of your own galaxy, and behold the universal examples of what we have found to be the perfect shape for an object which is to travel through what you still fondly refer to as 'empty' space."

In the center of the discus, gyroscopically controlled within a central sphere of the same transparent material, our control rooms revolve freely, accommodating themselves and us to flat or edgewise flight. Both methods are suited to your atmosphere, and when we convert abruptly from one to the other, as we are sometimes obliged to do, and you are watching, our machines seem suddenly to appear—or to disappear. At our possible speeds your eyes, untrained and unprepared for the maneuver, do make mistakes—but not the mistakes your scientists so often accuse them of making."

"We pass over your hilltops in horizontal flight. You see and report a torpedo-shaped object. We pass over, in formation, flying vertically 'edge-on.' Or we go over at night, jet-slits glowing, and you see an orange disc. In any event you see us, and in any event we do not care. If we chose to remain invisible, we could do so, easily, and, in fact, we have done so almost without exception for hundreds of years. But you must become accustomed to our shapes in your skies, for one day they will be familiar, friendly, and reassuring sights."

"This time, it is to be hoped that the memory of them, passed on to your children and their children, will be clear and precise. That you will not cause them to forget, as your ancestors forgot, the meaning of the diagrams and the instructions we will leave with you. If you do fail, as other civilizations have failed, we will see your descendants wearing wiring-diagrams for simple machines as amulets, expecting the diagrams to do what their forefathers were taught the completed article would accomplish. Then their children, forgetting even that much—or little—would preserve the amulet as a general protective device—or as an intellectual curiosity—or perhaps as a religious symbol. Such is the cycle of forgetfulness!" - The Anunnaki

We exopolitical investigators are encouraged to speculate based upon the evidence, and our general knowledge of extraterrestrials, that these ancient people were or are descended from ET humans. We and the tall blonde ET human extraterrestrials and others with dark hair and Eurasian features, may share the same ancestors. This would show just how closely related we really are to some ET humans.

Naturally if this is so, the human extraterrestrials would have a strong family interest in continued experimentation and tracking of bloodlines to the present day. If one takes time to run through the humanoid cases, these tall blond humans are frequently mentioned, indicating that they have been having a large impact on earth humanity for a long time.

The range of species within the human extraterrestrial collective or mega-population seems to be very large and it appears to run the gamut between at least several species of extraterrestrial humans almost exactly like ourselves. It runs from the Tall Whites, who stand out if not disguised, to quite different, as in the Fontes case. Others appear to be biological robots, partially constructed from human and other non-human species DNA, along with inorganic materials and machine technologies.

However, others like the well respected and credible George Filer, are also catching on and together we are bearing down on the truth from multiple individual perspectives and experiences. This even while other investigators and researchers find themselves bogged down in denial, or have become so loose minded that they go over the cliff into delusion. It seems to me that most people can't tolerate a high degree of uncertainty in their lives.

It seems to me many folks don't have the patience and or capability to mine and process all this UFO/ET ore in order to extract the facts properly through a lifetime of work. Many people take the easy way out and retreat, on the one hand into either denial beliefs, or on the other hand, irrational disinformation induced delusionary beliefs, when confronted by UFO/ET information.

Why in the world so many people in the UFO community would want to feed on copious amounts of false sensationalistic contactee garbage, when there are some really good credible cases of human ET contact available, is beyond me.

The following article written by the late Olavo T. Fontes, MD is an extraterrestrial human contact case that involves a healing. There are many such cases in the UFO/ET literature and I am reminded that Ben Rich once commented that not only do we secretly have the technology to travel to the stars, but that we also able to cure cancer. I would assume the cure for cancer is locked up just as tight by special interests as are the space travel and cheap clean exotic energy technologies.

Cure in Brazil Reported to Flying Saucer Review

On May I?, 1958, my friend Joân Marlins, who at that time was publishing in the magazine O Cruzeiro a series of cases on the Brazilian UFO "Flap" of 1957, received the following letter dated Rio de Janeiro, May I4, 1958:

"Dear Sr. Marlins. I have seen your articles and I wish to congratulate you. I believe in the existence of the so-called 'flying saucers` because I was a witness to an occurrence related with them. I don`t know if you are going to believe me, but I swear for everything that I am telling only the truth. I am poor but honest, and I am not going to mention the true names and you will understand.

"My name is Anazia Maria. I am 32 years old and living in Rio de Janeiro. I worked with Sr. X (my ex-master) until December 1957, he is a rich man from this city, forgive me for not giving his name. The daughter of my master was with cancer in the stomach. She suffered too much, and I was engaged to serve as a kind of housekeeper and mostly to look for Miss Laiz, the sick girl.

She had been submitted to all treatments, but the doctors had said there was no hope. In August, 1957, my master took all the family to his little farm close to Pelropolis hoping to see Miss

Laiz better in that good climate, but the days passed and nothing happened. She couldn't call, the pains were horrible and she was always taking injections of Morphine.

On the night of October 25, I remember well, Miss Laiz's pains were terrible, the injection was valueless, we were thinking that she was going to die, my master was crying in the corner, when suddenly a strong light illuminated the right side of the house (at the little farm close to Petropolis). We were gathered in Miss Laiz's room, which window was placed exactly on the right side, the room was lighted only by the small table light. Suddenly it got so much light as if the beam of a searchlight had been pointed to the inside of the room.

Sr. Julinho. son of my master, ran to the window first and saw the so-called saucer. It wasn't very big, I have no study to be able to tell what was the diameter and width. I know it wasn't very big, the upper part was involved by a yellow reddish light, and suddenly an automatic hatch opened out and two small figures came down. They walked in the direction of the house and another figure stayed in the hatch of the saucer. It became dark, and inside it-through the hatch-appeared a light-greenish light like we see in a nightclub.

The men entered the house and they were small in size and were 1.20 meters in height, smaller than the younger son of the master who was 10 years old. They had long hair reaching the shoulders, yellow-red hair, small eyes slanted like the Chinese, but of a strong green color. They had things on the hands, I think they were gloves, the cloth was white and seemed thick.

The Clothes were all white, but the chest, the back and the wrist glowed - I don't know how to explain. They approached the bed of Laiz, who was groaning with pain with her eyes wide open and not knowing what was happening around and was moving or talking, in a horrible expectation. I was in the room together with Sr. X and his wife, Sr. Julinho and his wife, and Olavinho who was the ten-year old son of the master.

The men looked silently at me and stopped beside the bed of Laiz, spread on the bed the things they carried and made a gesture to Sr. X, and one of them put his hand on the forehead of Sr. X who started to tell them all the case of Laiz, the disease, everything in telepathy. The room was in absolute silence.

The men began to illuminate the belly of Miss Laiz with a bluish white light, which showed everything inside; we all saw what was inside the belly of the girl. With another instrument that was making a creaking sound, "he" pointed in the direction of the stomach of Miss Laiz, and we could see the ulcer in the stomach.

That operation lasted for almost half an hour. Miss Laiz slept, and they went away, but before leaving the house, communicated to Sr. X, through telepathy that he should give a medication to Miss Laiz during a month; then they gave to Sr. X a hollow ball which was of steel. I think, and inside we found 30 small white balls, they were the capsules to be taken one each day, and she would be cured.

Really Miss Laiz was cured, and Sr. X, according to the agreement he had made with those men, avoided any publicity. In December, a few days before I left their house Miss Laiz went back to the doctor who verified she had no cancer anymore.

I left the house, but made the promise to keep absolute secret about the case. However, I am telling you about it, and I ask you to keep the secret. If the case is mentioned in your articles there will be no consequences because I will never disclose their names. However, l swear to you that everything really happened; my darling Miss Laiz was condemned to die of cancer of stomach and almost at the end she was saved by an instrument that looked like a flashlight, that emitted some rays that look off the cancer and she was cured. And those men have done many things of this kind to the people of the earth (planet), to show us that we must have no fear of them.

They saved Miss Laiz, and in the same night went back to the saucer and were gone forever. They are indeed from Mars and come here to search for magnesium, which they purify there in their planet, and this magnesium is used for their constructions and for the so-called Flying Saucers.

They have no intention of fighting against the people of earth, this I was informed hearing what Sr. X was telling the family. Please don't put me in a bad position; if you mention the case, never tell in your articles that you know about it from Anazia Maria. I don't want to pass for a blackmailer or be in a bad position with my ex-master. I am telling you this only to help you in your investigation of the problem.

Forgive me for not giving my address. I live in Río, in a suburban district. I am honest and but I don't want no press interviews because of my ex-master. Thanks for your attention. Anazia Maria.

The writer was obviously a person of little Culture, but in spite of that, her letter is sincere. Despite her bad use of the Portuguese language which I have tried to convey in this translation, she tells her tale so well that we can almost re-live the scene as if we were there ourselves. In my opinion this means that the letter was written with emotion; the emotion of something that might really have happened.

There are also technical details which are very interesting, such as the bluish while light which showed everything inside the body of the patient (an advanced form of X-rays); like the instrument looking like a flashlight, which evidently was emitting some kind of radiation capable of killing the cancer cells (an advanced form of cobalt ray therapy?) and like the chemical treatment to complete the cure, which also makes sense.

Another interesting thing is the telepathy through physical contact. There is also the description of the humanoid occupants of small size with long hair, light eyes slanted like the Chinese of which we have seen in other cases with disturbing frequency.

However, I was ready to reject this case mostly because of the part involving telepathy (in which I don't believe). I didn't, only because of another case (also in my 'reserve') which happened in the night of October 10, 1957 (15 days before). I will describe only a small part of it: Then a door was opened in the object automatically (like a Convair door).

There appeared two persons, then two more, then still two others and finally a seventh one, who passed between the two groups formed by the others. They watched the truck for three minutes, all of them; all those people looked like men of Earth but they were smaller in size, had long hair on the shoulders and the clothes were lumi-nous at the chest. "When those small men were looking at me I went into a trance-like state and had the strange feeling that they were saying: We come on a peaceful mission."

As the case of the "operation" was never published, the coincidence of another incident at the same period with similar details on the occupants, clothes, and mental communication again, is evidently disturbing. I decided to put both cases in the "special File" for future reference. The case of the "operation" is not closed yet. As a medical doctor living in Rio, I still hope to some clue (among my patients and other doctors) about someone who was cured from a gastric cancer in some unexplainable way.

While most cases of extensive extraterrestrial contact involve single or just several individuals at the most, there are a few very controversial contact cases that involve many people and that seem to span continents. Some believe these cases are real, others think they are cults, but it seems to me that the people being interviewed are sincere. I have been impressed as to the depth of the investigations especially the Chile case. A mainstream documentary was made that uncovered more witnesses and even exposed a fraudulent contactee hidden in the mist of the real contactees involved.

I am a bit reluctant to put these cases in this book but having thought on this a lot, I feel that the readers should be aware of these rare group cases in spite of the controversy surrounding them. I do find myself turning my spam filter up a bit when researching these cases because of the complexity of the cases and the possibility that these could be cult related. We just need to take these cases as part of the greater context within which this book has been written.

Recently I became aware of a longstanding extraterrestrial human contact case called Friendship, that if true involves many people both in Europe and in Chile, South America. The only other alleged contact case involving so many people that I am aware of is the controversial Ummo Case. What I found compelling about the following two videos was that the contactees seem very sincere. As the investigators investigated they found even more individuals that claimed contact especially in the Chile case.

In clips 11/12 and 12/12 there seems to be an Annunaki connection. While there is a huge amount of historical evidence of the Annunaki in the Bible, the Hindu Scriptures and the Sumerian clay tablets, modern cases are hard to come by. It's still a bit hard to determine if these two cases are really related, the one in Italy and the one in Chile. The Italian Friendship case.[125] The Chile Friendship case.[126]

The following article is from exopolitical investigator Paola Harris's website, who while not the writer of this article, has investigated the Italy Friendship case.[127]

Mass Contact-A Review, Aliens Among us!
By Barbara Barbatelli

In these days the Italian UFO community is under shock after the recent publication of a new, extraordinary book by Edizioni Nexus. Its title is "Contattismi di Massa" ("Mass Contacts") and was written by Professor Stefano Breccia, a famous and esteemed engineer from Abruzzi. His impressive curriculum shows us a long academic career in L'Aquila's and many other Italian and foreign Universities. He is also a founding member of the Italian Ufological Centre (CUN).

The author recalls and investigates many cases in which contacts with aliens did not occur to single, isolated individuals but, on the contrary, involved entire groups of people, more or less organized in communities, who lived together the same experiences. Some of these groups decided to reveal what was happening, some others preferred to keep everything secret.

This completely new and intriguing scenery will open to researchers the possibility, for the first time in Ufology, to investigate on crossed sources of information, to trace the many witnesses involved, verifying their reciprocal links, and to study facts, times and places from many and different points of view at the same time.

The book re-opens and deepens, with new and never published details, the famous case of "UMMO." This was the name of a race of self-defining extraterrestrials who sent for decades an incredible amount of letters to famous scientists and researchers living in Spain, France, and Italy etc. These letters were filled with extremely complicated notions denoting very advanced scientific knowledge. Many of the scientists who had received them later admitted they had been inspired by those letters, owing to that superior science many of their inventions and discoveries.

The book also shows a completely unknown corollary of the "UMMO case" involving central Italy and, more specifically, the town of Rome and the archaeological Etruscan ruins of Veio. During the seventies in those places acted, completely undisturbed, many extraterrestrials calling themselves "Italic Ummites." They looked like humans and for this reason could perfectly hide and integrate in our society. These beings, who possessed a technology well far beyond ours, produced many phenomena for us indistinguishable from magic and used their abilities to direct and manipulate a group of young UFO enthusiasts.

But the real "bomb" contained in "Mass Contacts" blasts when we read the third chapter: The Story of "FRIENDSHIP." In this chapter we assist to the fall of a secrecy that had enveloped for decades a case cited very sporadically and suspiciously only by few investigators (the best informed ones). They had some evidences suggesting that in Italy, from 1956 to 1978, something TREMENDOUS had happened, but all their efforts to discover the truth had failed. The fact was that the group involved in the case had decided to keep everything secret; many of them were famous and influent people and could not ruin their lives and careers saying they had met face to face with extraterrestrial people. They knew the world was not ready yet.

Now at last, Professor Stefano Breccia (a member of "Friendship" himself, as we can easily infer), providing many impressive documents and testimonies, discloses the truth on the entire story to give homage and justice to the memory of his big friend, the late Dr Bruno Sammaciccia, pivot figure in the "Friendship" group, and gives him the word publishing a long taped interview to his friend.

Professor Bruno Sammaciccia was a well-known Psychologist and Theologian from Pescara. He wrote many volumes on religious subjects including the study of miracles, holy relics, the Order of San Francis of Assisi and the history of compared Religions. His works have been translated in many languages and are well represented in all main religious libraries all over the world. He received the UNESCO prize "Man of the Year" in 1982, was friend of many important people and high prelates and the same

Pope Karol Woytila, at the time Cardinal of Cracow, wrote a friendly dedication on one of his books.

His public and irreprehensible image hid a fantastic and science fiction-like reality: From 1956 to 1978 Bruno Sammaciccia and many other people had continuative and intense contacts with extraterrestrial entities coming from planets orbiting around many different stars, many light years distant from our Solar System, forming part of a Galactic Federation.

Just like Enoch Wallace, the leading character of Clifford Simak's "Way Station", Bruno Sammaciccia found himself in the middle of an incredible passage of aliens on this planet Earth. They had many underground bases; the biggest one was under the Adriatic Sea and was long more than one hundred kilometers. Bruno Sammaciccia's duties ranged from buying and transporting goods to the underground bases, to organizing a selected group of terrestrials capable to understand the alien knowledge and to spread it more and more to humanity.

The whole operation had to remain secret. The total number of the lucky earthlings admitted to such a fantastic group is esteemed from Professor Breccia in no more than 200 people, including similar groups in Austria, Germany and Russia. They spontaneously called themselves "Friendship," "Freundshaft", "Amitiè" and, of course, "Amicizia", because the wonderful "human" warmness of the space visitors had suggested in everyone the same feeling.

Bruno Sammaciccia gave to his "Friends" the code-name of "W56" ("W" from the sign of victory and "56" from the year of the first contact). He describes them as human in the shape but very different in tallness, ranging from one meter to three meters and a half...in one occasion he and other people near Pescara saw from a distance some giants six meters tall!

The aliens "normally" tall showed to be perfectly fit in our society and had a knowledge of our world and our history much deeper than ours. They had technologies like teleportation or interstellar travel, but enjoyed themselves driving our cars or piloting our planes. They loved our foods and they loved smoking too! They knew that exceeding in some habits can be dangerous and used to take regularly some antidotes. Anyway the different atmosphere and gravity of their re-created environment could completely decontaminate bodies from toxic substances; this healing effect was experimented also from Sammaciccia and his human friends who had access to underground bases.

The "W56" aliens said they wanted to help humans to survive because, especially during the last decades, human civilization had chosen very dangerous paths, blindly trusting in science and forgetting morals. They said that the other civilizations, in space and on earth, who had made the same errors, had invariably perished. They could not interfere at a mass level with us because our culture would have been destroyed, but they could gently address with their teaching a little number of selected terrestrials to a better future, and their messages had to be spread in this way to more and more people, generation after generation.

Unfortunately the "W56" were fiercely struggled by a hostile race they called "our enemy brothers" and for this reason also our unaware human race was involved in some kind of "Star War." Sammaciccia re-named these enemies "CTR" (from "contraries" and one of the duties of the "Friendship" group consisted in helping W56's efforts to stop CTR's evil actions. The CTR are described like totally similar to us and this characteristic made them extremely dangerous, they were perfectly fit in our society, hyper technological and totally lacking in morals.

After almost thirty years of these fantastic interactions the history of "Friendship" came to a tragic end. The W56 were defeated, the CTR destroyed the enormous bases where also humans had gone many times and the Adriatic Sea erupted with many water columns, causing death and fear among fishermen in 1978. Sammaciccia states that humans too were culpable for this horrible end, because they had not trusted each other and they had not supported enough their alien "Friends."

Anyway W 56 promised they would come back at the beginning of the new century and Bruno Sammaciccia ends his long interview to Stefano Breccia hoping to see them again. Sadly the theologian died in 2003 not realizing his wishes, at least in this world. Now we have his extremely touching words and we have the duty to study the enormous amount of verifiable and concrete facts contained in Stefano Breccia's volume.

Talking about "facts," at the end of this book we can see a very clear photo of a W56. The person is in full light and all his body and face characteristics are perfectly detailed. For the first time in Ufology the image of a so-called "alien" is so clear, so "Human" (how tall is he?) and with no trace of photographic effects to make it more "exotic." Now researchers and debunkers will obviously try to verify the photo confronting that face with all similar faces they'll be able to discover and, in case, they will probably open also the police archives! That face is too recognizable; what happened if somebody would identify that guy saying: "HEY, I know him, he is my cousin! (or my brother, friend, husband etc...)?" The whole story would fall, of course.

So, why Dr.Breccia exposed his name and his career to such a great risk? Perhaps because he is totally certain that the person portrayed in that photo was not from this Earth. If the "Friendship" story is true it represents one of the most important cases in Ufology and an immense heritage for humanity.

Perhaps the reader may be wondering how mega-populations of extraterrestrials could organize themselves while traveling hundreds of light years or maybe even billions of light years away from each other using exotic propulsion systems that defeat space and time. The answer seems to already be out in the public domain and it is that of communication by quantum entanglement.

Quantum entanglement communications would seem to be the way ETs communicate and organize themselves across vast distances. Quantum entanglement communication is being proved to work with new developments happening on a regular basis. It's well known that many ET races are telepathic which seems to be based on quantum entanglement. Forget about primitive electromagnetic communications as the propagandists of SETI would have you believe in their false time line narrative to ET contact. In reality, I have been showing in this book that contact began long ago in the real narrative with classified shadow governments now interacting and coordinating with several ET civilizations.

The very fact that all this information about quantum communications is coming out in the public domain leads me to believe that just as in other areas, black technologies in the classified world are way ahead of public knowledge. I would suspect that the NSA already is far advanced in transmitting and receiving ET quantum communications. The Dan Sherman case indicates that. Also, if our secret space fleet is already traveling to the stars as has been suggested by credible people like Ben Rich, then we can expect that the fleet could already be using instantaneous quantum communications to communicate with and organize the fleet and to communicate back with the home planet just as ET seems to be doing.

The reader can see from the following article that entanglement communications are now far more advanced than from just sending messages via photons and other high energy particles. I would expect to hear any day that they can teleport matter via quantum entanglement and not just photons or other small high energy particles. I guess if intelligent beings become advanced enough, they could travel by teleportation rather than even using exotic propulsion systems.

"Scientists have linked two diamonds[128] in a mysterious process called entanglement that is normally only seen on the quantum scale. Entanglement[129] is so weird that Einstein dubbed it 'spooky action at a distance.'[130] It's a strange effect where one object gets connected to another so that even if they are separated by large distances, an action performed on one will affect the other. Entanglement usually occurs with subatomic particles, and was predicted by the theory of quantum mechanics, which governs the realm of the very small. But now physicists have succeeded in entangling two macroscopic diamonds, demonstrating that quantum mechanical effects are not limited to the microscopic scale.[131]

"If the two diamonds weren't entangled, the researchers would expect each detector to register a changed laser beam about 50 percent of the time. It's similar to tossing a coin, where random chance would lead to heads about half the time and tails the other half the time on average. Instead, because the two diamonds were linked, they found that one detector measured the change every time, and the other detector never fired. The two diamonds, it seemed, were so connected they reacted as a single entity, rather than two individual objects."

In this article scientists show we are well on our way in the public domain to use quantum entanglement communication over large distances.[132]

"Here we report a significant step towards satellite based quantum communication by transmitting an entangled photon over a distance of 144 km between the Canary Islands[133] of La Palma and Tenerife via an optical free-space link.

The transmitted photon was received in the Optical Ground Station of the European Space Agency,[134] and the entangled partner photon was detected locally at the transmitter. We have succeeded in establishing quantum correlations under experimental constraints and conditions characteristic for a Space-to-ground experiment."

More to the point the following article speculates that telepathy involves quantum entanglement.[135] "Some people have suggested that psychic powers do exist or other communication could exist, using quantum entanglement to allow instantaneous messages over any distance."

Quantum entanglement is an accepted part of quantum physics. The concept is often associated with an argument Einstein and others used to try to demonstrate limitations of quantum theory and the Uncertainty Principle. Einstein described an experiment in which two particles would be created by the same process, but would head in opposite directions. If at some time you were to establish certain attributes of one of the particles, you could use that to determine that attribute of the other particle. Einstein argued this could be used to get information on particles that was inconsistent with the Uncertainty Principle and would indicate that the particles actually have definite properties at all times rather than just probabilities of values.

However, what physicists have come to accept is that this does not mean that testing one particle tells us about attributes the other particle already had. Instead, it is believed that when one particle is tested that fact is instantaneously conveyed to the other particle which then is forced to acquire a particular property. This takes place by some means that does not involve exchange of photons or other means limited by the speed of light."

In summary the evidence for human and humanoid extraterrestrial contact is overwhelming as the reader has seen if they fully investigate these thousands of contact cases. I think the evidence is beyond a reasonable doubt that there is this megapopulation of humans and humanoids that most likely are spread across our universe. Who knows maybe if there is a multi-universe with many dimensions this human collective most likely has spread beyond our own universe and into these other dimensions and multi-universes. I am reminded by those with intimate inside knowledge of the classified world that tell us that the truth is beyond what we can possibly imagine.

CHAPTER NINE

EXTRATERRESTRIAL WARFARE

"Gurkha flying in his swift and powerful Vimana hurled against the three cities of the Vrishis and Andhakas a single projectile charged with all the power of the Universe. An incandescent column of smoke and fire, as brilliant as ten thousands suns, rose in all its splendor. It was the unknown weapon, the Iron Thunderbolt, a gigantic messenger of death which reduced to ashes the entire race of the Vrishnis and Andhakas." The corpses were so burned as to be unrecognizable. Mahabharata

By the time Lot reached Zoar, the sun had risen over the land. Then the Lord rained down burning sulphur on Sodom and Gomorrah – from the Lord out of the heavens. Thus he overthrew those cities and the entire plain, including all those living in the cities – and also the vegetation in the land. But Lot's wife looked back and she became a pillar of salt. Early the next morning Abraham got up and returned to the place where he had stood before the Lord. He looked down toward Sodom and Gomorrah, toward all the land of the plain, and he saw dense smoke rising from the land, like smoke from a furnace. Genesis 19: 23 – 27

If your very own brother, or your son or daughter, or the wife you love, or your closest friend secretly entices you, saying, "let us go and worship other gods" (gods that neither of you nor your fathers have known, gods of the peoples around you, whether near or far from one end of the land to the other), do not yield to him or listen to him. Show him no pity. Deuteronomy 13: 6, 7, & 8

I believe that warfare and conflict between extraterrestrial races go back in earth's history for tens of thousands of years as recorded in the Ramayana, Mahabharata and other Hindu texts and in the Bible. The Hindu texts speak in great detail of highly technical extraterrestrial civilizations during the time of the Rama Empire and of an incredibly destructive war some ten or twelve thousand years ago between Atlantis and Rama that could not be imagined until the second half of the 20th century. In this Link[136] there is some very interesting information. The author states:

>"The Mahabharata is a veritable gold mine of information relating to conflicts between gods who are said to have settled their differences apparently using weapons as lethal as those we have now. Apart from 'blazing missiles,' the poem records the use of other deadly weapons. 'Indra's Dart' (Indravajra) is operated via a circular 'reflector.' When switched on, it produced a 'shaft of light' which, when focused on any target, immediately "consumed it with its power."
>
>In one exchange, the hero, Krishna, is pursuing his enemy, Salva, in the sky, when Salva's Vimana, the Saubha, is made invisible in some way. Undeterred, Krishna immediately fires off a special weapon: "I quickly laid on an arrow, which killed by seeking out sound." Many other terrible weapons are described, quite matter-of-factly, in the Mahabharata, but the most fearsome of all is the one used against the Vrishis. The narrative records:

"Gurkha flying in his swift and powerful Vimana hurled against the three cities of the Vrishis and Andhakas a single projectile charged with all the power of the Universe. An incandescent column of smoke and fire, as brilliant as ten thousands suns, rose in all its splendor. It was the unknown weapon, the Iron Thunderbolt, a gigantic messenger of death which reduced to ashes the entire race of the Vrishnis and Andhakas." The corpses were so burned as to be unrecognizable.

The hair and nails fell out; pottery broke without apparent cause, and the birds turned white.... after a few hours all foodstuffs were infected.... to escape from this fire, the soldiers threw themselves in streams to wash themselves and their equipment..."Some say that the Mahabharata is describing an atomic war. References like this one are not isolated; but battles, using a fantastic array of weapons and aerial vehicles are common in all the epic Indian books. One even describes a Vimana-Vailix battle on the Moon!" Check this link for more good quotes from the Hindu texts of flying craft and battles.[137]

It seems that the reported destruction by God reported in the Bible of Sodom and Gomorrah by fire and brimstone was not an isolated incident, but part of a greater ET war in which we the indigenous people ended up as proxies and were drawn into these ET conflicts. The mysteries of the vitrified forts[138] provide additional evidence[139] of the use of modern weapons of mass destruction in ancient times.

Besides the vitrified forts there are also stretches of desert where glass sheets were found.

"One of the strangest mysteries of ancient Egypt is that of the great glass sheets that were only discovered in 1932. In December of that year, Patrick Clayton, a surveyor for the Egyptian Geological Survey, was driving among the dunes of the Great Sand Sea near the Saad Plateau in the virtually uninhabited area just north of the south-western corner of Egypt, when he heard his tires crunch on something that wasn't sand. It turned out to be large pieces of marvelously clear, yellow-green glass.

In fact, this wasn't just any ordinary glass, but ultra-pure glass that was astonishing 98 per cent silica. Clayton wasn't the first person to come across this field of glass, as various 'prehistoric' hunters and nomads had obviously also found the now-famous Libyan Desert Glass (LDG). The glass had been used in the past to make knives and sharp-edged tools as well as other objects. A carved scarab of LDG was even found in Tutankhamen's tomb, indicating that the glass was sometimes used for jewelry."

An article entitled "*Dating the Libyan Desert Silica-Glass*" appeared in the British journal Nature (no. 170) in 1952. The author, Kenneth Oakley said:

"Pieces of natural silica-glass up to 16 lb. in weight occur scattered sparsely in an oval area, measuring 130 km north to south and 53 km from east to west, in the Sand Sea of the Libyan Desert. This remarkable material, which is almost pure (97 per cent silica), relatively light (sp. gin. 2.21), clear and yellowish-green in color, has the qualities of a gemstone. It was discovered by the Egyptian Survey Expedition under Mr. P.A. Clayton in 1932, and was thoroughly investigated by Dr L.J. Spencer, who joined a special expedition of the Survey for this purpose in 1934."

The following article[140] quotes Oppenheimer.

"Interestingly, Manhattan Project chief scientist Dr J. Robert Oppenheimer was known to be familiar with ancient Sanskrit literature. In an interview conducted after he watched the first atomic test, he quoted from the Bhagavad Gita: "Now I am become Death, the Destroyer of Worlds." I suppose we all felt that way.
When asked in an interview at Rochester University seven years after the Alamogordo nuclear test whether that was the first atomic bomb ever to be detonated, his reply was; ancient cities whose brick and stone walls have literally been vitrified, that is, fused together, can be found in India, Ireland, Scotland, France, Turkey and other places. There is no logical explanation for the vitrification of stone forts and cities, except from an atomic blast."

In this article, *Ancient City Found in India, Irradiated From Atomic Blast*, is stated:

"Radiation is still so intense, the area is highly dangerous. A heavy layer of radioactive ash in Rajasthan, India, covers a three-square mile area, ten miles west of Jodhpur. Scientists are investigating the site, where a housing development was being built. For some time it has been established that there is a very high rate of birth defects and cancer in the area under construction

The levels of radiation there have registered so high on investigators' gauges that the Indian government has now cordoned off the region. Scientists have unearthed an ancient city where evidence shows an atomic blast dating back thousands of years, from 8000 to 12,000 years, destroyed most of the buildings and probably a half-million people. One researcher estimates that the nuclear bomb used was about the size of the ones dropped on Japan in 1945."

"When excavations of Harappa and Mohenjo-Daro reached the street level, they discovered skeletons scattered about the cities, many holding hands and sprawling in the streets as if some instant, horrible doom had taken place. People were just lying, unburied, in the streets of the city. And these skeletons are thousands of years old, even by traditional archaeological standards. What could cause such a thing? Why did the bodies not decay or get eaten by wild animals? Furthermore, there is no apparent cause of a physically violent death.

These skeletons are among the most radioactive ever found, on par with those at Hiroshima and Nagasaki. At one site, Soviet scholars found a skeleton which had a radioactive level 50 times greater than normal. Other cities have been found in northern India that show indications of explosions of great magnitude.

One such city, found between the Ganges and the mountains of Rajmahal, seems to have been subjected to intense heat. Huge masses of walls and foundations of the ancient city are fused together, literally vitrified! And since there is no indication of a volcanic eruption at Mohenjo-Daro or at the other cities, the intense heat to melt clay vessels can only be explained by an atomic blast or some other unknown weapon. The cities were wiped out entirely. While the skeletons have been carbon-dated to 2500 BC, we must keep in mind that carbon-dating involves measuring the amount of radiation left. When atomic explosions are involved, that makes them seem much younger."

Now let's fast forward in time a bit to Nuremberg, Germany, April 14th 1561 for evidence of extraterrestrial battles in the sky. The Hans Glaser wood-cut from 1566, 5 years after the event and in the same year as the Basle report says:

"At sunrise on the 14th April 1561, the citizens of Nuremberg beheld "A very frightful spectacle." The sky appeared to fill with cylindrical objects from which red, black, orange and blue white disks and globes emerged. Crosses and tubes resembling cannon barrels also appeared whereupon the objects promptly "began to fight one another." After about an hour of battle, the objects seemed too catch fire and fell to Earth, where they turned too steam."

A broadsheet that dates from 1561, held in the Wickiana Collection of Switzerland's Zurich Central Library, describes an ancient battle of UFOs over the skies of Nuremberg, Germany, on April 14th.

"At sunrise, many people witnessed large numbers of dark red, blue and black 'globes' or 'plates' near the sun, 'some three in a row, now and then four in a square, also some alone. And amongst these globes some blood colored crosses were seen.' The document also refers to two great tubes 'in which three, four and more globes were seen. They then all began to fight each other.' This went on for about an hour, until 'they all fell... from the sun and sky down to the earth, producing a lot of steam.' Beneath the globes a long object that looked like a great black spear was also described as being seen."

Quote from the Gazette of the town of Nuremberg reports:

At dawn of April 4, in the sky of Nuremberg (Germany), a lot of men and women saw a very alarming spectacle where various objects were involved, including balls "approximately 3 in the length, from time to time, four in a square, much remained insulated, and between these balls, one saw a number of crosses with the color of blood. Then one saw two large pipes, in which small and large pipes were 3 balls, also four or more. All these elements started to fight one against the other."[141] [142]

In 1608 the ETs were at it again with another aerial battle[143] between extraterrestrial craft in France. Occupants were seen as well. In August of 1608, people of southern France, from Marseilles to Genoa, witnessed a true wave of UFOs, as reported in a chronicle of the time entitled, "*Discours des terribles et espouvantables signes apparus sur la mer Gennes.*"

"In the sky over Martigues an aerial battle took place which left an odor of saltpeter (sulphur). The inhabitants of Nice saw three strange luminous vessels moving at high speed above the city. The vessels stopped close to a fortress then went down into the sea causing the water to boil and release a reddish-colored vapor. To the amazement of onlookers, two humanoid beings with large heads and large luminous eyes, and reddish scales connected to their vessels by tubes, passed several hours in some kind of strange work. Also off Genoa an aerial battle took place between flying objects and other craft emerging from the sea. The soldiers of the fortress delivered eight hundred blows from their guns to drive off the intruders."

I first began to hear about a war between ET factions in 2006 from my local contactee sources. They told me that what had been a cold war between ET races was now heating up. In 2008, I was told that one of my contact's female Nordic human ET friends had been wounded in a battle. Later, I was told that this ET had recovered and was back in action. I had no way of confirming this information at the time, so I just sat on it, but it did get me to researching cases of possible extraterrestrial warfare.

I have expressed the point before that I believe the evolutionary laws are not just limited to earth but extend across the universe. Wherever there is competition and cooperation here on earth, either in nature or human society, conflicts and alliances arise. The evidence accumulating in the UFO/ET field indicates that it's not any different on life evolving on other worlds and moving into space and across the universe.

I began searching the Internet, the first case of possible ET conflict I found was *UFO/ET activity Over Indiana*.[144] I read this article by UFO investigator Bill Knell and was told that this issue has been talked about on Coast to Coast radio. Investigator Bill Knell had the following to say about this activity in Indiana,

> "Lights similar to those seen over Phoenix also appeared on Tuesday and Wednesday (April 14-15, 2008) over the towns of Kokomo and Logansport in Northern Indiana. Those lights were accompanied by loud sounds, an odd metallic odor in the air, the appearance of military aircraft and debris falling from the sky. Earlier in the evening on Wednesday night (April 15, 2008), a fishing boat captain reported seeing a huge object split into smaller lights off the coast of Atlantic City, New Jersey and said that he felt a brief tremor after that event." The unexplained craft are back over Phoenix and the air traffic controllers have been muzzled.[145]

Obviously a lot is going on in the skies over Texas, Arizona and Indiana at the time and the public and the media do not have a clue as to what is really happening. After I wrote a first blog article the Open Minds Forum opened up a thread called War in Space, and as I had hoped more very interesting cases were posted. The following case I found on the OM thread from Kelowna, British Columbia region in 2007.[146]

Numerous eyewitnesses in different parts of Kelowna saw a cylinder shaped craft, with what looked like fins on it, and on fire, ripped down through the sky and finally hitting the water on Okanagan Lake, British Columbia. The sound was incredibly loud and like a deep bass "womp, womp, womp" sound as it came down. The same object then reappeared from where it hit the lake, rose up and then sat and hovered in the sky.

Meanwhile a cone or "possible" triangular shaped craft was stationary a short distance away from the cylinder shaped craft. What took place next dumbfounded all of the people who had watched the event unfold, the two objects started reacting to one another, and the best description given from the witnesses was like looking at tracer fire from automatic weapons, or in other words it was like the two UFOs were shooting at one another. After a short time of exchanging what looked like the two craft were firing on one another, a loud bang was heard and the cone shaped craft was nowhere to be seen.

The torpedo shaped object was still hovering in the sky. It started moving from side to side and then a loud sonic boom and it was now gone. Needless to say, some witnesses screamed loudly or when watching had their jaw almost hit the ground from watching such an unusual event unfold in front of their eyes.

Other witnesses on July 2 also saw UFOs fighting.[147] "Ok, so like I said I would I've been watching the skies. Not last night but the night before, I saw something out of this world (no pun intended). It was about 10:45ish at night and I saw two object(s) in the sky just hovering. They weren't doing much, but something new with most sightings, they were different shaped objects. One was thin and longish, and the other was like a triangular shape. They kept hovering there, so I got up quickly to run and grab my camera, but the next thing I know I hear a smallest bang, almost like a gun, and the longish one starts to hurtle towards earth on fire making a deep sound, kind of like a nuclear generator bass kind of sound. I'm thinking to myself what the hell!

I watched the object and it disappeared at low altitude behind a smallish hill between my neighborhood and the lake. I look up and I see the triangular object make a small circle, come a little lower and then I see it start to hurdle towards the sky at a fast rate, and the longish one reappears from behind the hill no more fire, and ascending at break neck speed and when it gets a little higher,

I saw it literally shoot something at the other object and then a very loud bang and the triangular one was no longer visible.

The longish one started to what looked like search the sky. It was going north, then south, then east and west, Very quickly, almost like a hummingbird when it goes side to side. Then the object disappeared and I suppose its departure broke the sound barrier immediately because I heard that sonic boom when the barrier is broken.

Anyways, like I said. This seems ludicrous, and after my many years of watching the skies, I finally saw what seemed like two E.T.s duking it out. The thing I find interesting about this sighting though, is that the objects were not glowing eerily like most UFO sightings refer to. It makes the sighting almost that much more "real" if you know what I mean. "

Here is yet another case[148] posted by Roger Marsh of a possible UFO dogfight over New Jersey. The witness said:

"Planes were traveling across the sky. In contrast to these planes, the objects were moving at incredible speeds...speeds that, as far as I know, are inhumanly possible. I'd estimate THOUSANDS of miles per hour. I can estimate these incredible speeds due to the known limited speed of commercial airliners. Furthermore, these objects were moving in MANY different directions.

I mean right angles, reversing direction "on a dime", vertically, horizontally, etc. during a sparing few instances these white lights would seemingly flash a red or orange hue as well. I would describe their movements; as if in a dogfight seemingly interacting with each other at times. Mind you, all the while planes are traveling through the sky."

This UFO Dogfight over Texas case is recent. I keep finding these cases for this Chapter by trying different search words and more cases keep coming to light.

"I walked outside at about 2 AM, on September 9, 2011, to make sure my car was locked and saw this weird blue glowing orb shoot across the sky towards a stationary white orb and a weird reddish glowing orb. Then the blue orb shot off a beam at the red orb. Then the red orb kind of shot off for about 30 seconds and the white orb turned a reddish color all about the same time.

The blue and red objects started shooting lights at each other. After about a minute of this battle, I watched the sky kind of flash like thunder for about five seconds and these objects were moving in weird directions stopping and then changing direction. After the flashing the red orb was gone, a second red orb appeared that I assume was the first red orb that disappeared. And they both shot off toward the northeast after a five minute dogfight."[149]

I found the following article, the *1989 Battle of the Saucers, in Russia*[150] from still another word search on the Internet.

"Subbotin claims that hundreds of people watched the group of six silver saucers fight against one golden UFO. The UFOs all made incredible moves in the skies-at times flying as low as 5,000 feet, giving a good view to onlookers. Beams of red light constituted the weapon of choice.

Witnesses who were interviewed by Sichenko claimed that the outnumbered golden UFO was finally defeated, although giving a gallant effort. The defeated UFO lost altitude, finally crashing to the ground. The six victorious UFOs disappeared into the clouds. Subbotin claims that the golden UFO crashed into a bog on a military test range, and the area was zoned off to everyone except military.

I received an email from Janice about a person who saw another UFO dogfight:

"Approximately 25 years ago the grandmother of my son's best friend watched an aerial dog fight between UFOs. It was way up in the sky. She saw UFOs explode and there was a lot more detail but I do not remember it."

In conclusion, let's not forget the five following cases alluding to extraterrestrial conflict that I already have in the book in other chapters. The Apollo 19 and 20 case refers to a battle on the moon. moonwalker1966delta says:

The origin of the two objects the mothership and the alien base were the same. Same materials and same age. We think they have been shot down during a sort of "lunar Pearl Harbor." The base has been completely destroyed and the mothership and the 2 spacecraft shot down during and emergency take off. That is what William and Leonov thought too.

Jeff Adams struck up a confidential conversation on the Internet with an individual who claimed to be the son of a MJ 12 Air Force general and he said that the ETs known as the Nordics have fought a war with the Greys.

"The Nordics and the Greys had an alliance which fell apart at this same time. The Nordics, who can be quite warlike when they want to be, opened up a can of whoopass on the Greys, and the war cost the Greys a lot of ground. The Greys were apparently using the Nordics for their own purposes, and the Nordics were not amused. The US/EU/UN still works with the Greys, so we all know where this is going to end."

Lyn Buchanan stated:

Pretty soon another Grey came up and asked him to hold up his hand. When Lyn did the Grey placed his hand against Lyn's and they had a long conversation. It took Lyn the longest time to figure out after he had remembered all this, what they talked about, but basically the Grey said they needed pilots and offered him a job. On this Lyn said: "Yes, but I will have to go back and get my family." Grey said; "No families, we are at war" at that Lyn replied that without his family he won't do it. The Grey did not say with whom they were at war with.

George LoBuono stated and this was confirmed by me from Charles Hall directly:

"Airman Charles Hall suggests that Air Force generals thought the Tall Whites were near-enemies of the Greys. Hall: "I am quite certain that the Tall Whites and the Short Greys hate each other. I am quite certain that the Tall Whites would never permit the Short Greys to come anywhere near their base areas or near to their housing areas or anywhere that their children might be playing, etc." But what is Hall's basis for that assumption? I asked him, and he replied, "I was with the Tall Whites for over two years. Various remarks were made, and in particular, the Teacher (a Tall White) made the point quite clear to me." (Charles Hall, personal email to the author 3-13-09)."

From the W56 article in Chapter 6:

"Unfortunately the "W56" were fiercely struggled by a hostile race they called "our enemy brothers" and for this reason also our unaware human race was involved in some kind of "Star War." Sammaciccia re-named these enemies "CTR" (from "contraries" and one of the duties of the "Friendship" group consisted in helping W56's efforts to stop CTR's evil actions. The CTR are described like totally similar to us and this characteristic made them extremely dangerous, they were perfectly fit in our society, hyper technological and totally lacking in morals.
 After almost thirty years of these fantastic interactions the history of "Friendship" came to a tragic end. The W56 were defeated, the CTR destroyed the enormous bases where also humans had gone many times and the Adriatic Sea erupted with many water columns, causing death and fear among fishermen in 1978."

It's been amazing working on this chapter that I have been able to continue to find cases of ET conflict and fighting adding to those I found years ago for my first two blog articles on the subject. Of course I am also running into lots of trash cases, but still there are still credible cases to be found across the Internet by coming at this from different angles using different combinations of search words and different search engines. I have no doubt that other credible cases can be found by diligent researchers.

CHAPTER TEN

PARANORMAL PHENOMENA THAT IMPERSONATE UFOs AND ETS

"O Oysters, come and walk with us!"
The Walrus did beseech.
"A pleasant walk, a pleasant talk,
Along the briny beach:
We cannot do with more than four,
To give a hand to each."

The eldest Oyster looked at him,
But never a word he said:
The eldest Oyster winked his eye,
And shook his heavy head--
Meaning to say he did not choose
To leave the oyster-bed.

Walrus and the Carpenter (Lewis Carroll)

Within the UFOET field, we have investigators that investigate phenomena that mimic UFOs and extraterrestrials. This kind of phenomena is well known and has been part of humanity's experience throughout history. Many researchers[151] are inclined to think that UFOs are not extraterrestrial and can be explained as paranormal phenomena[152] that originate in the vicinity of earth as psychological and poltergeist phenomena, perhaps intruding from other dimensions.

While I believe some UFO phenomena in the sky and so called 'extraterrestrial visitations' do fit into this category, I believe it is a mistake for exopolitical investigators to get sidetracked and deceived by this kind of paranormal trickster phenomena. I think I have shown very convincingly in this book that extraterrestrial life does exist and is coming here interacting with us in very major ways.

Paranormal phenomena that mimic UFOs and extraterrestrials can range from harmless mischief to possession, delusion and other dangerous and even deadly activity. Those of us investigating in the field of exopolitics simply can't ignore these phenomena and we have to be able to discriminate between this kind of paranormal phenomena and real extraterrestrial contact and activities.

A well respected investigator and researcher of trickster phenomena is Chris O'Brien author of the book, '*Stalking the*

Tricksters.'[153] The following is a review of Chris's book that sums up these phenomena quite well:

"The subject of Trickster-ism has permeated human belief for millennia but today, in the 21st Century, very little is publicly known about "The Trickster." Graced by many names including; fool, sage, coyote, Loki, men-in-black etc., tricksters have inhabited culture for millennia and this casual force has played pivotal roles throughout history.

Author/field-investigator Christopher O'Brien redefines this hidden subject of "tricksters" from a new, fresh perspective and he begins a journey down to the enchanted southwest desert to study the many elusive tricksters of North American indigenous myth and lore. He quickly realizes that for millennia, tricksters have been shrouded world-wide behind many guises such as skinwalkers, shapeshifters jokers, Loki, jinn, sorcerers, witches and other dark adepts.

They have burrowed deep inside human belief into the core of human culture. Cryptids, elementals, werewolves, vanishing hitchhikers, demons and dancing devils have been reported around the world for generations. But why? What are these forces? What is their agenda?

O'Brien journeys out into the field to determine whether these phenomenal masks worn by the tricksters can provide us a direct conduit to the unknown today in the 21st Century. Could it be that these denizens of phenomenal events may be attempting to communicate a warning to humanity in this uncertain age of prophesized change?

Chris reports from places such as the Navaho, Apache and Hopi Reservations of Arizona, the four sacred mountains of the Four Corners, Mexico's bizarre Zone of Silence and the Temple of the Inscriptions at Palenque in the Chiapan Highlands. O'Brien uncovers intriguing accounts that suggest there are beings walking among us able to utilize fantastic abilities. He realizes that subtle, deeply ingrained beliefs regarding these dark adepts with wild talents have subtly shaped cultural belief around the world for generations and today, these fantastic creatures continue to instill fear and awe."

One of the advisors on this book who has a background in the classified world became very concerned and initially tried to discourage me from getting further involved in the Michael Hill Case.[154] This advisor came to believe that the Michael Hill Case was most likely not an Annunaki case as Michael thinks, but rather a Jinn case. Personally, I think the case could still be an Annunaki Case because these beings seem to be cooperating with the American government to control release of UFO/ET related material. These beings became interested in Michael because of his involvement with Lockheed Senior Scientist Boyd Bushman.

That said I already had pointed out that Loki, the name of the alleged Annunaki in the Hill case, is the Norse god of mischief. I tend to waver between the two different explanations, but this advisor is quite adamant that this is a Jinn case and I value her informed advice. She writes:

> The REAL clue about the Jinns comes from the Tent "I dream of Genie" (JINN-ie) Michael Hill entered. He describes it as circular, well-furnished and difficult to exit. The Entities in there were Jinns, pretending to be Annunaki, their descriptions by Hill are pretty close to others, as Jinns can take any appearance they wish. Also they speak perfectly in whatever language needed. Their appearances vary, but Hill describes what he sees and it spells Jinns. They have a great sense of family and the comforting speech of the Son to the Father in the tent is also fairly typical Jinn. The words King, Sir, Father are good clues.
>
> They attract humans with orbs and are attracted to humans they feel they might possess. YES, we're talking possession and it is usually irreversible unless, as I've mentioned one goes to a Mullah who specializes in the language, mostly Arabic Koran prayers. The procedure is sometimes successful, the Jinn understand, but don't like to let the prey go. Total denial; of their existence, or making fun of them shows primary infestation, or readiness for an eventual contact.
>
> Hill is toxic, he's "theirs" but he is a victim like many others. Re-read carefully his trip into that tent, if you know Jinns, it's pretty much a classic. For more information you might have to

go to the sources, especially in Moslem countries, Saudi Arabia among others. The stupidest thing our American Intel tried in that country was to get in contact with Jinns to learn the secret of "portal" openings and trans-dimensional transportation.[139] This was discussed at the table of a Saudi Prince at a formal Embassy dinner and the Prince made it STOP immediately!

Gary Vey's then girlfriend got possessed by Jinns in Saudi Arabia chasing lights which wanted and granted communications. Despite the warnings of the Arab Guides, she became possessed and lost her mind. Her return to the States didn't help or cure her. I recognized the style of Jinn Communications in the Letter from the King and would guess that Ar Borden is also one of the victims. YES, they recruit! Do a thorough research, please.

There are male and female Djinn, and they do marry and have families. The family relatives are bonded together in clans that are ruled by a king. Good luck and watch out to get only good information, no matter how outlandish it reads. BTW, I don't care who else believes in the above, my wish is to spare some innocent from sticking his wet fingers in the Jinns' electrical outlets with the predicted results.

As we can see from the following article[156] by Philip Imbrogno that other UFO/ET investigators are well aware of the Jinns.

Who or What Are the Djinn

"God made the angels from light, he made man from the mud and the clay, and the Djinn from smokeless fire."

The passage above is from the Qur'an, and talks about a mysterious and ancient race of beings called Djinn. In the western world we are only familiar with man, angels, and fallen angels (often been referred to as demons). However, in the Muslim belief there are no fallen angels, but instead a different third race that is much older than the human race. The Qur'an makes it very clear that the Djinn existed before mankind; just how long before no one seems to know for sure. Some Islamic scholars say they lived on our planet a thousand years before humans, some say a thousand centuries. So just who are the Djinn?

The word "Djinn" (or Jinn) can be traced to the Persian word Janna or Jannu, which simply means hidden. This indicates that the Djinn are invisible to humans unless they want to be seen. According to Islamic belief the race of Djinn lived in desolate locations. These places are said to be haunted or cursed, and people kept away from these locations fearing they might invite the wrath of a Djinni for invading its privacy.

In modern terms the invisibility of the Djinn and living in a distant and hidden, desolate place could instead mean that they exist in a parallel dimension that is close to our own reality. They are out of reach and cannot be seen in the normal sense. It makes one wonder if shadow-like beings, which are reported around the world, are Djinn spying on us by pressing against the membrane that divides their world from ours.

In the Middle East, the Djinn race is considered to be very real. Even in the modern Arab world there are few who think the Djinn are simply legends. In Turkey, the Djinn are not only feared, but respected. From a very early age children are taught to stay away from them and never go to a place where their world borders our own.

In the western world we have little knowledge of this ancient race, but they have been mentioned in the media and some literature as the "Genie." Most of us in the United States are familiar with the 1960's television show I Dream of Jeannie. In this popular sitcom (which is still in syndication today), Barbara Eden plays a ditsy Djinni (Jeannie) who is released from captivity in a bottle by astronaut Tony Nelson (played by Larry Hagman). Jeannie falls in love with Tony and tries to help him in his life by granting wishes to obtain things that she thinks he may like or need. However, she always screws it up and makes poor Tony's life more complex.

As a result of this show, the animated Disney stories of Aladdin's Lamp, and other various tales of genies, we in the western world view Djinn or the genie as being harmless, even bumbling at times and easy to control. This could not be farther from the truth.

The people of the Middle East (in both ancient and modern times) consider the Djinn very dangerous and uncontrollable. The Qur'an states that, like a human being, Djinn have free will and can choose between good and evil. This means that not all Djinn are evil; some are good, and many are simply indifferent and don't want to be bothered by humans. The Qur'an has an entire Surah dedicated to the Djinn called Al-Jinn.

Djinn do not have a physical form, but they can take a number of different shapes. In the Arab country of Oman, residents in the villages near the Hajjar Mountains believe a Djinni can enter our world for an undetermined period of time. The Hajjar Mountains in north-eastern Oman are the highest mountain range in the eastern Arabian Peninsula. It is deep in these mountains that Arabs believe is one of the places in which Djinn can enter our world.

To go unnoticed Djinn like to take the shapes of a human or an animal. The mountain people of Oman believe you can tell a Djinni from a human by looking into their eyes (since, though they can mimic the human body, they have difficulty with the eyes). The eyes of a Djinn would be yellow with elongated pupils. Since they have this difficulty and don't want to be discovered, most of them will take the shape of a snake, dog, or some other animal that is common in the area.

There are male and female Djinn, and they do marry and have families. The family relatives are bonded together in clans that are ruled by a king. Djinn children seem to be very curious about humans, and will often appear as fairies, gnomes, elves, and other creatures prominent in mythology. Although Djinn children are taught by their parents to fear humans, their curiosity often gets the better of them, and occasionally they will attempt to interact with human children. Perhaps parents should take the stories of their child's imaginary friend more seriously.

Islamic law forbids humans to marry Djinn, but according to legend it has been done in the past. The offspring of such a union are said to be physical in form, but are sociopaths that do not know right from wrong. In Iran and Iraq crazed serial killers are thought to be the result of a union between a Djinn and human. It is also said that the children of this unholy union have great intelligence, strength, and charisma, as well as incredible powers of mind control, which comes from their Djinn half. The people of

Saudi Arabia believe girls who have very hairy legs are suspect of having Djinn as one of their parents.

Islamic historical accounts of the Queen of Sheba (known to the Arabs as Balqis or Balkis) say her father was a human and mother was a Djinn. Although she was not in line for the throne, she was able to rise to that position before her fifteenth birthday. Legend says she had great power over the minds of others, especially men, and controlled people to murder for her. Her powers of persuasion were so great that she was able to control the great king Solomon. Some say she did this out of revenge, since Solomon was given mastery over all the Djinn and subjected them to slave labor to build the Temple and his cities. The queen of Sheba's mother was one of the enslaved Djinn in Solomon's service.

In Islam there are no "fallen angels." This is because Muslims believe angels do not have free will, and since they were created by Allah from the purest of light they cannot be corrupted. The powerful beings who fell from grace were Djinn. One Djinn named Iblis who possessed the power of an angel refused to bow to man at the command of Allah. As a result, Iblis was cast out of heaven. The goal of Iblis is to corrupt other Djinn and destroy the human race.

Persian legends say the Djinn once lived in this world. They became very powerful and developed technology that was much greater than what we even have today. The Djinn race began warring with each other and polluting the physical universe. Allah, in an attempt to save the Djinn race from destroying themselves, sent an army of angels to remove them from this world and placed most of the Djinn in a world parallel to ours where they could do no more harm to themselves or other beings. Very powerful Djinn who fell from God's grace along with Iblis were imprisoned in bottles, rings, and great caves around the planet. One of these alleged caves is called Majis–Al Jinn, located in north-eastern Oman. My exploration of this cave is documented in The Vengeful Djinn.[157]

According to the legend, many of the Djinn race resent having to give up this world, which they still consider their home, to humans. They want their home back and will do whatever it takes. In our book *The Vengeful Djinn: Unveiling the Hidden Agenda of Genies*, Rosemary Ellen Guiley[158] and I, after years of research, unmask the Djinn and reveal the facts and legends about this ancient race of beings that have coexisted with the human race for countless centuries. If you choose to fear one thing in your life, fear the Djinn.

It would appear that the CIA, the Bigelow foundation along with its scientists and intelligence professionals, people like Eric Davis and John Alexander, still ignore warnings and retain a strong interest in understanding and developing the special powers of the Jinns to open portals and other manipulations of our perceptions and our reality.[159] Alleged Jinn activity monitored by scientists and intelligence professionals at the Skinwalker Ranch is well documented in the book, *The Hunt For The Skinwalker*, by Colm Kelleher, Ph.D., and George Knapp. The following is the book description at Amazon.

"The author of the controversial bestseller *Brain Trust,* brings his scientific expertise to the chilling true story of unexplained phenomena on Utah's Skinwalker Ranch - and challenges us with a new vision of reality. For more than fifty years, the bizarre events at a remote Utah ranch have ranged from the perplexing to the wholly terrifying. Vanishing and mutilated cattle. Unidentified Flying Objects.
The appearance of huge, otherworldly creatures. Invisible objects emitting magnetic fields with the power to spark a cattle stampede. Flying orbs of light with dazzling maneuverability and lethal consequences. For one family, life on the Skinwalker Ranch had become a life under siege by an unknown enemy or enemies. Nothing else could explain the horrors that surrounded them - perhaps science could.
Leading a first-class team of research scientists on a disturbing odyssey into the unknown, Colm Kelleher spent hundreds of days and nights on the Skinwalker property and experienced firsthand many of its haunting mysteries. With investigative reporter George Knapp - the only journalist allowed to witness and documents the team's work - Kelleher chronicles in superb detail the spectacular happenings the team observed personally, and the theories of modern physics behind the phenomena. Far from the

coldly detached findings one might expect, their conclusions are utterly hair-raising in their implications. Opening a door to the unseen world around us, 'Hunt for the Skinwalker' is a clarion call to expand our vision far beyond what we know."

Here is an example the paranormal activity at the Skinwalker Ranch indicating some kind of portal:

> The "Tunnel" - On August 25, 1997, two members of NIDS, Jim and Mike (not their real names) are on a night watch, on the edge of a bluff, a hundred feet above the pasture, where some strange events have taken place before. Around 2:30 A.M., they begin to see a faint light just above the ground, invisible to the eyes, but visible though powerful night vision binoculars, amplifying electronically low level ambient light. It's a dirty yellow light which expands to form a kind of "tunnel" about four feet in diameter.
> Suddenly, Mike perceives a dark creature, at least six feet tall, crawling out of it and walking away, whereupon the tunnel begins to shrink, and soon disappear. However, his companion, Jim, claims to have only seen the light. And although they have scientific equipment to measure radiation levels and magnetic spikes, they fail to record anything unusual. They have taken pictures, but "the photos were disappointing, showing only a single very faint blurry light in one and nothing on the rest of the roll of film."

In an article by Gary Bekkum, there is more information linking Dr Eric Davis, author of the Air Force teleportation report, to the activities at the Skinwalker Ranch. Now we see that that not only is the CIA into all this, but also the Air Force, DARPA and the DIA.

> "Last year the Air Force received a great deal of flak from the press about a research paper they commissioned to examine the use of teleportation for military purposes. Apparently the journalists didn't realize that quantum teleportation has been an active area of mainstream research, ever since it was discovered by a

team at IBM in the 1990's. MIT Professor Seth Lloyd has been researching the use of quantum teleportation for communication networks. Lloyd's support includes DARPA, the Defense Advanced Research Projects Agency. Recently he also developed an interest in quantum gravity, the elusive theory that would unite Einstein's theory of bending space and time with the foundation stone of all modern electronics and atomic engineering: the quantum theory.

In the mid 1990's, Dr Stuart Hameroff at the University of Arizona, and Oxford's Sir Roger Penrose proposed that quantum processes might be involved in the emergence of human consciousness. Penrose is well known for his work in mathematics and the physics of black holes. The idea of creating a synthesis of quantum teleportation and brain function quickly followed as a theory of telepathy. In the Penrose-Hameroff theory, the shape of certain structures in the brain are controlled by the location of single electrons, the quantum of electric charge, and these structures resemble quantum computing circuits.

Seth Lloyd's theory of quantum gravity is based on quantum computing circuits. In other words, Lloyd believes that spacetime is fundamentally a computational quantum process. Is this beginning to sound a little bit like "The Matrix?" It should. The STAR GATE legacy stands as evidence that the military will make operational use of anything appearing to offer a technical advantage, whether or not there is scientific support for the technology.

One unnamed high level source has confirmed that paranormal data was discussed by members of an elite government committee. Strange events investigated by Las Vegas businessman Bob Bigelow's National Institute of Discovery Science (NIDS) have been the topic of discussion between members at DIA sponsored meetings on the threats of emerging technologies.

Dr Eric Davis, author of the highly controversial report on teleportation commissioned by the U.S. Air Force, has been very forthcoming answering questions about observations of strange creatures and other anomalous phenomena made by NIDS personnel at Bigelow's Skinwalker Ranch. The Skinwalker is a shape shifting being said to haunt this remote part of Utah near Salt Lake City.

Strange creatures, strange objects, floating black triangles, animal mutilations, disintegrated dogs, telepathic messages - a smorgasbord of every strange and imaginable terror has been served to those unfortunates spending any period of time at the ranch. The strangeness is reported in "Hunt for the Skinwalker," by former NIDS staff scientist Colm A. Kelleher, and veteran UFO reporter George Knapp. In the Air Force teleportation study Davis examines potential scientific explanations for the weird phenomena, including space-time wormholes, teleportation, and manipulation of the quantum vacuum.

If Star Gate was any measure of the interest displayed by the DIA in this kind of weirdness, it wouldn't be surprising to learn that the Utah ranch is the subject of at least a few confidential memos for the record. Perhaps DIA would like to 'read in' a Skinwalker or two as part of their secret paranormal war on terror."

My friends at Open Seti have been very helpful in finding links for this book and for this Chapter. As I worked on this Chapter they sent me this helpful link. William J. Baldwin Ph.D.'s book called *Close Encounters of the Possession Kind.*[160] *Close Encounters of the Possession Kind,* goes way beyond the Jinns and gets into spirit possession and other kinds of phenomena that he as a clinical therapist finds in his practice.

Edith Fiore wrote a small forward to Baldwin's book that pretty much sums up this work for those that may have an interest in this area of research. This is beginning to get into the really big picture that I intend to sum up on my Chapter on, Reincarnation, OBE and NDE so I don't want to get into it in detail here. Dr Edith Flore, Ph.D. said:

"Dr William Baldwin's book, CE- VI: Close Encounters Of The Possession Kind, systematically shows the reader the various kinds of spirit attachments, including dark force entities and earthbound lost souls. However, he goes beyond what has been described before by clearly examining case histories that involved attachments, or take-overs, by aliens or extraterrestrials. Not only that, he demonstrates how some attachments by ETs have been manipulated by dark forces intervention. Besides showing the reader what has happened, he demonstrates the effectiveness of his releasement therapies in eliminating any of, and all of, these types of attachments.

His stunning case histories, showing him at work in resolving those debilitating conditions, gives the reader not only information, but hope. The knowledge that one does not have to be burdened by these, at times life-threatening, intrusions. His book is also a manual for any mental health worker open-minded enough to put the client's welfare above previously accepted belief systems or what is currently accepted as conventional therapy. He shows that these conditions do, indeed, happen, and, best of all, they can be resolved in a loving, human, and effective way. Dr Baldwin's work is another of his contributions to the understanding and relief of human suffering. Bravo! Dr Baldwin.

Dr Baldwin himself had this to say about his book.

"This book describes the conflicts which seem to be produced by the intrusive, selfish, opportunistic, sometimes confused, often malevolent entities and energies that interfere with living people. Humans are sovereign beings, and have the right to live without such interference from aliens, entities, other human beings, or government agencies of any kind.

Most of the case histories and dialogues in this book have been taken from actual sessions with people in our counseling practice and training courses. The general information is pieced together from the clinical sessions of many clients. There is a consistency in the personal narratives, a pattern which can neither be denied nor ignored. The material is organized here in a coherent picture; the details have not been embellished in any way. My own conclusions, assumptions, and speculations are identified as such."

It's obvious to me that modern psychology and psychiatric practice have a long way to go in understanding the human condition and the nature of the really big picture, and for that reason they are often not able to effect cures, but are only able to diminish the symptoms with drugs and therapy if they are fortunate. As we can see from the Skinwalker and other cases, the national security services are also coming at all this from their own security perspectives, just as the therapists are attempting to do from their healing perspectives.

We can only hope that the knowledge of these, for lack of a better word, spiritual entities with special powers, will be used to protect and preserve human sovereignty and alleviate human suffering. This rather than increase the suffering of humanity if the investigators and globalist power brokers become enamored by the seductive power over others and so surrender to these powerful dark forces. The danger here is that those that investigate become possessed, but the opportunity is that we may one day free ourselves and others of these psychic predators and parasites that inhabit our bodies, our emotions and our minds, that seem to be obstructing our evolutionary development.

CHAPTER ELEVEN

TAKING BACK OUR FUTURE

"Fifty men have run America and that's a high figure." Joseph Kennedy

"Every man is equally entitled to protection by law, but when the laws undertake to add... artificial distinctions, to grant titles, gratuities, and exclusive privileges, to make the rich richer and the potent more powerful, the humble members of society; the farmers, mechanics, and laborers, who have neither the time nor the means of securing like favors to themselves, have a right to complain of the injustice of their government." Andrew Jackson.

"The refusal of King George III to allow the colonies to operate an honest money system, which freed the ordinary man from the clutches of the money manipulators, was probably the prime cause of the revolution." Benjamin Franklin

If we are to take back our future it is important to understand how the Western Global Oligarchy operates, and how it undermines and destroys democratic principles. The accelerating erosion of the secrecy surrounding the Bilderberg Group, thanks to alternative media and social activism, now gives us names, faces and addresses of the globalist mafia. There has been an almost total mass media blackout, of even the name of this group from its inception, until only recently. Bilderberger's David Rockefeller said:

"We are grateful to The Washington Post, The New York Times, Time magazine and other great publications whose directors have attended our meetings and respected their promises of discretion for almost forty years. ... It would have been impossible for us to develop our plan for the world if we had been subject to the bright lights of publicity during those years. But, the world is now much more sophisticated and prepared to march towards a world government."

The name of the Bilderberg Group comes from its first annual meeting in 1954 at the Bilderberg Hotel. The group has Nazi and fascist roots, but the roots go back hundreds of years. There are around 100 regular members, and perhaps forty more invited participants, that are rotated in and out of the Group. It seems to operate as the action arm of even more secret family groups; the Rothschild's being the most powerful and influential. Professor Mike Peters writes the following in, *The Bilderberg Group and the Project of European Unification.*

"Bilderberg' takes its name from the hotel, belonging to Prince Bernhard of the Netherlands, near Arnhem, where, in May 1954 the first meeting took place of what has ever since been called the Bilderberg Group. While the name persisted, its meetings are held at different locations. Prince Bernhard himself (who, incidentally, was actually German not Dutch) was chair until 1976 when he was forced to resign because of the Lockheed bribery scandal.

The possible significance of this group may be gleaned from the status of its participants: the membership comprises those individuals who would, on most definitions, be regarded as members of the 'ruling class' in Western Europe and North America-In particular, the conferences brought together important figures in most of the largest international corporations with leading politicians and prominent intellectuals (in both academia and journalism).

Moreover, virtually all the European institutions we take for granted today, or treat as if they 'emerged' as a matter of course, from the ECSC, EEC and Euratom down to the present European Union, were conceived, designed and brought into existence through the agency of the people involved in Bilderberg."

Prince Bernhard was a member of the Nazi SS but he claims that he became a member out of necessity. We also have discovered that the fascist Allen Dulles also plays prominently in the formation of the Bilderberg Group. Some even claim that the covert Bilderberg Group was the covert Plan B that the Nazis followed after their overt attempt at world dominion failed with World War Two.

Its members are some of the most influential and powerful people on the planet, that include high level politicians, royalty, wealthy industrialists and bankers, high level military, and intelligence operatives. The group has a steering committee, and at its annual conference, the group breaks down into many different committees that are expected to promote individual committee agendas globally.

While the Group as a whole only meets on an annual basis, investigative conspiracy investigators and activists are aware of sub-groups that meet more frequently. I very much expect that one of these sub-groups has close ties to the MJ 12 committee, and what I call the alien resource cartel corporations, like General Electric.

Kissinger a regular Bilderberg attendee has long been rumored to be chairman of the MJ 12 committee. The present day NSA director attended the 2012 meeting, so let us not forget the comments on UFOs that former NSA director Bobby Inman made. More than likely he was a past Bilderberg attendee.

Fortunately for global society, the Russian and other oligarchies around the world are suspicious of, and even hate the western oligarchies. These deep divisions are now contributing to slow down the western push toward global dominance and dominion. English Pravda soon after the 2012 Bilderberg meeting had this to say:

"The end of the Bilderberg meeting means impending trouble for the world. The good news is that Independent journalists are digging the mainstream media's grave as each day passes. Who needs the mainstream media when you have videos from educated people? The protesters that gather with them are wrecking the plans of these global elitists."

So we have the Russian oligarchy upset with western oligarchy meddling in their affairs, complementing the American and UK alternative media and activist's exposure of the 2012 Bilderberg meeting in Virginia. They thank conspiracy investigators reporters and activists, like Alex Jones of infowar.com, theintelhub.com, as well as long time investigator Jim Tucker and the UK Guardian's Charlie Skelton, for their coverage and demonstrations to expose the Bilderberg Group. Pravda says:

"You can bet that Putin will not let the Bilderbergs interfere. He swore at his inaugural address May 7th, "to protect the sovereignty and independence" of Russia. I'm sure he's on the same list as Ron Paul. Vladimir Putin is the only one besides China who is not afraid to physically oppose the Bilderbergs agenda with military force."

Paul Hellyer, former Canadian Minister of National Defense, really understands not only global politics but exopolitics as well. In this address called, Global Fraud: Global Hope, to the International UFO Congress on March 01, 2011 he discusses the macro context of global politics and economics within which stellar exopolitics is exerting considerable influence on people's everyday lives and those of their children.

Paul even discusses the Tall White Extraterrestrials and a two hour long conversation he had with Charles Hall. Paul has the credentials and has done such a good job in this article exposing the corruption within our global society, that has resulted in the complete lack of transparency, and the Breakaway Civilization, that I am publishing this article in its entirety in this chapter.

Global Fraud: Global Hope
By Paul Hellyer

The world financial system is a total fraud. It is one gargantuan Ponzi scheme, no better than the one Bernie Madoff used to swindle his friends and neighbors, and thousands of times worse if you add up the total number of victims it has ripped off over countless generations.

The principal difference between the two schemes is that Madoff was acting outside the law while the international banking cartel has persuaded generation after generation of monarchs, presidents and prime ministers to provide legislative protection for their larceny.

The banks Ponzi scheme is alarmingly simple. They lend the same money to several people or institutions at the same time and collect interest on it from each. What the banks really lend, however, is their credit, and what they take back in compensation for that privilege is a debt that must be repaid with interest.

The number of times they lend the same money is called leverage. The practice is as old as the hills but for our purposes we can start with the goldsmiths of Lombard Street in London, England, who accepted deposits for which they issued certificates redeemable on demand. They paid their depositors a nominal interest rate on the understanding that they could lend the money to their customers at higher interest rates. They soon found that they could lend more than they had in their vaults because only a few depositors came in to redeem their gold or silver at any one time. It was a scam. It was illegal.

Nevertheless they got away with it for a long while and the scam was legitimized when the Bank of England was chartered to help King William finance his war. Rich people subscribed £1,200,000 in gold and silver, as capital, to found the bank, which then was lent to the government at 8 percent. To show his appreciation the King allowed the bank to print £1,200,000 in banknotes and lend them at high interest rates. In effect, the bank was allowed to lend the same money twice – once to the government and once to the people.

Over the years, due to the avarice of the banks and the complicity of the politicians, that ratio has increased dramatically. In the early days of the 20th century, federal chartered U.S. banks were required to keep gold reserves of 25 percent. That means they were allowed to lend the same money four times. I remember when Canadian banks were required to maintain a cash reserve of 8 percent. That means they were allowed to lend the same money 12½ times.

Today, thanks to Milton Friedman's irrational flip-flop from being a proponent of 100% cash reserves to the opposite extreme of zero reserves, and the adoption of his ideas by the major central banks of the world in 1974, multiples have increased dramatically – in some cases to as much as 20 to 1 or more. Banks only keep enough cash to meet day-to-day demands for those few customers who go in and request it, and consequently the fraud is virtually total.

The system works this way. Suppose that you want to borrow $35,000 to buy a new car. You visit your friendly banker and ask for a loan. He or she will ask you for collateral – some stocks, bonds, a second mortgage on your house or cottage or, if you are unable to supply any of these, the co-signature of a well-to-do friend or relative. When the collateral requirement is satisfied you will be asked to sign a note for the principal amount with an agreed rate of interest.

When the paperwork is complete, and the note signed, your banker will make an entry on the bank's computer and, presto, a $35,000 credit will appear in your account which you can use to buy your car. The important point is that seconds earlier that money did not exist. It was created out of thin air – so to speak.

The banking equation is a species of double-entry bookkeeping where your note becomes an asset on the bank's books, and the new money that was deposited to your account is a liability. The profit for the bank comes from the difference between the low rate of interest, if any, you would be paid on your deposit if you didn't spend the borrowed money immediately, and the much higher rate you would be obliged to pay on your note – the technical term is "the spread."

At some point, however, you have to pay off your note and any interest owing. And not only you but everyone else who has borrowed "money" from banks – including governments which, by the way, own the right to print money but that have irresponsibly handed the right over to an elite group of private bankers. Anyone who defaults is in big trouble. Individuals who default will have the assets they pledged as collateral seized by the bank. A government that is in danger of defaulting will be forced to borrow from the International Monetary Fund, which will then tell that government how to run its affairs including cutting back on services and selling off public assets to the international vulture capitalists.

In reality, then, the banks have turned the world into one humongous pawn shop. You hock your stocks, bonds, house, business, rich mother-in-law or country and the bank(s) will give you a loan based on the value of the collateral.

A world system where all the money is created as debt is a perpetual disaster in the making. It is like a giant balloon that the banks pump full of debt. The balloon gets larger and larger until the debt load becomes too heavy to carry, and then it is like a balloon with a pin stuck in it. The system crashes and thousands or sometimes millions of innocent people lose their jobs, homes, farms and businesses.

Almost any high school student should be able to see that any monetary system based on debt creation is totally insane. The total world debt, mathematically, is always tending toward infinity – and there is no possible way of paying it off. The real money (legal tender) to do so doesn't exist and the real economy that depends on cash to grow shifts into low gear whenever the supply of credit money dries up.

Not surprisingly, there have been 25 recessions and depressions in the United States since 1890. In several cases, including the Great Depression of the 1930's and the current Great Recession, the evidence indicates that the meltdown was anticipated by a few insiders who helped trigger the catastrophe.

In the wake of the Great Depression, the U.S. Senate Banking and Currency Committee Report that became widely known as the Pecora Report on the Practices of Stock Exchanges indicated that there were insiders who benefitted from the crash. "Legal chicanery and pitch darkness were the banker's stoutest allies," Pecora wrote in his memoir. Similar allegations were evident in Charles Ferguson damning documentary "Inside Job," relating to the 2007-2008 meltdown. These reports and other historical evidence prove beyond any doubt that much of Wall Street is rotten to the core. It has become one gigantic millstone around the neck of both the American and world economies.

The collateral damage from the recent meltdown has been staggering. The U.S. Bureau of Labor estimated that 8.4 million jobs were lost in the U.S. alone. Most countries experienced similar dramatic losses. The reduction in asset values worldwide has been estimated at $20 trillion U.S. dollars, yet not a single one of the culprits is in jail. You would think that someone would have had the decency to launch a class action for at least $10 trillion against every individual and every organization that contributed to the catastrophe in any way.

It boggles the mind that a system so vulnerable to manipulation would ever have come into existence in the first place. The evolution did not happen by accident. It was not guided by the mythical invisible hand of Adam Smith. On the contrary, for more than a century-and-a-half, it was engineered by the barely visible hand of the Rothschild family and its allies, and since World War II by the Rockefeller family. The two dynasties combined forces to exercise influence on many fronts sheltered by the cloak of secrecy established by the Bilderberg Group.

The long term influence of the banking cartel is incalculable. Their biggest coup was the establishment of the Federal Reserve System in the United States. The big New York banks really didn't like the idea of genuine competition, so a small group held a secret meeting at the private resort of J.P. Morgan on Jekyll Island, off the coast of Georgia. Their scheme, devised by Paul M. Warburg, and subsequently adopted by Congress, is a legal private monopoly of the U.S. money supply operated for the benefit of the few under the guise of protecting and promoting the public interest.

It is a tribute to the skill of the international bankers that they were able to draft a bill, revise it, change its name and make the few window dressing compromises necessary to get it adopted by Congress just before Christmas when quite a few Representatives must have been dreaming of sugar plum fairies instead of exercising due diligence. Only Charles Lindberg Sr. seemed to grasp the essence of what was going on.

To put it bluntly, the Congress transferred its sovereign constitutional right to create money to the sole custody of a group of private bankers. The magnitude of the hoist is unprecedented in the history of the world – the numbers now are in the high trillions.

Soon after the bill was passed the magnitude of the tragedy began to be recognized. William Jennings Bryan, who acted as Democrat whip, later said: "In my long political career, the one thing I genuinely regret is my part in getting the banking and currency legislation (Federal Reserve Act of 1913) enacted into law." President Woodrow Wilson, just three years after passage of the Act, wrote: "A great industrial nation is controlled by its system of credit. Our system of credit is concentrated (in the Federal Reserve System).

The growth of the nation, therefore, and all our activities are in the hands of a few men.... We have come to be one of the worst ruled, one of the most completely controlled and dominated governments in the civilized world." But the bill was not repealed; almost 100 years later the sell-out is still the law. This makes you wonder what the people's representatives have been doing to earn their salaries.

The people in charge of the original deception were very far-seeing. They realized that when future governments had to borrow from them they would need a constant income stream to pay the interest on the bonds. So they persuaded the government to introduce income taxes, first as a temporary measure, but later permanently, so it would be able to meet its obligations to the bondholders. In fiscal year 2005 total individual income taxes in the U.S. totaled $927 billion. Of that amount $352 billion, or 38%, was required just to pay interest on the federal debt. The figure would be higher now.

The banksters, as they were often called, then decided that an independent press might catch on to the chicanery. Oscar Callaway is reported in the Congressional Record of February 9, 1917 as follows.

"In March, 1915, the J.P. Morgan interests, the steel, shipbuilding, and powder interests, and their subsidiary organizations, got together 12 men high up in the newspaper world, and employed them to select the most influential newspapers in the United States and sufficient number of them to control generally the policy of the daily press of the United States... They found it was only necessary to purchase the control of 25 of the greatest papers. The 25 papers were agreed upon; emissaries were sent to purchase the policy, national and international, of these papers; an editor was furnished for each paper to properly supervise and edit information regarding the questions of preparedness, militarism, financial policies, and other things of national and international nature considered vital to the interests of the purchasers [and to suppress] everything in opposition to the wishes of the interests served."

It has been suggested that the Bilderberger Group may have taken a leaf from the Morgan precedent to protect their interests in the late 20th and early 21st centuries. That is impossible to prove because its members are sworn to secrecy, and the press won't report on its meetings. Could it be mere coincidence that the monetary system, the downside of globalization and the decades-long cover-up of the extraterrestrial presence and technology (especially the clean energy sources that would impact the value of oil stocks), the three subjects of most direct beneficial interests of the banksters, are the three subjects that are avoided like the plague by the mainline press?

I am not willing to go so far as to say that the men behind the international banking system are evil men because their thoughts are private. But Sir Josiah, later Baron Stamp, a former director of the Bank of England, has given us a rare snapshot of the truth.

"Banking was conceived in iniquity and was born in sin. The Bankers own the earth. Take it away from them, but leave them the power to create money, and with a flick of the pen they will create enough money to buy it back again. However, take that power away from them and all the great fortunes like mine will disappear, and they ought to disappear, for this would be a happier and better world to live in. But if you wish to remain the slaves of Bankers, and pay the cost of your own slavery, let them continue to create money."

In the latest meltdown of 2007-2008, the Fed acted quickly to prevent the Ponzi pyramid from collapsing completely. It printed trillions of dollars to bail out the banks and a few industries that were highly indebted to banks.

But what did the Fed do for the taxpayers whose money was so wildly diluted to save the banks? Nothing! They were left to fend for themselves. Millions of people lost their jobs, their farms, their houses, their hopes, and their dignity as a result of circumstances beyond their control. The taxpayers bailed out the banks, but got nothing in return.

The same is true of governments who came so quickly to the rescue. As a result of the meltdown their revenues were decreased so they were forced to incur or increase their deficits, as well as to start cutting back on essential services.

The Fed pretended to be helping stimulate the economy by reducing interest rates to near zero. It would be an interesting exercise to find out what happened to all of this low-cost money. It would be a good subject for Congressional attention. How much did the banks use to buy up domestic and foreign assets at fire-sale prices? Was any of it used by financial institutions to try to corner world food markets and raise prices at a time when millions are starving?

No doubt some taxpayers did take advantage of the low interest rates available but were they warned about the old bait and switch game? Anyone who acquires assets with cheap money runs the risk of losing their property when the Fed ultimately raises rates. It's all part of the boom-bust cycle inherent in our infinitely silly monetary system.

The Economics Profession

What does all this have to say about the economics profession? What it really says isn't fit to print. Someone once said that if you put 20 economists in a room you will get 21 opinions.

That is not my experience. If you get 20 economists together they are likely to give you one stock answer, or at most two. And if there is one dissenter he or she is likely to be drowned out by the 19, squawking like a flock of parrots the words memorized from what their professors taught them.

I have witnessed this herd-like mentality firsthand. When I was first elected to the House of Commons in 1949 there were only a handful of Keynesians in Ottawa. Twenty years later nearly everyone was a Keynesian including, I am told, Richard Nixon.

At that time there were only a few monetarists around. But they spread like mushrooms and soon dominated the economic landscape. It reached the stage when Keynes was anathema, and it was almost impossible to get a tenured position in a school of economics unless you were part of Milton Friedman's monetarist revolution.

Apparently little if any thought was given to the possibility that neither Keynes nor Friedman had got it right. The former was a bit closer to reality than the latter, but both theories foundered on the rocks of one inescapable truth. Both assumed that the economic system is self-correcting, yet more than two centuries of experience has demonstrated clearly that it is not! Someone has to be at the tiller charged with steering clear of the shoals and rocks of economic disaster and that person has to be someone who is responsible to the people and not the self-serving boom-busters.

Global Warming

While bank reform is the most urgent problem facing the world today, it is global warming that has equally or even greater long term consequences. It is a total fraud to pretend that we have thirty, forty or fifty years to reduce greenhouse gas emissions. There are reputable scientists who think we may already have crossed the Rubicon. Even if that is true, we can't roll the clock back; we can only influence the present and the future. Each of the past three decades has been the hottest on record, according to a report released in July 2010 by the U.S. National Oceanic and Atmospheric Administration. The report pulled together data from ten climate change indicators, measured by 160 research groups in 48 countries.

The data shows sea levels are rising; snow cover in the Arctic melts earlier; the average air temperature is rising; ocean surface temperatures have also been rising; the summer sea ice cover is declining; sea air temperature has been rising; for 19 years glaciers have lost mass; land air temperature has been rising – a global trend.

All of this puts the lie to the propaganda of the oil industry aimed at creating doubt about the reliability of scientific data. Taking a leaf from the tobacco industry, which managed to create doubt about the safety of their products years after they privately knew the facts, the oil industry has been attempting to raise doubt about the urgency of replacing fossil fuels with clean energy, and with considerable success. In their case, however, the stakes are higher. It was a tragedy that so many people lost their lives through lack of sound information about the consequences of smoking. In the case of global warming, however, many times more people will have their lives put at risk.

Still the oil cartel is making plans as if nothing is going to change, and that we are going to be stuck with a fatal oil economy for decades until the damage is irreversible. It is too late to begin more offshore drilling. It is too late for new developments in the Alberta oil sands. It is too late for more noisy windmill farms. The transition must start now, with a 10-year deadline.

Is that possible? Of course it's possible but only with the kind of mobilization essential to win a war for survival. One excuse for inaction has been the lack of money due to government deficits and debt. But that obstacle can be overcome in less than a year if governments and legislatures change the system and exercise their sovereign right to make what is physically possible financially possible. Heaven knows there are millions of unemployed workers worldwide waiting to rise to the challenge.

The other major obstacle has been a lack of consensus on the form of clean energy to use to replace fossil fuels. And that brings me, finally, to the subject of the day, the extraterrestrial presence and technology.

The Extraterrestrial Presence and Technology

It is a fraud for the U.S. government to pretend that it is not interested in UFOs. In fact, it has been a matter of high and probably pre-eminent interest for decades.

An early Canadian ufologist, Wilbert Smith, who was a senior employee at the Department of Transport, where I became minister not long after his retirement, wrote a top secret memorandum to the Controller of Communications dated November 21, 1950 asking permission to set up a group to study the geomagnetic aspects of UFOs propulsion systems.

As part of his memorandum Smith said that he had made discreet enquiries through the Canadian embassy staff in Washington where he obtained the following information.

(a) The matter is the most highly classified subject in the United States Government, rating higher even than the H-bomb.
(b) Flying saucers exit.
(c) Their modus operandi is unknown but concentrated effort is being made by a small group, headed by Doctor Vannevar Bush.
(d) The entire matter is considered by the United States authorities to be of tremendous significance.

So, Dr Vannevar Bush, one of America's pre-eminent scientists, and a team of experts he had assembled, were already working on back-engineering by 1950. (Back-engineering is the combined art and science of analyzing an object, in this case parts of a crashed vehicle, in order to determine its characteristics for possible replication or adaptation.)

Many people who are interested in the subject of UFOs use one of the Roswell crashes of July 1947 as their starting line. Recent evidence, however, confirms that the U.S. Army Air Corps was in the crash retrieval business before that. Paola Harris, on July 5, 2010 interviewed two men, Jose Padilla and Reme Baca, aged 9 and 7 at the time, who witnessed a saucer crash on Padilla land near San Antonio, New Mexico, in August 1945. In her new book Exopolitics: Stargate to a New Reality, Paola gives the detailed account of what these men saw as children, the actual crash, the creatures' appearance, the pieces of the craft they took, the military clean up, and an in-depth analysis of the significance of the case.

I had the opportunity to chat with Reme Baca by telephone recently and the thing that stuck in my mind was that when Sgt Avila came to ask Mr. Padilla's permission to enter his land to retrieve the "object," he referred to it as "an experimental weather balloon." That was exactly the same ruse that Brigadier General Roger Ramey used in reference to the Roswell incident two years later. Apparently there was a considerable lack of imagination on the Army's part.

In later years the Air Force, that had succeeded the Army Air Corps, became much more sophisticated in its misinformation and disinformation techniques. These include having the Star Visitors portrayed in movies as sinister beings that we should be fearful of – probably without justification.

Another fascinating case that Paola brought to my attention not long ago was that of Charles Hall, the physicist and information technology professional, who worked as an airman meteorologist at the USAF bombing and gunnery range at Indian Springs, Nevada, in the 1960s.

Charles worked in close contact with Tall Whites, a species that I had been previously unfamiliar with. Over a period of months he learned to lose his fear of the aliens who lived, worked and played on Air Force property.

In a two-hour telephone conversation he gave me many of the characteristics of the Whites, described the scout ships in which they travelled and said most of them were assembled in the U.S. Furthermore, he talked about the mother ship arriving on the nights of the full moon and sliding into its hangar cut into the side of a mountain nearby.

It was all fascinating stuff that included the fact that the Tall Whites were working closely with the USAF and exchanging technology in the mid-1960's. So it is very difficult to imagine how much has been achieved in 60 years of back-engineering alien technology that was much more advanced than our own. There is no doubt that myriad scientists, technicians, and many of America's most advanced aircraft and weapons corporations must have achieved what would have been classified as miracles just a few years ago.

It is alleged that the U.S. engineers working in one of the vast underground facilities have built vehicles that are virtually indistinguishable from those of other planets. If this is true, to what purpose will they be put, and will it be for good purposes or military purposes?

The area of discovery that is most relevant to this presentation, however, is the question of exotic energy sources. Years ago it was reported that both zero point and cold fusion energy had been developed. These are energy sources that could facilitate the 10-year target date and not only revolutionize the world for the better, but help preserve it as a happy habitat for Earthlings.

In the unlikely event that these sources are not yet commercially viable, all we would have to do is ask one of the friendly species to help us and they would because they are deeply concerned about our stewardship. In the event that we are still treating them as enemy aliens, and doing our best to shoot them down, we would have to curb our lust of conflict and adopt an acceptable level of intergalactic civility.

Better People

The third essential change is for us as individuals. A just and peaceful world is not possible when it is riddled with graft, fraud and corruption of all kinds. Greed is king and mammon rules the world.

Institutions have to change too. For centuries major religions have been selling their alleged superiority or exclusiveness at the point of a sword, leading to the deaths of thousands of innocents. The three Abrahamic religions, for example, all claims the inside route to paradise. Mathematically that is impossible. It is far more probable, mathematically, that they are all wrong and that the truth is larger and more inclusive.

Ancient and modern history both suggest that there is no hope of a just and peaceful world unless all religions, and those with no religion, forget their differences and start working together to build the Kingdom of God on Earth. I define this as a world where every child can expect food to eat, clean water to drink, adequate clothing to wear, a roof overhead, access to medical support and enough education to be able to determine how best he or she can serve humankind positively, with dignity and self-fulfillment.

What a wonderful world that would be! But it would require a 180-degree change in policies and priorities and a serious effort to apply the Golden Rule that all religions claim as a common thread.

The application of the Golden Rule would mean an end to empire building, and the pursuit of military power and advantage. The U.S., for example, would have to stop being its own worst enemy. The declaration of the war on terror was the biggest strategic blunder I have seen.

On the 11th day of September 2001, following the attacks on the World Trade Center, the United States enjoyed the sympathy of the world, including Arab states and populations. The threat from al-Qaeda was limited and quite within the potential of police and intelligence operations to cope with.

The situation changed dramatically with the launch of a war on Iraq. The goodwill began to evaporate overnight. Soon, instead of a few dozen insurgents the numbers of young Muslims willing to die for their cause multiplied to thousands and a great chasm of hate and mistrust enveloped much of the world.

The U.S. has consistently refused to be even-handed in the Israeli-Palestinian dispute, and the Israelis deceive themselves, and the world, when they claim to be the victims. For a long while peace has been within their grasp if they could have agreed to a just settlement, and establishment of a vibrant Palestinian state. But a handful of fundamentalists have always succeeded in disrupting the peace process because they are not willing to accept the great Rabbi Hillel's admonition. "So always treat others the way you would like them to treat you; that is the message of the Law and the Prophets." Meanwhile the peace and stability of the world remains in jeopardy.

The world community must adopt principles and practices that override fundamentalists of any stripe whether they be, Christian, Muslim, Jewish or Economic. In addition, religious people should pay more attention to their holy books. There is nothing in the Bible that would legitimize a preventive war, with its carpet bombing, or the launch of a drone or missile intended to kill one person when there is risk that innocent bystanders will also die. Similarly, there is nothing in the Qur'an that would justify suicide bombing that result in the random death of innocents.

Global Hope

If you get the impression that the world is going to hell in a hand basket you have heard me correctly. But it doesn't need to be so. There are remedies but they involve massive change in the areas discussed – none of which are even on the political radar at present. There is light at the end of the tunnel but, as Sir John Quinton, a former chairman of Barclay's Bank said, "Bankers sometimes look on politicians as people who, when they see light at the end of the tunnel, order more tunnel."

What we are really talking about is restoring democracy to countries that not only claim they have it, but also take pride in trying to export it, even though they don't really qualify as democratic as defined in the dictionary. In Webster's it is: "government in which supreme power is vested in the people and exercised by them or their elected representatives." To begin, Wall Street has been the dominant power in the U.S. for decades, and still is. Add to that the fact that the Commander-in-Chief of the Armed Forces, the President of the United States, does not have the security clearance for a number of projects controlled by troops under his command, and you have to conclude that the U.S. is not really a democracy.

The same can be said about Canada, the United Kingdom, Germany and myriad countries that are really puppets of the International Financial System. In each case the real interests of citizen voters is subjugated to the demands of international finance.

There is a sad irony in reading U.S. history of the pre-revolutionary and revolutionary days. Historians often attribute the revolution to the tax on tea. On the other hand, "[Benjamin] Franklin cited restrictions upon paper money as one of the main reasons for the alienation of the American provinces from the mother country." The U.S. won the revolutionary war but then lost the next critical one when it adopted the British banking system instead of pursuing the better model their provinces had been experimenting with.

For the U.S. now to inflict the British practice on countries around the world, using the International Monetary Fund and World Bank as enforcers, is comparable to the King's edict that gave birth to the United States. So the financial chains of oppression have to be broken and freedom restored to citizens everywhere.

It's time to forget the tea party and address the critically important issues facing the U.S. and the world. All of these issues are non-partisan by definition and deserve the attention and support of all genuine patriots without distinction of race, color, religion or political affiliation – both in the U.S. and worldwide. We must unite to preserve and enhance the beautiful satellite that is our birth right.

An Agenda for Action

The first and most urgent project is to clip the wings of the banksters and democratize the money-creation function. In the U.S. the Federal Reserve System must be abolished and its alleged function of regulating the money supply be assumed by the federal government or an agency under its direct control. The most powerful and valuable tool in the economic arsenal must be available to the representatives of the people who can be held responsible for their success or failure.

Some monetary reformers recommend that governments create 100% of new money in a debt free form, greenbacks or equivalent. In the interests of a fast and smooth transition I am suggesting that a ratio of 34% government-created money to 66% bank-created money would work satisfactorily. Banks would be required to maintain 34% cash reserves against their deposits.

The important thing is that governments must immediately create the large sums necessary to balance their budgets and get their economies running at maximum output again. I am talking about an infusion of perhaps $10 trillion U.S. dollar equivalent to start and more if needed to get economies up to speed and to reduce unemployment worldwide by at least half, with the creation of millions of new jobs.

Is this likely to cause massive inflation, as the financial cartel will immediately allege, because it is one of its longest running and most successful bugbears? The answer to their phony phonetics is a resounding "no." As any economist should know, it is the amount of money that is created that influences prices, and not who prints it. So as long as governments limit what economists call "the multiplier effect" there will be no problem.

Certainly the present system has been inflationary. A 1950 U.S. dollar is only worth 7.5 cents today. A common sense monetary system should produce better results than that. So there is no reason why the banking system should not be fundamentally reformed – at once!

There are four other actions that I think we, the people of the world should demand of our politicians.

1. A law must be passed at once to prohibit all politicians, candidates for political office and political parties from accepting money from any financial institution as well as make it a criminal offense for any such institution either directly or indirectly to offer it.
2. World leaders must adopt a 10-year time frame to reduce greenhouse emissions by 90 percent.
3. That will only be possible if the U.S. discloses its knowledge of the ET presence and technology, and what has been accomplished in 60 years of back-engineering.
4. The U.N. should declare 2012 the year of forgiveness and reconciliation – a new era of cooperation and (agape) love between races, tribes, religions, nations, and regions both mondial and intergalactic. We have so much to learn from our star visitors in many areas including medicine and food production.

So the U.S. must relinquish its privileged position as the center of "the loop" as part of a new kind of leadership in creating the better world we all dream of.

International Finance vs. the People of the World

None of this vision of a just and peaceful world will be possible unless the all-pervasive power of the international banks has been broken. In 1999 I wrote a book in which I said the next world war would be between the banks and the people of the world. There have been skirmishes for centuries and, so far, the banks have always come out on top. They are now taking advantage of the recent meltdown, and the resulting sovereign debt crisis to line up their heavy artillery including the International Monetary Fund, the World Bank, the Federal Reserve System and the Bank for International Settlements for a final conclusive battle.

As always the aim of the game is to rob the people of the world of their sovereign right to govern their own affairs, and to entrench the power of the international banks, their elite industrial allies and a small cabal of military insiders who run the world as their private fiefdom. The word "unjust" is too small a word by far to describe what they are up to.

If any skeptics think I am overstating the case don't take my word for it. Go to 'victoryfortheworld'[161] and read some of the books that can be used as references. A hundred pages of The Web of Debt, for example, setting out the history of money, will probably be enough to make you sick at your stomach. I stopped reading it at night because if often made me so angry I couldn't sleep.

I entered politics more than 60 years ago because I thought recessions were quite unnecessary. They were monetary phenomena with a relatively easy fix. I have made hundreds of speeches on the subject and convinced a few thousand people. But never the movers and shakers. And the mainline press were less than helpful. They were so jaundiced that they were not interested in a maverick speaking truth to power. So it was always a case of David vs. Goliath, to use a Biblical analogy.

Now, for the first time, the power exists to turn the tables and go for the jugular. The internet is providing power to the people that they have never enjoyed before. The young people of the world, in concert with the thousands of their parents and others who care about the state of the world can use the power of social networking to affect a miracle on their own behalf and that of succeeding generations.

The valiant people of Tunisia and Egypt have shown the way by achieving what was believed to be impossible. We share their euphoria. At the same time they, and we, must acknowledge that it is only the beginning. Real freedom will only be possible when they have escaped from the tyranny of international banks, and Wall Street is no longer able to manipulate the price of their daily bread.

A good start might be to distribute a million copies of this speech and translate it into a number of languages. Then the rising generation can bombard the barricades through their social networks. Regime change is not necessary except for leaders who refuse to see the light. But concerned citizens of the world should band together and rattle the cages of all federal politicians. Tell them bluntly that they must vigorously support the above agenda or face inevitable defeat at the next election. It is a simple message, but the only one they understand.

At a press conference on March 29, 2001 announcing the U.S. was backing out of the Kyoto Protocol, President George W. Bush said; "A friend is someone who tells you the truth." That is what I have been doing today. It is a message of global hope for every race, color, religion and nationality in the world and of peaceful relations with visitors from other realities.

CHAPTER TWELVE

THE REALLY BIG PICTURE:
Reincarnation, OBE and NDE Experiences

Then death, so call'd, is but old matter dress'd
In some new figure, and a varied vest:
Thus all things are but alter'd, nothing dies;
And here and there the unbodied spirit flies. . . .
From tenement to tenement though toss'd,
The soul is still the same, the figure only lost:

And as the soften'd wax new seals receives,
This face assumes, and that impression leaves;
Now call'd by one, now by another name;
The form is only changed, the wax is still the same.
So death, so call'd, can but the form deface,
The immortal soul flies out into empty space;
To seek her fortune in some other place.

Ovid - Roman Poet (43 B.C. – A.D. 17)

In my life I have come to believe that we are eternal beings existing in a greater immaterial universe of which the material world is a subset. We enter into a body in order to experience from the inside this virtual reality field. This virtual reality program acts as a school where one chooses moment by moment lessons to be learned mostly on an unconscious basis. The determining factor is to become aware of the unconscious choices we make so as to exercise our free will. We have free will, but it is up to us to exercise that free will and take responsibility for our thoughts and actions.

This esoteric idea of a greater reality in which our material universe is embedded has a long historical history and is now beginning to be embraced by science. I watched a series by Brian Green on PBS in which he stated that some physicists are beginning to think that what we experience as three dimensional reality is some kind of holographic projection from a two dimensional surface. He speculates that everything that we know is on this two dimensional surface, perhaps something like the inside of an event horizon surrounding a black hole in a universe that is part of an even larger mega-universe.

I think just as we can't understand terrestrial politics without understanding exopolitics because both are so intertwined, we can't really understand both of these without understanding an even greater domain that involves life after death and reincarnation. I believe that when UFO/ET insiders say it's all more than can possibly be imagined, that they are talking about this greatest domain.

The yogis have divided this larger domain into planes of existence where intelligent beings reincarnate in and out of this larger domain into vast numbers of physical worlds. The evidence also seems to suggest that there is incarnational transmigration of intelligent beings between physical worlds to further complicate matters. All this tends to make the beliefs, ideas and perceptions of earth-centric yogis and Buddhists downright providential.

I was first exposed to reincarnation and life after death by the little metaphysical book store in down town Fairbanks Alaska when I was around seventeen years old. Later Patricia Degal an individual who considered herself a reincarnation specialist came to lecture on reincarnation at the University of Alaska. I got a mini reading from her right after the lecture and a few years later a very detailed report on myself and my past lives. She made some predictions about by life that came true, as well as gave the first names of people who would become significant to me later in fife that also came true.

It did not make much sense to me at the time when she told me that I had 144 lives on earth and seven before that on another star system. She said that I had been on earth for hundreds of thousands of years from the very beginning of the extraterrestrial colonization of earth. At the time I really had no idea of the overall context of these statements, but today they fit neatly into what I have learned over the years. It's interesting how things tend to come together for the truth-seeker over time, but tend to fall apart over time for the deceiver.

There are plenty of good books providing evidence for reincarnation. I would suggest the very popular books, *'Many Lives, Many Masters'* and *'Only Love Is Real'* by Brian Weiss to begin with. The following Amazon book review by Subhamoy Das not only describes the book *Many Lives, Many Masters*, but pretty darn well sums up this whole concept of reincarnation and past lives.[162]

"*Many Lives, Many Masters* is the true story of a prominent psychiatrist, his young patient, and the past-life therapy that changed both their lives. As a traditional psychotherapist, Dr Brian Weiss, M.D., graduating Phi Beta Kappa, magna cum laude, from Columbia University and Yale Medical School, spent years in the disciplined study of the human psychology, training his mind to think as a scientist and a physician.

He held steadfastly to conservatism in his profession, distrusting anything that could not be proved by traditional scientific method. But when he met his 27-year old patient, Catherine, in 1980, who came to his office seeking help for her anxiety, panic attacks, and phobias, he was taken aback at what unfolded in the therapy sessions that followed, which jolted him out of his conventional ways of thought and psychiatry. For the first time, he came face-to-face with the concept of reincarnation and the many tenets of Hinduism, which, as he says in the last chapter of the book, "I thought only Hindus... practiced."

For 18 months, Dr Weiss used conventional methods of treatment to help Catherine overcome her traumas. When nothing seemed to work, he tried hypnosis, which, he explains, "is an excellent tool to help a patient remember long-forgotten incidents. There is nothing mysterious about it. It is just a state of focused concentration. Under the instruction of a trained hypnotist, the patient's body relaxes, causing the memory to sharpen... eliciting memories of long-forgotten traumas that were disrupting their lives."

During the initial sessions, the doctor regressed her back to her early childhood and she strained and stretched her mind bringing out isolated, deeply-repressed memory fragments. She remembered from age five when she swallowed water and felt gagged when pushed from a diving board into a pool; and at age three when her father reeking of alcohol molested her one night. But what came next, catapulted skeptics like Dr Weiss into believing in parapsychology, and in what Shakespeare had said in Hamlet (Act I scene 5), "There are more things in heaven and earth... than are dreamt of in your philosophy."

In a series of trance-like states, Catherine recalled "past life" memories that proved to be the causative factors of her recurring nightmares and anxiety attack symptoms. She remembers "living 86 times in physical state" in different places on this earth both as male and female. She recalled vividly the details of each birth – her name, her family, physical appearance, the landscape, and how she was killed by stabbing, by drowning, or illness. And in each lifetime she experiences myriad events "making progress... to fulfill all of the agreements and all of the Karmic (from Hindu concept of Karma) debts that are owed."

Dr Weiss's skepticism was eroded, however, when she began to channel messages from "the space between lives," messages from the many Masters (highly evolved souls not presently in body) that also contained remarkable revelations about his family and his dead son. Often he had heard his patients talk about near-death experiences when they float out of their mortal bodies guided towards a bright white light before re-entering their discarded body once again.

But Catherine revealed much more. As she floats out of her body after each death, she says, "I am aware of a bright light. It's wonderful; you get energy from this light." Then, while waiting to be reborn in the in-between-lives state, she learns from the Masters great wisdom and becomes a conduit for transcendental knowledge.

Here are some of the teachings from the voices of the Master Spirits:

1. Our task is to learn, to become God-like through knowledge... By knowledge we approach God, and then we can rest. Then we come back to teach and help others.

2. There are many gods, for God is in each of us.

3. We have to be on different planes at different times. Each one is a level of higher consciousness. What plane we go to depends upon how far we've progressed.

4. We must share our knowledge with other people. We all have abilities far beyond what we use. You should check your vices, if you do not, you carry them over with you to another life. When you decide you are strong enough to master the external problems, and then you will no longer have them in your next life.

5. Everybody's path is basically the same. We all must learn certain attitudes while we're in physical state. Charity, hope, faith, love. We must all know these things and know them well.

6. Everything is energy. Humans can only see the outside, but you can go much deeper. To be in physical state is abnormal. When you are in spiritual state that is natural to you. When we are sent back, it's like being sent back to something we do not know. In the spirit world you have to wait, and then you are renewed. It's a dimension like the other dimensions.

7. The fear of death, that no amount of money or power can neutralize, remains within us. But if people knew that life is endless; so we never die; we were never really born, this fear would dissolve. We have lived countless times before and would live countless times again, and spirits are around us to help while in physical state and after death, in spiritual state. We and our deceased loved ones would join these guardian angels.

8. Acts of violence and injustices against people do not go unnoted, but is repaid in kind in other lifetime.

9. Everything comes when it must come. A life cannot be rushed, we must accept what comes to us at a given time. Life is endless, we just pass through different phases. There is no end. Time is not as we see time, but rather in lessons that are learned.

10. After death, we get to the spiritual plane, we keep growing there, too. When we arrive, we're burned out. We have to go through a renewal stage, a learning stage, and a stage of decision. We decide when we want to return, where, and for what reasons. Our body is just a vehicle for us while we're here. It is our soul and our spirit that last forever.

Dr Weiss believes, under hypnosis, Catherine was able to focus in on the part of her subconscious mind that stored actual past-life memories, or perhaps she had tapped into what the psychoanalyst Carl Jung termed the Collective Unconscious, the energy source that surrounds us containing the memories of the entire human race.

Reincarnation in Hinduism:

Dr Weiss's experience and Catherine's transcendental knowledge might be awe inspiring to the Occidental, but to a

Hindu, the concept of rebirth, cycle of life and death, and this divine knowledge is natural. The holy *'Bhagavad Gita'* and the ancient Vedic scriptures embody all this wisdom; and these teachings form the primary tenets of Hinduism. Therefore, Dr Weiss's mention of Hindus in the last chapter of the book comes as a welcome acknowledgement to a religion that has already established all of his new-found experience.

Reincarnation in Buddhism

The concept of reincarnation is not new to Tibetan Buddhists, too. His Holiness the Dalai Lama believes that his body is like a garment, which when time comes, he will discard and move on to accept another. He will be reborn, and it is the disciples' duty to find him out and follow him.

Reincarnation in Christianity:

Dr Weiss also says that there were indeed references to reincarnation in the Old and the New Testaments. The early Gnostics – Clement of Alexandria, Origen, Saint Jerome, and many others – believed that they had lived before and would again. In A.D. 325 the Roman emperor Constantine the Great and Helena, his mother, erased references to reincarnation in the New Testament and the Second Council of Constantinople declared reincarnation a heresy in A.D. 553. They thought this would weaken the growing power of the Church by giving humans too much time to seek their salvation.

Many Lives, Many Masters makes for an unstoppable read and, like Dr Weiss, we too realize that "life is more than meets the eye. Life goes beyond our five senses. Be receptive to new knowledge and to new experiences. Our task is to learn, to become God-like though knowledge."

If you are a scholar or scientifically inclined, I would recommend the three extensively researched books on Reincarnation compiled and edited by Sylvia Cranston. I have her third book called *Reincarnation, the Phoenix Fire Mystery*, and it's got just about everything available on reincarnation down through the ages to the present day. Whew! The material about reincarnation and Christianity probably came from her book. I also see Sylvia has even another book out on the subject.[163]

According to Sylvia Cranston the greatest contribution to reincarnation research has been done by Dr Ian Stevenson. She says;

> "He now apparently has over 1,700 cases in his files of people, mostly children, from all parts of the world, who appear to have memories of previous lives. He has found 90% of their memories to be accurate, and thus far four large volumes of his case histories have been published by the University of Virginia Press." This Wikipedia entry on Dr Stevenson has a higher figure of 3000 cases and seems to have more up to date information on Dr Stevenson.[164]
>
> Wikipedia says, "Stevenson considered that the concept of reincarnation[165] might supplement those of heredity and environment in helping modern medicine to understand aspects of human behavior and development. He travelled extensively over a period of 40 years to investigate 3,000 childhood cases that suggested to him the possibility of past lives. Stevenson saw reincarnation as the survival of the personality after death, although he never suggested a physical process by which a personality might survive death. Stevenson was the author of several books, including; *'Twenty Cases Suggestive of Reincarnation'* (1974), *'Children Who Remember Previous Lives'* (1987), *'Where Reincarnation and Biology Intersect'* (1997), *'Reincarnation and Biology'* (1997), and *'European Cases of the Reincarnation Type'* (2003)."

Okay so how are we to place exopolitics and terrestrial politics into this greatest possible perspective. My thinking is that there are three types of individuals incarnating on earth. A few seem to be highly intelligent predatory old soul individuals that lost a war in space, maybe even an Anunnaki civil war as described in ancient religious texts. I suspect that these few individuals and their families incarnating together could be the elite globalists whose agenda is to maintain dominion over earth and its peoples out of predatory self-interest. These individuals seem stuck in a lower state of consciousness that of a feudal nature that takes a win-lose approach to life.

A second type involves a few highly evolved old soul altruistic individuals who are incarnating to counter-balance the first type, so that free will can be maintained on earth for the large third group. These altruistic individuals and their families have a higher evolved state of consciousness and indulge in a win-win approach to life and living.

The third type and by far the largest type are all these young soul individuals caught in the middle between the first type and the second type. Their consciousness shifts back and forth between the first and second type consciousness as they gain experience and develop the free will necessary to evolve further.

It's important to note that we do not seem to incarnate alone, but with our support networks, unless we are just entering this earth system and have to build our networks from scratch. I really think of the big picture as a school, a learning experience for the development of character. The prime motivators seem to be the carrot and the stick. If we learn our lessons we get the carrot and if we don't we get the stick. If we learn, we find peace and happiness in life and if we don't, we continue to suffer no matter how clever we get at covering up our suffering!

It's still unclear to me that if we refuse to learn and continue to fault the lessons, what happens to us. Do we eventually destroy ourselves by indulging in destructive processes or are the destruction and suffering only temporary until we give up the path to destruction? I somehow suspect it could both and this seems to be indicated in books like, The Journey of Souls. Journey of Souls talks about how souls are created, so maybe if one is determined enough one can undo what has been done.

Closely connected with reincarnation are Out of body experiences where the person finds themselves floating outside their body or up out of their bodies.[166] While skeptics can come up with all kinds of conventional reasons to account for OBE experiences these conventional reasons just as with UFOs often come up short. Consider on case, for instance, where the person dies on a hospital table and floats up through several floors to find three sets of shoes next to a window. When resuscitated, they tell a nurse about the shoes and when she goes up to inspect, she sees the shoes exactly as described. To say that this can be explained by unconscious brain activity just does not cut it with me.

It has been reported that perhaps as many a 1 in 10 people have experienced an OBE or Near Death Experiences (NDE). Actresses Jane Seymour and Elizabeth Taylor cases illustrate a typical OBE or NDE. Jane reportedly experienced a NDE when she delivered her twins.

> "I literally left my body. I had this feeling that I could see myself on the bed, with people grouped around me. I remember them all trying to resuscitate me. I was above them, in the corner of the room looking down. I saw people putting needles in me, trying to hold me down, and doing things. I remember my whole life flashing before my eyes, but I wasn't thinking about winning Emmys or anything like that. The only thing I cared about was that I wanted to live because I did not want anyone else looking after my children. I was floating up there thinking, "No, I don't want to die. I'm not ready to leave my kids."
> "And that was when I said to God, "If you're there, God, if you really exist and I survive, I will never take your name in vain again." Although I believe that I "died" for about thirty seconds, I can remember pleading with the doctor to bring me back. I was determined I wasn't going to die."

During an interviewed by Larry King on CNN's Larry King Live, Elizabeth Taylor shared how she had been pronounced dead for five minutes while on the operating table during one of her surgeries. She relayed that while she was clinically dead, she had encountered the spirit of Michael Todd, one of her former husbands. She had wanted to stay with Todd, she said, but he had told her that she had work and life ahead of her, and he "pushed me back to my life." Ms. Taylor told the medical team who brought her back to life about her experience.

"I went to that tunnel, saw the white light, and Mike [Todd]. I said, oh Mike, you're where I want to be. And he said, 'No, Baby. You have to turn around and go back because there is something very important for you to do. You cannot give up now.' It was Mike's strength and love that brought me back."

Over my life I have talked to people personally who have had these experiences and they tell me that when one really experiences this, there is no doubt in one's mind that it really happened. A friend of mine even found himself starting to float out of his body while driving a car. Fortunately even though it scared him half to death, the fear caused him to snap back into his body. This was the first and only time he ever had an OBE.

I have never had a OBE even thought I had at one time trained myself to become fully awake while dreaming. Being awake in a dream is really a lot of fun because one can manipulate mental imagery at will to fly, float about and even change landscapes at will. In lucid dreaming one is not really out of the body but simply awake in the dream landscapes. One time I reached down and felt the sand on a beach and realized that the sand I was seeing and feeling was constructed from all the perceptions of sand I had had in my life. I think a lot of people confuse real OBEs with lucid dreaming.

The Monroe Institute[167] investigates these kinds of consciousness phenomena. Here on their website they give links to other organizations that support OBE and Near Death Experiences (NDE). An important site referenced here is that of:

"Dr Raymond A. Moody[168] who is a leading authority on the "near-death experience"—a phrase he coined in the late seventies. Dr Moody's research into the phenomenon of near-death experience had its start in the 1960's. He is the best-selling author of eleven books on the subject of NDEs, and continues to capture enormous public interest and generate controversy with his ground-breaking work on the near-death experience and what happens when we die."

A person who understands very well how UFO/ET material intersects with the really big picture is astronaut Edgar Mitchell who founded the Institute of Noetic Sciences. He has talked openly about the reality of extraterrestrial life. On the Noetic Sciences website[169] is the following:

> "Traveling back to Earth, having just walked on the moon, Apollo 14 astronaut Edgar Mitchell had an experience for which nothing in his life had prepared him. As he approached the planet we know as home, he was filled with an inner conviction as certain as any mathematical equation he'd ever solved. He knew that the beautiful blue world to which he was returning is part of a living system, harmonious and whole—and that we all participate, as he expressed it later, "in a universe of consciousness."
>
> This experience radically altered his worldview: Despite science's superb technological achievements, he realized that we had barely begun to probe the deepest mystery of the universe—the fact of consciousness itself. He became convinced that the uncharted territory of the human mind was the next frontier to explore, and that it contained possibilities we had hardly begun to imagine. Within two years of his expedition, Edgar Mitchell founded the Institute of Noetic Sciences in 1973."

Edgar Mitchell is right, the deepest mysteries of the universe are to be found in the evolving field of consciousness investigation and research and we have yet to even scratch the surface of the really big picture. As I finish up this exopolitics rough draft I see yet another book in the wings waiting to be written which may be called, '*The Long Hard Road to Enlightenment.*'

On this rainy Christmas day in late 2011, I sit alone in body in my small cabin, but next to me real or imagined, I sense the presence of my long dead father who watches over my shoulder approvingly holding that book yet to be written. Dad was unable to pull all that he learned in life together in books before old age caught up with him and I am determined that the same will not happen to me.

    I would hope that every person would write up an account of what they have learned in life to pass on to today's youth to build upon. Everybody has an important story to tell and I mean everybody! Maybe someday soon, technology will allow the compilation and transfer of knowledge, wisdom and experience from the older generation to the young in some very surprising and fantastic ways.

Footnotes
Supporting document hyperlink index

1. Ben Rich biographical information: http://en.wikipedia.org/wiki/Ben_Rich
2. Lockheed CEO Admits on Deathbed: ET UFO Are Real: http://xenophilius.wordpress.com/2010/09/14/ben-rich-lockheed-ceo-admits-on-deathbed-et-ufo-are-real
3. The Globalist Agenda: http://globalistagenda.org/who.htm
4. Admiral Roscoe Henry Hillenkoetter: http://en.wikipedia.org/wiki/Roscoe_H._Hillenkoetter
5. UFOs over Washington prompted policy of denial and ridicule: http://archive.alienzoo.com/conspiracytheory/ufosoverwashington.html
6. Former UFO Project Chief Apologizes for Dirty Spin & Tricks: http://www.huffingtonpost.com/2011/08/17/uk-releases-ufo-files_n_927351.html?/
7. NASA Employed Photo Artists To Airbrush Out Apollo Anomalies!: http://www.ufos-aliens.co.uk/airbrush.htm
8. Philip J. Corso: http://en.wikipedia.org/wiki/Philip_J._Corso
9. The Day After Roswell: http://www.amazon.com/Day-After-Roswell-Philip-Corso/dp/067101756X
10. Operation Paperclip: http://greyfalcon.us/restored/Operation%20Paperclip%20Casefile.htm
11. Paul Hellyer: http://en.wikipedia.org/wiki/Paul_Hellyer

12. Global Fraud; Global Hope:
    http://adventuresinnewparadigms.blogspot.com/2011/03/global-fraud-global-hope.html
13. Edgar Mitchell:
    http://en.wikipedia.org/wiki/Edgar_Mitchell
14. Buckminster Fuller:
    http://en.wikipedia.org/wiki/Buckminster_Fuller
15. Exopolitics World Network:
    http://www.paradigmresearchgroup.org/ExopoliticsWorld.htm
16. Exopolitics: http://www.exopolitics.org
17. 50 Billion Alien Planets: http://www.space.com/10982-kepler-alien-planets-billion-galaxy.html
18. UFO Crash at Aztec: http://www.amazon.com/UFO-Crash-Aztec-Well-Secret/dp/093426905X
19. Insectoid Encounter in Poland:
    http://www.ufodigest.com/news/0906/insectoid.html
20. Karla Turner 'Into the Fringe':
    http://www.bibliotecapleyades.net/archivos_pdf/karlaturner_intothefringe.pdf
21. Linda Moulton Howe:
    http://www.amazon.com/Glimpses-Other-Realities-Facts-Eyewitnesses/dp/0962057053
22. Reptilian Encounter in Nevada:
    http://www.ufodigest.com/article/ufo-spotlight-onreptilian-encounter-nevada-desert
23. Missouri Caver Encounters Reptilian:
    http://naturalplane.blogspot.com/2011/10/missouri-caver-encounters-under-ground.html?utm_source=feedburner&utm_medium=em

ail&utm_campaign=Feed%3A+PhantomsAndMonsters APersonalJourney+%28Phantoms+and+Monsters%29&utm_content=Yahoo!+Mail
24. An Interview with Johnny Sands: http://www.mysterious-america.net/johnnysands.html
25. Aquatic Humanoids: http://en.wikipedia.org/wiki/Greek_sea_gods
26. Johnny Sands: http://www.myspace.com/johnnysands
27. Udo Wartena Case: http://thechurchofufology.blogspot.com/2011/08/contact-in-1940.html
28. Charles Hall Case: http://openseti.org/Hall.html
29. UFO Crash and Retrieval, Missouri, 1941: http://www.ufocasebook.com/missouricrash.html
30. Unidentified Crash Retrieval: http://www.seekingmoinfo.com
31. UFO Crash 1936: http://greyfalcon.us/restored/1936.htm
32. Boyd Bushman Testimony: http://www.youtube.com/watch?v=VzwOFCSFms4
33. Majestic Documents: http://majesticdocuments.com
34. Military Industrial Complex: http://en.wikipedia.org/wiki/Military-industrial_complex
35. Eisenhower's 1954 Meeting with ET: http://www.bibliotecapleyades.net/exopolitica/esp_exopolitics_Q.htm
36. Milton Torres Account: http://colinandrews.net/UFO-MiltonTorres2.html
37. Fatal Encounter At Fort Dix: http://www.nicap.org/fortdixSYM.htm

38. Alien Being Shot Dead By MPs: http://www.ufocasebook.com/ftdix.html
39. Richard Dolan - Secret Space Program: http://www.youtube.com/watch?v=DsJDsxmzMDw
40. Paul Hellyer – Global Fraud, Global Hope: http://www.globalresearch.ca/index.php?context=va&aid=23431
41. Electrogravitics Systems: http://www.padrak.com/ine/INE24.html
42. Bob Lazar: http://www.ufo-blogger.com/2011/10/robert-bob-lazar-ufo-worked-on-alien.html
43. Cash-Landrum Case: http://www.ufocasebook.com/Pineywoods.html
44. Richard Dolan, Peter Levenda: http://pindz.blogspot.com/2011/07/secret-space-program-richard-dolan-and.html
45. Reagan, Space Command: http://www.examiner.com/exopolitics-in-honolulu/reagan-records-space-command-antigravity-fleet
46. NASA Decline and Anti-gravity Space Fleet: http://www.examiner.com/exopolitics-in-honolulu/nasa-decline-and-antigravity-space-fleet
47. Star Trek vs. Solar Warden: http://www.examiner.com/exopolitics-in-honolulu/star-trek-vs-solar-warden-the-real-starfleet
48. Secret UFO Propulsion Systems: http://www.youtube.com/watch?v=VzwOFCSFms4
49. Bob Lazar, Element 115: http://www.youtube.com/watch?v=NUfY2L3Q8xs

50. Phil Corso and The Truth About UFOs:
https://www.facebook.com/video/video.php?v=108296962543535&comments&ref=mf
51. UFO Over Nellis:
http://www.youtube.com/watch?v=1oCl2kROv1Y&feature=player_embedded
52. X-22A Description:
http://www.gotthatonline.com/x_22a.htm
53. Buzz Aldrin Encounter:
http://www.youtube.com/watch?v=XlkV1ybBnHI&feature=share
54. NASA and UFO Secrecy, Edgar Mitchell:
http://www.youtube.com/watch?v=Zu_7hd5B-dc
55. Gordon Cooper and UFOs:
http://www.youtube.com/watch?v=dvPR8T1o3Dc
56. An Alien Spaceship On The Moon:
http://www.angelismarriti.it/ANGELISMARRITI-ENG/REPORTS_ARTICLES/Apollo20-InterviewWithWilliamRutledge.htm
57. An Interview With Apollo 19 Commander:
http://www.angelismarriti.it/ANGELISMARRITI-ENG/REPORTS_ARTICLES/Apollo19CDR-interview.htm
58. Apollo 20, The Disclosure:
http://www.amazon.com/Apollo-20-Disclosure-Luca-Scantamburlo/dp/1445273977/ref=sr_1_1?ie=UTF8&qid=1327048767&sr=8-1
59. Technological Singularity:
http://en.wikipedia.org/wiki/Technological_singularity

60. Singularity, Physicist Explains:
http://www.physlink.com/Education/AskExperts/ae251.cfm
61. Scientists Create Animals that are Part Human:
http://www.msnbc.msn.com/id/7681252/ns/health-cloning_and_stem_cells
62. Human/Machine Integration:
http://www.surroundingsignifiers.com/blog/2011/3/13/the-future-of-uxui-and-human-machine-integration.html
63. Could Hackers Develop Computer Virus to Infect Human Minds?:
http://www.dailymail.co.uk/sciencetech/article-2073936/Could-hackers-develop-virus-infect-human-mind.html
64. Flying Shields of the Hopi:
http://www.mondovista.com/flyingshields
65. Ancient Star Cities and the Hopi:
http://www.bibliotecapleyades.net/esp_leyenda_hopi21.htm
66. Gavin Menzies: http://www.gavinmenzies.net
67. Majestic Documents:
http://www.majesticdocuments.com
68. Special Access Program:
http://en.wikipedia.org/wiki/Special_access_program
69. Admiral; Never Looked For UFO Data:
http://www.heraldtribune.com/article/20080806/BLOG32/525095430/2121&title=Admiral__Never_looked_for_UFO_data?p=2&tc=pg
70. Richard Dolan on the Admiral Wilson UFO Story:
http://www.ufodigest.com/news/0808/wilson.html

71. Jesco Von Puttkamer:
http://en.wikipedia.org/wiki/Jesco_von_Puttkamer
72. Operation Paperclip:
http://en.wikipedia.org/wiki/Operation_Paperclip
73. Extraterrestrial Life; Where Is Everybody?:
http://www.bigear.org/vol1no3/life.htm
74. Walter Dornberger:
http://en.wikipedia.org/wiki/Walter_Dornberger
75. German Americans Honor Rocket Engineer:
http://www.germerica.net/Puttkamer-German-American-Rocket-Scientist
76. List of German Rocket Scientists in the US:
http://en.wikipedia.org/wiki/List_of_German_rocket_scientists_in_the_United_States
77. Gunter Wendt:
http://en.wikipedia.org/wiki/Guenter_Wendt
78. Operation Paperclip Case file:
http://greyfalcon.us/restored/Operation%20Paperclip%20Casefile.htm
79. Burned Memo:
http://majesticdocuments.com/documents/1960-1969.php#burnedmemo
80. Kennedy's UFO Involvement Led To Assassination:
http://www.examiner.com/exopolitics-in-honolulu/president-kennedy-s-ufo-involvement-led-to-assassination-order
81. CIA Director Denied Kennedy Access To UFO Files:
http://www.examiner.com/exopolitics-in-honolulu/cia-director-issued-secret-directive-denying-president-kennedy-access-to-ufo-files

82. Review of MJ-12 Activities: http://www.majesticdocuments.com/pdf/kennedy_ciadirector.pdf
83. TW craft, satellite image: http://brumac.8k.com/DMSP/DMSP.html
84. Russian Navy encounter: http://www.alieneight.com/alien-encounters-the-russian-navy-and-aquatic-ufos.htm
85. Colin Andrews: http://colinandrews.net/UnexplainedPhenomenaAlert.html
86. Titanium on the Moon: http://news.discovery.com/space/moon-titanium-111012.html
87. Titanium on the Moon II: http://www.huliq.com/12092/titanium-moon-resources-spark-new-space-race
88. China's Moon Ambitions: http://news.discovery.com/space/china-moon-resources-bigelow-111020.html
89. Battelle, Memory Metal: http://ufocon.blogspot.com/2010/08/roswell-battelle-memory-metal-new.html
90. Lunar Mining: http://www.thelivingmoon.com/43ancients/02files/Moon_Mining02.html
91. Building on Mars: http://paranormal.about.com/od/marsanomalies/v/mars-biostation-alpha.htm
92. Bio-Station Alpha: http://www.youtube.com/watch?v=BeN8bSvYv0U

93. MJ-12 AF General's Stepson Talks ET:
http://exopolitics.blogspot.com/2011/01/mj-12-af-generals-stepson-talks-et-by.html
94. Richard Sauder Ph.D.:
http://keyholepublishing.com/Sauder.html
95. Dr Richard Sauder on Veritas:
http://www.youtube.com/watch?v=93NKocM58_g&feature=related
96. White House; No ET:
http://www.homelandsecuritynewswire.com/white-house-no-evidence-contact-extra-terrestrials#.TrmD3lE8as.facebook
97. Dr. Kary Mullis' Encounter:
http://thenightsky.org/mullis.html
98. Kary Mullis bio:
http://en.wikipedia.org/wiki/Kary_Mullis
99. Bill Uhouse: http://www.area51et.com/bill-uhouse
100. Bill Uhouse Area 51 video:
http://www.youtube.com/watch?v=3-ICRApPMzQ&feature=related
101. Humans Working Alongside ETs:
http://www.youtube.com/watch?v=xXIWKQOu-k8&feature=related
102. SAIC: http://www.answers.com/topic/science-applications-international-corporation
103. Bob Oechsler:
http://www.americanchronicle.com/articles/view/226510
104. Dan Sherman:
http://www.bibliotecapleyades.net/exopolitica/esp_exopol_aboveblack.htm#menu

366

105. Solar Storm Warning: http://www.foxnews.com/story/0,2933,478024,00.html
106. NASA Warns of Solar Flares: http://www.telegraph.co.uk/science/space/7819201/Nasa-warns-solar-flares-from-huge-space-storm-will-cause-devastation.html
107. Lyn Buchanan Abduction: http://www.deepspace4.com/pages/ufo/abductionstory.htm
108. Aaron Russo Interview: http://www.youtube.com/watch?v=7nD7dbkkBIA
109. William Pawelec's Widow Reveals Secrets: http://beforeitsnews.com/story/873/183/William_Pawelecs_widow_reveals_national_security_secrets.html
110. William Pawelec Interview: http://www.youtube.com/watch?feature=player_embedded&v=yytSNQ2ogD4
111. Levengood's Research Reports: http://www.iccra.org/levengood/allotherpub.htm
112. 1954 Humanoid Reports: http://www.ufoinfo.com/humanoid/humanoid1954.shtml
113. Father Gill, Papua New Guinea: http://www.ufoevidence.org/cases/case67.htm
114. 1959 The Papua New Guinea UFOs: http://ufos.about.com/od/bestufocasefiles/p/papua.htm
115. Neil Gould Interviews Major George Filer: http://www.educatinghumanity.com/2011/07/ufo-ufo-video-interview-with-major.html
116. Reform MUFON: http://reformmufon.org
117. National UFO Reporting Center: http://www.nationalufocenter.com

118. Are Humans Part Alien?:
http://www.nationalufocenter.com/artman/publish/article_427.php
119. Peter Khoury, Mary Rodwell:
http://www.youtube.com/watch?v=QUznIAGy_n8&feature=autoshare
120. Tall Caucasian Mummies in China:
http://www.youtube.com/watch?v=lRj-IR5Aqbg&feature=related
121. Vril Women of WWII:
http://www.viewzone.com/vril22.html
122. Lake Eerie UFOs: http://www.alien-ufos.com/ufo-alien-discussions/40855-jaime-maussan-latest-ufo-sightings-recent-ufo-sightings-lake-erie-2011-report.html
123. UFO Base Under Lake Eerie:
http://beforeitsnews.com/story/1124/854/Claim:_Giant_UFO_Base_Under_Lake_Erie.html
124. Anunnaki Message from FSR:
https://www.facebook.com/notes/michael-lee-hill/an-actual-message-from-the-anunnaki-mankind-in-amnesia-flying-saucer-review-maga/2017197393092
125. The Friendship Case: http://www.ufo-blogger.com/2011/05/project-il-caso-amicizia.html
126. ETs Live in Patagonia: http://www.ufo-blogger.com/2010/06/extraterrestrial-humanoid-had-lived-in.html
127. Mass Contacts, A Review:
http://www.paolaharris.com/masscontact.htm

128. Diamond Linked by Quantum Entanglement: http://www.livescience.com/17264-quantum-entanglement-macroscopic-diamonds.html
129. Spooky Physics: http://www.livescience.com/2785-spooky-physics-signals-travel-faster-light.html
130. Spooky Physics Gets More Entangled: http://www.livescience.com/5499-einsteins-spooky-physics-entangled.html
131. Quantum Physics Could Power the Future: http://www.livescience.com/7547-quantum-physics-power-future.html
132. Entanglement Based Quantum Communication: http://www.quantum.at/research/quantum-teleportation-communication-entanglement/entangled-photons-over-144-km.html
133. Canary Islands: http://en.wikipedia.org/wiki/Canary_Islands
134. European Space Agency: http://www.esa.int/esaCP/index.html
135. Quantum Entanglement Communications: http://www.hardsf.org/HSFTEnta.htm
136. Vimanas: http://www.crystalinks.com/vimanas.html
137. Quotes From Ancient Indian Texts: http://www.inquiring-mines.com/ancient_aircraft_quotes_from_indian_texts.htm
138. Vitrified Fort: http://en.wikipedia.org/wiki/Vitrified_fort
139. Vitrification: http://www.ancient-wisdom.co.uk/vitrified.htm

140. Ancient City Found in India, Irradiated from Atomic Blast: http://veda.wikidot.com/ancient-city-found-in-india-irradiated-from-atomic-blast
141. UFO Battle Over Nuremburg Germany 1561: http://www.ufoevidence.org/cases/case486.htm
142. 1561 News Article: http://www.youtube.com/watch?v=eOgwhvmwUKM&feature=player_embedded
143. 1608 UFO Aerial Battle, Southern France: http://www.inquiring-mines.com/ufo_1608_aerial_battle_france.htm
144. UFO Alert, Explosion, Strange Lights, Northern Indiana: http://www.opednews.com/maxwrite/print_friendly.php?p=7083
145. Air Traffic Controllers Who Saw UFO Muzzled: http://blogs.phoenixnewtimes.com/valleyfever/2008/04/air_traffic_controllers_who_sa.php
146. Canadian UFO Sightings: http://www.americanchronicle.com/articles/view/36243
147. UFOs Fighting Thread: http://www.unexplained-mysteries.com/forum/index.php?showtopic=197629
148. Witness Describes UFO Dogfight Over New Jersey: http://www.examiner.com/ufo-in-national/witness-describes-ufo-dogfight-over-new-jersey
149. UFO Dogfighting Over Texas: http://www.godlikeproductions.com/forum1/message1665300/pg1
150. 1989, Battle of the Flying Saucers: http://ufos.about.com/od/ufofolkloremythlegend/p/battle1989.htm

151. The Jinn: http://www.thejinn.net/world%27s_greatest_hoax.htm
152. True Nature of the UFO Entities: http://www.thejinn.net/true_nature_of_the_ufo_entities.htm
153. Stalking the Tricksters: http://www.amazon.com/Stalking-Tricksters-Shapeshifters-Skinwalkers-Adepts/dp/1931882924
154. Wes Penre, Michael Lee Hill: http://wespenre.com/remarkable-michael-lee-hall-case.htm
155. Who Or What Are The Djinn?: http://www.llewellyn.com/journal/article/2182
156. The Vengeful Djinn: http://www.llewellyn.com/product.php?ean=9780738721712&utm_source=llewellynjournal&utm_medium=article&utm_campaign=llewellynjournal
157. Rosemary Ellen Guiley: http://www.visionaryliving.com
158. Portals A Step Closer To Reality: http://www.telegraph.co.uk/science/science-news/6016857/Invisible-doorways-or-portals-a-step-closer-to-reality-claim-scientists.html
159. Psychic Intelligence Agents: http://www.urigeller.com/articles/psi_spy.htm
160. Close Encounters of the Possession Kind: https://www.dmt-nexus.me/doc/William%20Baldwin%20-%20CEVI.pdf
161. Victory For The World: http://www.victoryfortheworld.net

162. Many Lives, Many Masters:
http://hinduism.about.com/od/reincarnation/fr/weissbook.htm
163. Reincarnation; The Phoenix Fire Mystery:
http://www.theosociety.org/pasadena/ts/reincbks.htm
164. Ian Stevenson:
http://en.wikipedia.org/wiki/Ian_Stevenson
165. Reincarnation:
http://en.wikipedia.org/wiki/Reincarnation
166. Out-Of-Body Experience:
http://en.wikipedia.org/wiki/Out-of-body_experience
167. The Monroe Institute:
http://www.monroeinstitute.org/research/out-of-body-experiences
168. Life After Life: http://www.lifeafterlife.com
169. Institute Of Noetic Sciences:
http://noetic.org/directory/person/edgar-mitchell/

3371305R00204

Printed in Great Britain
by Amazon.co.uk, Ltd.,
Marston Gate.